Breakthrough into Recovery

Rory MaGrath

Onwards and Upwards Publishers

3 Radfords Turf, Cranbrook, Exeter,
EX5 7DX, United Kingdom.
www.onwardsandupwards.org

This first edition published in the United Kingdom by Onwards and Upwards Publishers (2018).

ISBN:	978-1-78815-637-0
Typeface:	Sabon LT
Editor:	Sharon Fletcher
Graphic design:	LM Graphic Design

Printed in the United Kingdom.

Endorsements

Having met Rory and heard a little of his story, I am glad that he has now written it down. It will help many struggling with addiction find sobriety, serenity and sanity.

Trevor Hudson

Methodist minister who has served in pastoral roles in southern Africa for over 35 years. Author of multiple books, Hudson travels widely, teaching and lecturing on the areas of spiritual formation, spiritual direction and pastoral therapy.

Self-reflection can be a powerful tool towards healing and growth, and helps one gain perspective and insight, and this is exactly what Rory has achieved in this gripping story of the betrayal of alcohol that has caught many people from different walks of life.

Prof. Wim Roestenburg PhD

Professor of B Soc Sc (Social Work) (Currently at NWU; North West University, RSA), MA (Clinical Social Work – Cum Laude), D Litt et Phil (Social Work); non-alcoholic trustee board member of Alcoholics Anonymous South Africa.

Rory's story pulls no punches and is sobering in more ways than one. Read it and be inspired – even transformed, by seeing what happened when Rory began to depend not on alcohol but on Jesus Christ.

Matt Wright

Baptist minister (MA) – Lister Hill Baptist church in Horsforth, Leeds, UK – and author ('The Roman Road' and others.)

This book shows the fire Rory has for the Lord and the amazing journey he has been on. It's a testimony of what God can do in a person's life. Rory has a passion to see this transformation made available to any who needs it.

Anne Lawrence BA, MA, MBA, PGCE
Paul Lawrence Dip Mgt, MA & MBA

Former Centre Directors of Ellel Grange – Ellel Ministries (Currently reside in Leeds, UK.)

About the Author

Rory was born in 1972 in Port Elizabeth, Eastern Cape, South Africa, and grew up in the province of Natal, in a town called Ladysmith. His father was an Assemblies of God pastor (currently retired) in various South African towns.

Rory was involved in the SCA (Students Christian Association) at school and was made chairman of the SCA in his final year. He then went on to do courses in both Homiletics and Hermeneutics within the church. After completing his military conscription in the South African Defence Force's Engineering corps, he studied for three years as a Medical Tech., then after six years switched careers and went into construction. In 2010, he completed a certificate in Bible Theology through SATS (South African Theological Seminary).

Rory married his wife Pauline in May 2009, and they moved to the UK in October 2016. They now reside in Leeds, West Yorkshire, where Rory is actively involved in their local Baptist church, Lister Hill. He works full-time as a Construction Site Manager, whilst in his free time he works to help people overcome various dependencies, as well as continuing to write.

From 1990 to 2006, Rory drifted away from the Lord, and for seventeen years his life changed to one of 'living hell'. The road back was painful and long, but through it, he experienced an amazing miracle that brought him into the close and personal relationship that he has with God today. Since then, he has been involved with, and supported, many recovery institutions and has started a few of these Christian support groups in various churches. With it has come an overwhelming desire to help people struggling with dependencies and those who seem to battle to experience a closeness with God.

The author can be contacted at: *rmagrath2@gmail.com*

This Book is dedicated to my Lord
and Saviour, Jesus Christ;
in gratitude.

"For in Him we live and move,
and have our being."
(Acts 17:28a)

May Your glory shine!

Acknowledgements

First, I want to thank my Father God through Jesus Christ for what He has done in my life. If I hadn't been an alcoholic, I would not have come to the point of desperation where I was truly willing to seek Him; I was so self-centred. I want to thank Him for the pain and hardship He gracefully granted me. I now know that while I went through 'living hell', He was looking after me the whole time. Ego makes you feel consciously separated from God, and I believe this must be a bit of what hell is like. If it were not for this experience, I would not have the wonderful relationship I have with Him today. Because of His love, mercy and grace, I am living a life of peace, joy and contentment.

Secondly, I would like to thank the organization Alcoholics Anonymous that took me in, loved me, and placed a spiritual set of tools before me, which ultimately helped me find God and sobriety. To all its members: guys, you saved my life; may God richly bless you all. I wish to state emphatically that the organization of AA as a whole has no opinion on any of this book's writings; they neither endorse nor oppose anything written here. I write this to honour their 10th Tradition.[1]

I would like to thank the following people:

- *My mother and father.* Thank you for your unceasing prayers; I believe that they did more for me than anything else. I know it must have been difficult to let go and to keep interceding in love while I did my thing. I love you both dearly.
- *Daniel M.* I want to thank you for allowing God to use you to introduce me to the Program. If it were not for your simple, unpressurising approach, I would never have come into the Program.
- *Raj I, Blackie H and Vossie D.* I'd also like to thank you for sponsoring and mentoring me; your support and raw love has been invaluable.

---

[1] See *www.aa.org/assets/en_US/smf-122_en.pdf* for a list of the AA traditions.

- *My wife, Pauline.* Thank you for being so patient and gentle with me over the years. Thank you for your pledge not to drink either and for participating in the recovery Program and finding your own freedom while learning to understand me. I am glad you never knew me in my drinking days. I love you with all my heart.
- *Mike C.* I want to thank you for working through the steps of the Program with me for so many months at 05:30 in the morning. The sessions spent in the car have brought me into a much closer relationship with God. I pray there is a special place reserved for you in heaven.
- *The many people whom I fought and clashed with over the years.* I thank you for being there so that I was able to break my old nature down. I want you to know that I love you all and have prayed deeply for each and every one of you.
- *Professor Wim Roestenburg.* I want to thank you for your timeless input, for your dedication and love for alcoholics, and for your wonderful, clearly-stated explanation of our Program. May you too find the peace and serenity you so freely aid others in finding.

I would also like to thank the following authors and speakers:

- *The late Charles Chamberlain.* I thank him for his living example of sobriety. His talks have revolutionized my entire outlook and have given me a sobriety of unparalleled joy.
- *The late C S Lewis.* I thank him for his simple explanation of Christianity. Because of this, I have found my own relationship with God and not that of someone else.
- *The late Oswald Chambers.* I thank him for his God-inspired writings. His daily readings have birthed a new love and focus into my walk with God.

There are many people that have had input into my life over the years: family, friends, members, organizations, authors and clergy. I thank each and every one of you. May God bless and keep you all.

Contents

Preface

The first thing that I'd like the reader to understand is my total powerlessness. I do not want this to come across as false humility, but in order to emphasize that all power and glory belongs to God, I am willing to take that chance. The awareness of my powerlessness has ended up being my greatest asset.

> For in _Him_ we live, and move, and have our being.
>
> Acts 17:28 (emphasis added)

I thank God for the grace to see this. Letting go practically, however, is much tougher; I have to surrender on a daily basis.

If any person has absolutely no skills in an area of their lives, God is in total control. My final school mark for English was a D; nothing exceptional. My spelling leaves something to be desired (thank the Lord for spellcheck), and I tap away at the keyboard two-fingered. I have never written anything that has been published. I therefore want to give all the power, honour and glory to my God and Saviour, Jesus Christ.

I would never have dreamed of attempting a book on my own. It just never entered my mind. Maybe dreams of owning my own company, swimming for South Africa or becoming a top lawyer – nothing big, you know! Writing a book was just not on my list of 'hip' things to do. I really love the Lord, though; if you let go of everything and take a chance trusting Him, most times there is a big surprise waiting – how can anyone say that following Jesus is boring!

I sobered up on 29th May 2006, and my sponsor said I should not attempt anything else in that first year of sobriety except to work the Program and not to _drink_. Towards the end of that first year, I had written down a few things during my quiet times and time spent working the Program; nothing major. I started to go back to church and recommitted my life to the Lord; I simply told Him that I wanted to live for Him and help others. It was around September 2007, and I remember talking to the pastor about my recovery from alcoholism. He started to share a little of how there were people in the church who were suffering terribly with alcohol-related disorders: wives with alcoholic husbands at home who did not want to come to church, women who drank on the sly and were too scared of ridicule to ask for help, and then there were people who came to the pastor for help with drinking – both Christian and non-Christian. He told me of the many other addictions and disorders that afflicted people in the church; things such as drugs, sex, pornography, gambling, over-working, overeating and the like. There were those, too, who suffered agony and abuse from alcoholic spouses, parents, family members or other loved ones. I felt that something was needed to cover all these disorders and many reoccurring problems people were battling with; problems that they just couldn't seem to break free from.

There is a cry and prayer that goes out daily to God, to deliver people suffering with some addiction or dependency disorder, both by the person afflicted and by their church leadership and families; but this is most often to no avail. The fear of judgement and rejection – both perceived and experienced by addicted Christians and non-Christians in the church – seems too heavy to many of us to ask for help.

There are many reasons why church leaders and members may judge or reject alcoholics. This is not intended as a criticism; I am merely stating the fact. Indeed, I believe that in 99% of these cases, the response does not come from a sinful heart or from evil intent. Most of this 'rejection' and 'judgement' is no doubt subconscious and not of a malicious nature at all. The churches as a whole do love us 'alkies' – I believe there are many churches praying for us – but they often do not know how to help us or do not understand our disease properly. Therefore, it is difficult for them to relate to us and people often keep an 'emotional' distance. We are extremely sensitive people; we pick up on the 'uneasiness' of others, who may just be feeling helpless, and this makes us feel rejected or judged. We start feeling that God is not there for us, that the church is hypocritical, and we may decide there is no point in pursuing any kind of help from God or His church. We can feel that, for whatever reason, His power and help are unavailable to us. Christians who suffer from alcoholism or other dependency disorders often do not want to entertain recovery Programmes, as they view many of these organizations as cultish, or at the very least, non-Christian.

A deep sadness came over my heart at that time. I understood how all these suffering people were feeling – I'd been there. I felt empathy for the church and their leaders, as they wanted to help but just seemed to have little or no success in this area of addiction. My heart bled for the many spouses and family members who were being abused or had to watch their loved ones slowly die. I know now that God had placed this burden on my heart.

I woke one morning in the first week after speaking to the pastor of our church; I was going to write a book. I often used to think of diet books as 'another one of *those* diet books'; each year, it seems, a few more come out. I had doubts as to whether God really wanted another 'help book' and so I prayed about it. Amazingly, I remember seeing the whole layout of the book and reasons for writing it come to mind in a strong way. It is for those people in, or with some connection to, the church, who have approached the church or the Lord Jesus Christ – either if they are the sufferer or are involved with the sufferer – and have not found any deliverance from a dependency disorder. *I was that person!* My journey had taken me away from the church for this reason, and it was a difficult and extremely painful journey back – I fought myself and God all the way.

It doesn't have to be this way for others. As long as the reader is completely *honest,* entirely *willing* to do the simple work required in the book, and *persists,* even in the face of possible initial 'failure', God will remove the desire to drink from them (or whichever dependency disorder they may have). The content of this book is not revolutionary or complicated; but it is God-inspired and powerful. I do not believe this approach to be the only way to recovery, but it was how I found sobriety, and I do believe it to be the most successful way.

People are all too often faced with ridicule and dismissal, and they can be in such a fearful, dark place that rejection is just too unbearable to think of. This book can be read and worked through without anyone else having to know about your business, so that you can get well without any fear of discrimination whatsoever. There are parts of the book where interaction will be necessary, but I believe that the Lord's grace will be granted to the sincere reader such that a sufficient amount of fear will leave them at the appropriate time, allowing them to make the connection with the relevant people – it certainly worked that way for me. As the reader is most likely to be tackling their recovery alone at first, I felt that the book had to be precise; there had to be a step-by-step, exact method to follow which would remove most of the difficulties in understanding the process. I have aimed to do this, answering as many potential questions as possible. I have taken most of these from the questions I asked, and also from questions that have been asked of me over the years.

I have included tables and templates that I used in working through the steps, so that the person doing the work can break it down for themselves and see where they are headed. I have also given as much of an explanation of my understanding of each step as possible. This will be read long before coming to the actual working part of the Program but should be re-read while going through each step. Just remember that if you don't agree with something, that's OK, you don't have to. I didn't agree with a lot I have written at the beginning of my journey. The main thing is to press on and see what you can identify with.

This book is not just for those with drinking problems; the content will help any and every reader. You see, the philosophy contained herein is not new. It goes back to the times before the Bible. I believe the nature of our problems on earth come from the original sin: *self*[2]. This book is merely my personal experience of the journey God took me on to help me overcome my alcoholism – and self, to a degree. It is very practical and shows you step-by-step *exactly* what you need to do to overcome your obstacles. I have tried to make it that simple because it was that simple when I did it. You do not need to understand; you need to do the work. Reading the book might bring some understanding and relief, but it is only when you *do* the work that the miracle takes place; that's biblical:

> *But wilt thou know, O vain man, that faith without works is dead?*
>
> *James 2:20*

Do not get anxious at the thought of working something; this time it is laid out step-by-step in a simple format. I used to be so afraid during my drinking that I could not even go and pay my electricity bill, which is why I have given easy suggestions to follow all the way through the working section of the book.

It will be mentally tough at times, but we have God; and we can pray. I believe this book will benefit anyone struggling with any problem or issue that recurs: people who want to know more about the disease concept of addiction, anyone battling through personal involvement in the lives of people suffering from dependency disorders, and of course those suffering themselves from any such disorder. More than anything,

---

[2] Here 'self' refers to selfishness, self-centeredness, self-focus, self-attention, self-obsession, self-absorption etc.

I pray that some of what is written here will help bring you into a closer, more meaningful relationship with God.

You will notice that I have made mention of other people by either names and initials, or pseudonyms. This is to protect their anonymity and the organizations to which they belong. There will be quotes from other authors and books, but I have put nothing in here that I have not found to be true in my own personal experiences. God teaches us things in life mainly through other people, and when I have quoted others, it's because it was impossible for me to rewrite their words without losing the effect or meaning of what they said. God gave them the words and sometimes it's best to leave it just like that. Also, I would like to mention that all Bible quotes are from the King James Version, unless otherwise stated.

I firmly believe in God's timing. I praise Him for the patience He has shown towards me. I am over nine years sober as I finish putting this book together, and I praise Him for every sober minute. During this time, I have written and put together pieces as I felt God lead or inspire, and I have sat and edited as I've compiled the book. I did not want to have it edited too much because I wanted God's inspiration to come through. I have tried to put the words in simple 'easy' style English. It is a miracle that happened to an ordinary person, and it can happen to you. I trust His light will shine through those 'cracks'. May the grace of God's Spirit touch you and heal you as you read this book. Amen.

Foreword by Wim Roestenburg

Rory's story is one heard so many times all over the world in so many different places; towns, communities and at AA groups; involving so many friends, family members, loved ones, employers, doctors, clergy, therapists and ordinary community members. Yet this particular story about the debilitating effects of alcoholism is different – it is not about the end, but about a new beginning, a journey into sobriety, and it has a positive and constructive twist to it. His story is one of hope, of change, of making amends in relationships that at some stages were totally hopeless.

Self-reflection is a powerful tool towards healing and growth and helps one gain perspective and insight, and this is exactly what Rory has achieved in this gripping story of the betrayal of alcohol that has caught many people from different walks of life.

As a former addiction counsellor, an educationist and university professor in social work, it remains a mystery to me how some people are able to turn away from alcoholism and lead lives of sobriety whilst others completely lose themselves in alcohol and are unable to quit. Much of what is known about alcoholism is that its causes are multiple and complex, that it is a chronic condition that has characteristics of an illness. If untreated, alcoholism eventually leads to death or severe impairment, and leaves a path of destruction in the lives of those who consider them significant to the alcoholic. The alcoholic needs help, requires another human being who mirrors reality to them at the right moment, time and place when they are vulnerable, and who is willing to offer a glimpse of insight. The mystery of recovery is greater than the mystery of causality. For here we have a person, desperate, yet stuck and unable to see, who somehow manages to turn away and restart life. Needless to say, such recovery depends on the person him/herself, on the love of fellow human beings who understand the phenomenon, and most of all, on God, who is almighty and can change any person's life permanently. These three elements – the *self,* the *family* and *God* – can offer hope to anyone who is a desperate alcoholic.

Of the multiple treatments currently available, most have only some measure of success, but success is relative to the alcoholic's personal circumstances, his self-motivation, support systems and the sources he relies on for the future sustainability of a sober lifestyle. One such treatment is the 12-step self-help Program, or the Alcoholics Anonymous (AA) approach to alcoholism. 12-step programmes are aimed at acceptance of alcoholism as a chronic disease with no outcome and chance to be cured. This approach regards the only alternative to drinking as staying sober, even if it means for one hour, one day or one week; and then working through a programme that is based on sound principles of behaviour change. The AA approach has helped many people and Rory's story gives an account of how the 12-step Program has helped him survive and begin on the road towards recovery. The beauty of the AA approach is that it is run by alcoholics for alcoholics, and support by fellow group members is a major component of the success of the Program. Working through the AA traditions, the Big Book and applying these to your life leads the recovering alcoholic towards self-examination, making amends and healing oneself from the devastating effects of social and relationship failures.

Read Rory's story and discover one person's road to recovery...

Prof. Wim Roestenburg PhD
Professor of Social Work and non-alcoholic trustee of Alcoholics Anonymous, South Africa

Introduction

As I mentioned in the preface, my writing skills left something to be desired. I thank the Lord that he uses the weak in his plans:

> *But God hath chosen the foolish things of the world to confound the wise; and God hath chosen the weak things of the world to confound the things which are mighty.*
>
> *1 Corinthians 1:27*

I would therefore like to give a few little hints and explanations in order that you may get the most out of reading this book and doing the work needed for this vital connection to God's power.

Before you read or work each time, I suggest you pray. The power comes from God, and praying is our most direct communication with Him. Pray for grace, understanding, peace and willingness. If you do not believe in a God, that is alright; I was convinced I didn't believe in Him when I did the Program and it still worked. Just keep an open mind to the idea that there may actually be a being or spirit with a power that is greater than your own. I had gone the atheist route, and what helped me to grasp this concept of something wielding a power greater than myself was to understand the power that the bottle wielded over me. If I'd had a drink or two under the belt, and there was a bottle in front of me, I could not leave it alone. The fact that the bottle with liquid in it was just an inanimate object and I never had enough power to leave it alone made me realize that even a lifeless object wielded more power over me than I could resist. This realization helped me open my mind up just enough to the possibility that there might just be a 'being' of sorts that held more power than I did as well. I found this to be enough. (The exact expression of this understanding was not known to me then, as you will see later in the book.) If you are desperate enough, as I was, you will probably be willing enough to continue reading.

You will see that I have made reference to alcohol and my recovery from it. Please make a mental note to replace 'alcohol' with whatever dependency disorder you may have. If you have an eating disorder, replace 'alcohol' with 'food'. Remember that if you have a spouse addicted to gambling, for instance, you are *also* powerless over gambling in his life. This means that you too fall victim to the power of gambling, albeit indirectly. You will read in my story that I delved into narcotics of numerous types, and I touch briefly on my sordid sexual past as well. I have needed recovery in both these areas of my life. I have also found recovery from rejection, fear of economic insecurity, loneliness, boredom and a few others. On my first-year sobriety birthday, God's grace allowed me to stop smoking cigarettes using this same Program. I had to want to stop, of course. The road to freedom from other character defects, such as anxiety, anger, frustration and bad language, is one that is still 'under construction'. I am in construction by profession, and sometimes the language that I use is shameful. The thing that upsets me the most about it is that it is not a very good witness for Christ, and I'm sure this hurts the Lord. But I understand and hang on to this scripture:

> *There is therefore now no condemnation to them which are in Christ Jesus, who walk not after the flesh, but after the Spirit.*
>
> Romans 8:1

I need to live by this, otherwise guilt will destroy me; I am not where I want to be, but, thank God, I'm not where I was! I have also had to deal with addictions within my family and have been hurt and warped by it. I have needed to recover from this. In my recovery from all these things, I have used the Program contained in this book, and it has worked. Not all at once, however; some things have taken six years to recover from, like the fear of economic insecurity. However, this time there is a new, underlying, almost subconscious, excited trust and hope in me that things will be OK. This was never there before I actually did the work outlined in the Program. In short, no one is excluded from benefitting from this Program. I pray that even if you are just reading this book out of curiosity, God will touch your life; and I believe He will.

I found that the most crucial aspect to doing this work was an attitude of total willingness. In order for me to be this committed to anything, I had to be convinced that I was in the same category as the people who had recovered – the ones telling me that their recovery was found in this Program. That is why I have put so much of my own personal experience into the book; I cannot give away what I don't have. I know this is not the only path to recovery, but I have tried many others and this is the only one that has worked for me. When reading these experiences, you are unlikely to find an exact match to your own, but try to identify with as much as possible of what you read; try to relate to the outlook and 'feelings' described. You will probably find that you can relate to quite a few of the stories. Once you make this connection, you are ready to do the work. However, I recommend that you continue to read the book in the sequence and format in which it is laid out. There might be a few misgivings that will rarely be dispelled *properly* before you start the working part of the book. Whether you are someone who has a dependency disorder or not, please read everything and try not to skip chapters or sections; this will give you a broader picture of everyone involved and how they are viewing the situation.

Another important principle I discovered was not to get too serious when reading the book and working through the steps. Sure, this is a serious business, as we are dealing with life and death and insanity, but I found a serious approach to be not much help. If you make mistakes, don't get down on yourself, just maintain an attitude of willingness and continue. One of the most liberating feelings for me was the freedom from guilt. I'm far from perfect and that is why I need God. This understanding allowed me to 'be cool', as they say. Laugh at yourself because, even if you don't think so, you're very funny! Your openness, willingness and honesty are all that are required from you – the rest is God's job. You might experience a lot of fun in this journey which you never thought possible.

I have included a personal story of a woman who lived with someone suffering with a dependency disorder. I hope to create a bit of diversity so that you may see different outlooks on the same solution, and I also hope that those who have not been able to fully relate to my experience might do so in another's story. You may very well be able to relate to her, and hopefully see where you might have become unwell by another person's disorder.

Once you start doing the work, I suggest doing it to the best of your ability. I urge you to remain willing and not to lose heart. Do not worry if it is going slowly and not 'working', or if you feel you are missing things, or that you might not be doing it 'perfectly' enough to attain this vital spiritual experience. You do not even need to understand what is going on to do the work. The key lies in your willingness and honesty. Remember, God looks at your heart. As long as the sincere desire to recover is there, and you continue with the work, God will do the miracle.

Keep at it. If you are like I was, you will have nothing to lose. It might take time but ask God for the strength to stick at it and not to get despondent.

You will see that I have written a piece about working with others and how to set up a recovery group in your community. I cannot over-emphasize the importance of trying to do this as part of maintaining your sobriety and well-being. This is also scriptural:

> For where two or three are gathered together in my name; there am I in the midst of them.
>
> *Matthew 18:20*

Remember this very important suggestion when all else fails (this includes praying, fasting, counselling etc.), trying to help another person with whatever they may need will save your life. As I wrote in the preface, our true problem is self-centredness. Even though I am recovering from my disease, ego, pride and self[3] sometimes consume me to the point where contact with God is just impossible. By working with another, I am able to 'get out of myself', and in that time, there is enough levelling of pride for God to be able to step past my self-will and help me. It sounds funny, but that is exactly how it worked in me.

---

[3] Throughout the book I will often refer to these three together, as they are very closely related and, in certain contexts, even synonymous. All of them have one key element that is destructive: they are all self-focused. I believe that this element is the biggest problem facing people, and the main hinderance to recovery. Even if you cannot see all three of these issues in yourself, you might be able to identify one or two of them. For example, you might not consider yourself to be proud, but perhaps you can admit that you have a bit of an ego. 'Self' is an attitude of, "This is all about me." Sometimes the book will use words such as 'self-centredness' or 'selfishness'. Ego means (quoting Charles Chamberlain), "The feeling of conscious separation from God (in other words their creator), good (being able to do the right thing in any given circumstance) and life (the normal everyday things people do and are involved in)." This kind of thinking is very self-centred, effectively, "I am a very special case – different to the entire universe by being so good/bad/different." This is also a form of pride. In this book, the word 'pride' means thinking, "I am more special than anyone else, and therefore in a category of persons all on my own." Again, such thinking is self-centred. Here, 'pride' has nothing to do with one's dignity, which is a different meaning of the word. So, in summary, 'self' focuses on 'me' and believes me to be unique ('ego') and supremely different ('pride').

Note that I said, *try* to start a recovery group or work through the Program with another who wants help – but don't force the issue. God is in control and His timing is always perfect!

Finally, we need to consider the right attitude when going into something 'new'. I believe that right attitude comes from right thinking, and right thinking comes from proper understanding. Understanding comes best through experience, simply because we humans generally don't like to follow advice – even more so those of us with dependency disorders. Trial and error is the usual order of the day. Think about it; if there were another way that you knew you hadn't tried, like a special new pill on the market or something, do you think you'd be reading this book? I know for myself, I never would have. I first had to try every single easier way before I'd give this Program a try. We humans are like a stream of water; we always try to follow the path of least resistance. The irony is that the true path of least resistance is often the one that appears most obstructive to us. My prayer is that you read this book and realize that you are dealing with life and death here; *yours.* I pray that the Holy Spirit will open your eyes to be able to see where you are headed. I believe that a person can reach a point of desperation without having to lose everything (the so-called 'rock bottom'). This is as long as they can clearly see that they are on the same path of destruction as someone else was and identify with another who also has a dependency disorder up to the point they are at in their own lives; after which they can follow the other person's story of destruction to its eventual 'rock bottom'. I believe that as long as they can see themself on the same path, the reader will become willing and desperate enough to try the Program.

One of the biggest hindrances to recovery is an attitude of expectation. I don't mean you should work through this Program thinking nothing will happen, but rather, try to keep your mind neutral as to the 'how' and 'when' of it all. Expecting God to work in such-and-such a way, or in a certain time frame, is all part of our sinful self and cuts us off from God (the true power). An expectation becomes another expression of our self-will. Our God is awesome, majestic and all-powerful, and we, as His small-minded creations, try to put Him in a box. We want to 'plan' our recovery in our minds. "Right," we say, "first, I will battle off the hangover; then, I will be a bit ill; then, I will feel fine and the cravings won't be there anymore. And if it doesn't work like that, then I'm not going to waste my time on the stupid Program anymore." Most of us that say this haven't even worked past the third step of the Program. If you read the New Testament part of the Bible, you will notice the number of different ways in which Jesus healed blind people, for instance. He even used some very unconventional methods, like spitting in the mud and caking a guy's eyes with it.[4] Oswald Chambers wrote:

> *When we are certain of the way God is going to work, He will never work that way anymore.*[5]

I have found this to be true so many times in my life. We must not let expectations rob us of a miracle; 'let go and let God,' as they say.

The last attitude to consider is that of 'having the right motive'. Do not place yourself under any illusion as to what might happen when you sober up; the only thing guaranteed is sobriety. I have experienced sobriety in the way that the late Charles Chamberlin (Chuck C) defined it at his talks at a men's retreat at Parla Mesa:

> *Sobriety is the ability to live peacefully, joyfully and comfortably with oneself.*

I found this to be the case, no matter what the circumstances were. Yes, there were scary, worrying times, but underneath all that fear there ran a current of peace and comfort. This Program often brings much more to a person's life, but it promises nothing more. Therefore, you need to adopt the attitude that you are doing this Program because you do not like the person you are becoming or have become. In other words, you are doing it for yourself, not for anyone else.

The reason I say this is that you can sober up for your wife who might be threatening to leave you, and when you get sober, she might still leave you. Then you have lost the reason you actually stopped drinking for in the first place, so what stops you from going back to it again? It might not be that severe a scenario – you might stop drinking because your kids don't respect you. One day your frustrated kid might turn to you when you're telling them to clean their room and say, "Shut up and leave me alone. You're just an old drunk anyway!" You might say to yourself, "I stopped for them and this is the thanks I get? I'll show them who's an 'old drunk'!" Before you know it, you're off to the races again. The gambler might say, "I want to visit my folks in New Zealand, so I'll stop

---

[4] See John 9:6.
[5] Oswald Chambers; *My Utmost For His Highest;* daily reading, 1st August

gambling in order that I can save enough money." When they call their family to say they want to come and visit in December, they are told that their parents already have guests coming to visit over that period and they cannot accommodate them. This person will probably go straight into the nearest casino for a little 'consolation'.

There are hundreds of variations on these examples. Do the Program for *yourself*, because you have come to the realization that you do not want to be the person you've become. I believe this to be one of the strongest motivations.

Do not get me wrong, though; those who have stuck with the Program and have done it thoroughly usually reap wonderful rewards in other areas of their lives – I have, and still do. I've seen all kinds of relationships restored, good jobs landed, promotions; even material gain. But I don't know of a case where anyone achieved any of these *things* when these *things* were the actual motivation for doing the Program. Rather, these came as a by-product after change occurred.

Always remember that self was the problem. Alcohol was the solution that turned sour (excuse the pun) and stopped working.

May the Lord our God do for you what you could not do for yourself.

PART ONE

Understanding Recovery

Breakthrough into Recovery

The Miracle

My Miracle (written in September 2008)

My dad became a Christian when I was three years old, he became an ordained minister a few years later, and I have grown up in a Christian home ever since. I never saw my parents drinking alcohol in all the time I lived at home; not even once by either of them.

I made my personal commitment to God at age eight, was baptized at twelve, went to church twice a week, went to youth on Fridays, did an Alpha course, Homiletics course, Hermeneutics course, and was made chairman of the S.C.A. (Students' Christian Association) in my final school year. I once witnessed my dad cast a demon out of an Indian woman, for real. In all this time, though, nothing special had ever happened for *me*. I remember asking my mom why miracles never happened to us. She just said that they did in all sorts of little ways, which I then just put down to 'pot luck', so to speak, and not actual miracles. So, I knew there was power, but it was just not available for me, it seemed. This is why I have called my story 'My Miracle'.

I remember feeling different to everybody else at the tender young age of three. I went to a nursery school from this age and remember all the kids wearing woollen mittens when the winter came.

I thought, "I gotta get me a pair of these gloths [gloves]."

So I went home and asked my mom if she could knit me a pair. She asked me what colour and I said dark green, my favourite colour, and she proceeded to knit me a beautiful pair of dark green woollen gloves. According to my mom, when she gave them to me, I looked at them a little apprehensively and asked why these gloves had so many 'fingers'. She realized then that I had wanted mittens and said that she was sure some of the other kids would have 'fingered' gloves and not to worry.

Off I went to school sporting my new dark green gloves, only to run into hordes of kids all wearing mittens! They, of course, laughed and teased me; the usual banter one would get from horrible little 'rug rats' of that age. But it shattered me; I felt devastated and shameful inside, out

29

of place and *different!* Needless to say, I never wore them again. I took them off, threw them in the bin and sat in the sandpit crying. I was burning inside with humiliation and this turned to anger at the other kids. Believe it or not, I started 'bunking'[6] nursery school by hiding in a bush at the bottom of the garden. My mom's feisty friend in her clapped-out old white Peugeot 504 would come to take me to the school, but when I didn't appear after she tooted her horn a few times, she would drive on. I would later go indoors and tell my mom that I had been waiting but the woman hadn't turned up.

This feeling of being the odd one out persisted throughout my schooling; the continual feeling that I never quite fitted in, that all the other kids were 'normal' and that I had to do my best to become 'normal' and fit in. So, I used to try all sorts of weird shenanigans to be accepted or noticed; I guess, what people would call showing off. I see now that this just added fuel to the fire. If there was a sports day and the kids were all in vests, I inevitably rocked up in a T-shirt. If black shorts were the order of the day, guess what? I would be wearing a nifty pair of dark blue shorts. Some awful little individual would usually say something like, "Ha, ha, ha! Look, Rory's parents must be colour blind or something!" To hide the embarrassment, fear turned to rage, and I'd punch the little bully right in the 'snot box'! I would get caned and the other kids would dislike me even more. They sometimes sent some abnormally advanced adolescent who was shaving already (in grade 8[7]), to come and pulverize me! I sat once more outside the circle of normality feeling very sorry for myself.

I just couldn't get it; I did well at sports, got good grades and generally did all the things that seemed right and yet I felt so isolated, even with all the kids around. Looking back now, it sends shivers down my spine when I realize the power of perception. The real truth was that I was just like all the other kids, and they actually didn't consider me too different from the rest; they teased each other equally. The difference was in the way I felt about myself. What I now realize is that this feeling is *ego*. One of the best definitions of ego that I have ever heard was by Chuck C, at a talk to a group of recovering alcoholics at a retreat at Parla Mesa. He said that ego was…

---

6 skipping
7 year group for children aged 12-13

...the feeling of conscious separation from God, good and life.

This was exactly me. This, I believe, made me a prime candidate for alcoholism.

During my high school years, I started to resent all the 'hypocrites' in the church. I was no fool and carefully analysed the situation in the greater scheme of things. We went to an extremely charismatic church, which started to look more and more like a show to me. The same elderly lady in her pink and white floral dress would, Sunday after Sunday, go to the front for prayer. Every time the pastor laid his hand on her forehead, she would keel over backwards in as graceful a swoon as is possible for a five-and-a-half foot, hundred kilo woman. I always felt for the poor church usher who had to wrestle with this 'mound' and lay it down in as dignified a manner as possible! There would be the ones who would start speaking in tongues and everybody would get fully involved; chanting, wailing and singing in different tongues. It would always end in a mass crescendo and then die down for the preaching.

I never felt anything in all this. I wanted to 'feel' something and took my turn to get prayed for. But when the pastor prayed for me to receive the Holy Spirit and to speak in tongues, I felt him steadily trying to ease me off my feet with the palm of his hand against my forehead. I stood my ground and pushed with my forehead! He said I was resisting the power of the Holy Spirit entering me – the manifestation of which would be that I would be able to speak in tongues. I said that he was trying to push me over. He got highly irate and told me that I had a spirit of rebellion in me. I thought he was a schmuck! The people in the church would always talk about the 'ones who had received the Holy Spirit' in a sort of hierarchical way. It seemed they viewed the ones who hadn't as not quite having 'arrived' – not godly enough. I remember feeling very hurt, shamed, rejected and once more 'out'. I thought straight away that this stood to reason because I *was* different, remember? I had so badly wanted to 'receive the Holy Spirit' and to be part of it all that I did everything I thought I was supposed to do. I thought it was that problem of 'being different' that kept me out of it, and I couldn't stand the feeling of shame. I vowed there and then that when I left home, I would never go back to church if I could possibly help it. I couldn't 'get the Holy Spirit' in me, and I wasn't considered for miracles by God, and I felt ashamed at not being able to be *normal* with these Christian people.

I went into the army in February 1990 after receiving a university exemption. I wasn't sure what to study, and military conscription had just been dropped from two years to one year. In the army there was no way to tell whether I fitted in or not because we came from all walks of life, dressed the same and ate the same. One thing I did find out, like I'd realized at the odd school party, was that I could not drink properly! This added to my feelings of inadequacy straight away. After training as a Sapper (Military Engineer) and making the Military Band, I was moved to Regimental Headquarters. We answered only to the Regimental Sergeant Major (RSM), and apart from parades and various events, we did our own thing. There were a few 'jols' (parties) we had on the base with ample cheap booze.

We drank like hooligans and within the first hour, I was vomiting and passing out. I would consume about half a bottle of Cane (white rum) semi-diluted with Coke. I remember wishing that I could just hold out better so I could join in the fun. They would tease me at each party, by calling me 'Kots-Kop MaGrath' in Afrikaans, which directly translated meant 'Puke-head MaGrath'!

Things changed after the army when I moved to Jo'burg[8], the big city, to study. I studied Haematology (Med. Tech) through the Medical and Dental Council of South Africa, and a lot of our practicals and exams were done at Wits University. It was there that I found that missing 'something' that had kept me from being normal and fitting in. It was a 'Magic Muti' (medicine) called Snake bites and Pumplemuse shots! Snake bites were half a litre of beer with a shot glass of Blau (a sweet blue liqueur) dropped into the beer mug and then downed; Pumpelmuse was a German grapefruit liqueur. When I had drunk one of each of these in tandem, the most amazing thing happened to me! A warm, 'fuzzy', self-contented feeling enveloped my entire body from head to toe. It gave my mind a rest from worrying whether I fitted in or not. It unleashed my tongue with wit, charm and exceptional vocabulary that must have been hidden in me all along. The effects of this combination were incredible! I was the joke-telling funny guy, the daredevil, the friendly guy, the philosopher and... the *lover!* All the guys liked me, and the girls seemed to take a keen interest in me as well. But the most important revelation was that I felt *normal,* like I fitted in properly for the first time ever! I could even get up on the bar counter, drop my pants and 'moon' the

---

[8] Johannesburg

crowd and still feel very normal. It became a *must* thing I did with all the lads... *my* group!

I analysed the whole thing and sold myself on an idea: that I was suffering with some kind of chemical imbalance that caused me to act stupid and weird; that is why people couldn't accept me. When I consumed a few drinks, something about the alcohol managed to right this chemical imbalance and this allowed me to function and feel normal. Clearly, after that, people were responding to me positively as they would do anyone else. I was sure there was some medication that a doctor could prescribe for me that would do the same thing, but why should I change a winning formula? Meanwhile, to keep up the confidence to continue with this circus act, I was consuming more and more. The lovely thing about all this at that time was that I could carry on until 7am, go home and shower and be at work or lectures at 8am. All this with no hangover (I thought that was normal at the time)! I honestly had the time of my life, lots of friends and any girl I wanted (and there were a few). Of course, there were always copious amounts of booze involved!

Something changed when I reached about twenty-five years old... I woke up one morning and I thought someone must have hit me on the head with an iron bar, which was quite possible in those days. My head was pounding! In the latter days of my drinking 'career', I used to refer to it as "a bastard betwixt the eyes". This was to be my first of many terrible hangovers. I remembered drinking a glass of red wine at a meal before the 'jol', and upon mentioning this to one of my drinking pals, he said that that was why I had this sore head. He said once you started on red wine, you had to stick with it, otherwise you ended up with a 'thick head' like the one I was experiencing.

From then on, I always had hangovers of varying degrees of severity, depending entirely on the quantity drunk and the duration of the spree. I implemented a few of the famous alkies' changes to my drinking habits, mainly to combat the hangovers. I used to switch to a lighter beer; eat a can of sardines and drink the oil before a 'session'; only start drinking at 5pm; make the first beer last an hour. Nothing worked; the 'barbies'[9] would still hit me with a force.

It was around this time that a couple of the 'chicks'[10] we hung out with started mentioning that I might be drinking a little too much. This

---

[9] hangovers
[10] girls

seemed absurd to me and I laughed it off. But it started to spread to one or two of the lads as well, who wanted to know before a 'jol' whether I was going to "take it easy" or not. I very seldom took it easy because it took more and more booze to get the 'normal' feeling. So, they slowly stopped hanging out with me and the chicks that knew me started warning the others to steer clear of me because I got too drunk and obnoxious. I was invited to less and less 'braais'[11] and parties. This then awakened the old feeling of being left out, which, in turn, awoke three terrible 'demons' which would haunt me for a long time to come: Rejection, Fear and Resentment...

I changed my friends and started to hang out with people who drank the same as me and whose social standards weren't as high as those of my other friends. However, I still let that unrighteous indignation seethe within me – they had left me out and pushed me away. I drank more and I drank hard. With these new characters I was a hero because I drank a lot and bought lots of rounds for them. They forgave me the next day when I had been an a*** in many different ways, and I loved this. I kept saying to myself that these were genuine guys because they understood and forgave, and never held grudges. When I look back now, I realize that half of them couldn't remember what had happened the night before, a quarter knew they would fly off the handle and need to be forgiven themselves, and the other quarter knew if they said 'no problem' a free drink would come their way.

My morals started to be affected; stupid flings, drugs, lying, verbal abuse towards others, fights and laziness. This would make me feel morose. I would wake up *dying* of a hangover – hot and cold sweats, pounding head, the shakes, heartburn, dry mouth but not thirsty, vomiting until blood came up – and still continue to have a nauseous feeling all day. Added to this, I had feelings of total guilt, dread, self-pity, misery, fear it would never end, anxiety, depression and disgust: disgust at what I had actually become, what I stood for and what people thought of me.

I started to justify my behaviour by convincing myself that it was always someone else who had caused me to react with whichever inappropriate behaviour I had shown.

For instance, someone might have, in a 'well oiled' state, said, "Ah, c**p, man, you talk a load of rubbish! That bloke is a bastard anyway;

---

[11] barbeques

how can you associate with him?" I would take offence to this and say to him something like, "Shut up or I'll bliksem[12] you!" Naturally he would start to argue and patronize me and I would 'bliksem' him. The bouncers would grab me, give me a few 'love taps' and try to get me outside. I was feeling totally justified in hitting the "parasitical oxygen thief" and would squiggle and perform with the bouncers. They would push; I would hit; they would hit back and bundle me outside just in time to see the cops arriving. The police would ask me to calm down and I would refuse, explaining that I was the victim of verbal assault from the drunk in the bar and had been beaten up by the two "gorillas" at the door. I then proceeded to tell them that if they did not remove the drunk from the bar and arrest the two bouncers, I would call my attorney and lay a charge against them for being "absolutely incompetent" in doing their jobs; I never even had an attorney, of course. They would try to get me into the van for creating a public disturbance. I would resist; they would push; I would hit; they would hit again and then bundle me into the van. I would shout obscenities at them about how they were cowards and that if they came one on one, I would hit them so hard that their mothers would feel it. This never helped my cause, and after spending a night in the cell, I had charges of disturbing the peace, assault of a civilian, assault of a police officer and resisting arrest. This all happened several times, although with slight variations in the course of events. The anger, resentment and hatred grew each time I felt I had been unjustly treated!

At this stage, my father was telling me I was an alcoholic, and I fought him all the way on that one. He had said that I was a "raging alcoholic" and that I would never be able to touch booze again. I guess that's why I fought him so fervently. How was I going to feel normal without my 'Magic Muti'? The other reason was that he always had to be right and I wanted to prove him wrong. But I was worried... I knew that, somehow, I had a problem which needed attention. I just felt too 'tired' all the time to address it.

When I did pluck up the courage to address the problem, I was twenty-eight years old; the year 2000. It was three years since I had sighted this hiccup in my drinking career, and ten years since I had started drinking. I went to a psychiatrist and told him of the *feelings* and *issues* I'd had; things from the past involving heavy bullying and abuse of a

---

[12] hit

sexual nature, which I won't go into (I have received the right counselling since and have got over it). I told him that because I was dealing with all this stuff, I was hitting the bottle a little too heavily, and that I wanted to stop for three months. The real reason I wanted to stop for three months was to prove to my father that I wasn't an alcoholic, and I thought that giving my system a break would be good for me as well. He gave me anti-booze which I took in the morning when I least felt like a drink, knowing later that if I did drink I would be violently ill. I kept it up for three months, mainly due to the discovery of taking ecstasy and smoking 'Zol'[13]. But I nearly died after the doc told me I had to wait another week for the anti-booze to work out my system before I could have a drink!

Now, having rejuvenated my liver and proven my dad wrong about me being an alcoholic, I hit the bottle with a vengeance! Within a week or so, I was right back where I started. In the meantime, I met a bloke who became my buddy, and he introduced me to the weird and wonderful world of cocaine. I never became a regular user of ecstasy or weed because of the feelings of paranoia they created in me, but I liked this 'cocaine stuff'. The fact that I never got addicted to cocaine can only be attributed to God's grace. When I was feeling 'finished' from drinking too much and was slurring and stumbling, a line of coke sobered me up instantly so that I could drink more. It also made me into quite the professor and it was brilliant for the libido (even if the equipment needed a little more coaxing than usual). But the subsequent hangovers from the heavy drinking and the cost of the cocaine (R250 for a gram of about eight lines) made me stop. It was about this time that I moved down to the Natal South Coast from Johannesburg. I would take cocaine once in a blue moon, but the drinking never stopped. This all happened to me in October of 2004.

Before I moved down south, I had an argument with my mother about a disturbance I'd caused with her neighbour. She now wrote me a letter saying she loved me but that I was not welcome at her house any more. This affected me very badly. The guilt ate at me terribly! But, being a true alcoholic, I drank more and put the cause of the argument down to my mother being stubborn. The reason it hurt me so much is that my mother is one of the sweetest people I know. The guilt and depression were almost unbearable!

---

[13] marijuana

I was what they term a 'social binge drinker', although I don't know how 'social' I was when I was drinking. Basically, I never drank alone at home and I didn't need to drink everyday… yet! I normally went to the pub every third day or so and drank myself into a stupor. If it was the weekend, I drank for three days and staggered around half-dying for the next two days. This would allow me to recover nicely for a midweek session, battle through Thursday and Friday, and give it 'horns' from Friday night again. Of course, it hadn't always been like this; it had got to this stage over many years of drinking – it was most definitely *progressive.*

Then the *blackouts* started. I know that people who are not alcoholic think that this is a brilliant cop-out used by the drunk to get away with despicable behaviour, and in many instances, they'd be right. The alcoholic is good at manipulation and grabbing at any opportunity to get out of a sticky situation. But a blackout is something quite real and very frightening!

I was in my local pub one Saturday evening getting nicely *toasted.* I was feeling surprisingly good considering I'd been drinking pretty solidly since the night before. I was enjoying myself immensely and then things tapered down at about 22:00. The Sharks (my provincial rugby team) had had a good win, we'd all had a good time, and the bar was emptying out for the evening. I played one or two more games of pool against some of the die-hards, and then ambled my way home in a merry mood at around 23:00. I specifically remember feeling quite pleased with myself for getting home so early, because I knew I wouldn't feel so rough in the morning. This meant I could have a couple of 'civil' drinks from midday on Sunday and be in bed early evening with no repercussions the next day.

Well, I woke the next day feeling as if I'd been knocked over the head! I was parched, dizzy, disorientated, nauseous, shaky, cold and sweaty. I couldn't understand it; I was in the throes of a full-blown grade 10 hangover! Somebody must have spiked my drink, I thought, because I hadn't drunk that much! When I lifted my head up, I hurled my guts out for about five minutes until just blood was coming up. Finally, after a cold shower and half a bottle of Gaviscon antacid, I managed to calm down to a cold, shaky sweat.

I could not deal with a hangover of this magnitude and knew exactly how to sort the problem out. I threw on some clothes and staggered down to the bar just in time for opening at 10:00am.

I flopped down on a bar stool and grunted an order at the barman. I ordered a beer shandy to start with because I knew that the bitterness of a straight beer would make me vomit and spirits would do the same. He was the barman from the night before, filling in for a colleague who never turned up. He looked very offish and asked me how I could sit here again so early. I told him I felt like death warmed up, and I didn't know why because I'd gone home early. He laughed and said that I'd left at 03:30am after telling him to "stick [his] pub where the sun don't shine" because he wanted to close. Apparently, I'd told him that my friends and I would never come back again and he'd go out of business. I told him that he was lying, so he produced my tab, signed by me! I had drunk two draught beers, two-and-a-half bottles of Vodka and three quarters of a bottle of Jagermeister!

I was gobsmacked, and all I could say was, "Thank you!"

"Thank you for what?" he asked.

"Thank you for not putting the bar up where the sun don't shine," I replied, "because it would have been a messy job to get it back out, and I really needed that shandy!" Still the funny guy!

Anyway, I proceeded to get back on the vodka after the second shandy and was 'tight' again by 12 noon. I'd like to say I learnt my lesson that time, but it was just the first of many blackouts to come.

Then, on 12th July 2005, my nineteen-year-old sister was tragically killed in a car accident with her boyfriend. Now I had a real reason to drink unhindered, and I did. I had started taking the morning drink as a cure for the "old bastard betwixt the eyes"; it was the only thing that worked. I'd forgotten my promise to never drink first thing in the morning like "all those other filthy alkies". The irony of that statement was staring me in the face and I just couldn't see it. It was all still circumstantial in my mind, and everything would come right as soon as my situation improved. I was swimming in a river of poo, and I'd got used to the smell.

I was drinking one rainy day (no work, supposedly) at 12 noon, completely 'blotto'. One of the plumbers that knew me came in and asked how I could be so drunk so early. My reply still disgusts me today. I said, "P*** off, you d***-head; my nineteen-year-old sister was killed in a car accident!" He humbly apologized, bought me a drink and left. As I raised the drink to my lips, a thought struck me: it was ten months after her death! How low can a person go? I was literally using my sister's death as an excuse to sit and get blotto in the middle of the day. I convinced myself that this was why I was drinking and that I needed it to get through this tough time. That 'stinking thinking' is the mind of an insane alcoholic!

I had reached the end, in my mind. I had tried all the tricks in the book to stop drinking and I couldn't. This *thing* had me; I was now 100% sure that I could not stop drinking or even moderate it. The fear of this realization was almost unbearable. I could not keep this pretence up any longer. The pretence I wanted everyone to see was that things were under control. I hated everything about myself and it was getting worse! I couldn't bear hurting people anymore, but I kept doing it.

I had seen the movie *Leaving Las Vegas* in which Nicolas Cage plays a man who loses his wife and then his job. He decides to cash in everything, move to Las Vegas, and drink himself to death. He actually achieves this, but not before he really hurts a prostitute who falls in love with him (played by Elizabeth Shue). I couldn't hurt another person; I just couldn't bear that thought. So, I thought I'd do a similar thing but without the chance of hurting anyone. I would get a piece of land in the old Transkei[14], with a hut on it. The only necessity would be that it needed to be near the bottle store and near the sea. I would drink myself to death away from anyone I could hurt. I look back now and smile at the irony of the fact that I'd never got drunk all by myself before!

Around this time, I had been playing league pool for my local pub. A fellow whom I'd seen a few times 'floating' around the games machines in the bar was asked by the owner to play for us, as one of our team members had left. The second week we were playing, this 'floater' was teamed up with me in a doubles game. We won a tight game that night and I had cause to celebrate and get inebriated. (Of course, I would have had just cause to commiserate and drown my sorrows if we'd lost!)

I asked him what 'dop'[15] he wanted; I was buying.

He told me he didn't drink and that I could get him a Coke.

I said, "OK, and what shooter do you want with it?" How crazy an alcoholic is, as if a shooter wasn't a drink!

He told me once again that he didn't drink.

I asked him, "What, not at all?"

He was very patient and assured me that he didn't drink at all. I remember that I couldn't believe what I was hearing and thought he must

---

[14] in the bush
[15] drink

be one of those mentally challenged weirdos you often find drifting around the South Coast. The funny thing was that he seemed very normal and quite at ease.

I made it my mission to ask another of the drunks who played league pool and hung around the bar about this non-drinker (Daniel M), because they always greeted each other. A few days later he and I got to chatting. When I asked him how well he knew Daniel M, he said that he knew him well enough, as they had both been on the coast a good few years. I started 'fishing' by saying it was crazy that this Daniel M fellow never touched booze ever. He laughed and said, "He ussshhed to get ssho drunk in here that he fell off hisshh bar sshhtool alomsshht every time!" (This guy had a very funny slur when he'd had a few in.)

Now I was interested. I asked him how he had just stopped, or if he was brain-damaged or something. He told me that he'd heard this guy went to "some kind of meetings" but didn't know much more than that. I immediately thought that it couldn't have been Alcoholics Anonymous (AA) meetings, because those were for those "miserable old bastards" whose livers were about to pack up, and he was too young!

In my mind, mainly due to the way television portrayed it, I had always likened AA to a dry dock for ships. You know, when a ship has been on the water for too long they crank it up out of the water by pulley into the docking bay. Then they get to work scraping off the barnacles, fixing the leaks and giving it a fresh coat of paint underneath. Finally, when it is in tip-top shape, they push it back out into the sea for another ten years or so, or until it springs a fresh leak. I pictured these old drunks suffering with peptic ulcers, liver failure, renal failure and general fatigue being hauled into AA. Here they were given medication, a bath, clean clothes, good food, a lot of rest and some good wholesome pep talks. When they were well and in good spirits once more, they were sent off back into the world to resume their drinking careers for the next few years, or until they 'sprung a fresh leak'! The television never seemed to paint a fair picture of AA. There were always old bullets[16] sitting around with a look on their faces like the next-door neighbour's dog had just taken a 'dump' on their freshly-mowed lawn! Just picture a weather-beaten old man with a long-drawn-out monotone voice, irritated with life and everybody, and bored out of his mind saying, "Hel-lo ev-'ry-bo-dyyy... Myyy naaame is Norrr-maaan... aaand I... aaam aaan al-co-hol-

---

[16] men

40

ic..." Now picture the others, all looking very similar, saying, "Hiii... Norrr-maaan..." Who in their right mind would want to join that lot?

Daniel M wasn't ill, and he was only twenty-seven years old, so as far as I was concerned, it wasn't AA meetings he was attending. But I was going to find out which psychiatrist or group he was going to if it was the last thing I did.

I caught up with Daniel M a week or so later. It was a Sunday, late afternoon, on 28th May 2006, and I was 'on like a scone', merrily drunk! It was the aftermath of a bender that had started on the Friday afternoon, and it had been a *biggie*. I hadn't eaten, and I was slurring and battling to stand up straight. Almost everybody had left the pub for the day and had gone home. Daniel M came into the pub for his daily Coca Cola and golf machine game 'fix', and a bit of company, I guess. I had just stuffed a greasy burger and chips down my throat, but I still felt ravenous! I had also drunk so much that I wanted a change of drink and was trying to figure out what it would be. I was actually feeling sick to death with drinking, but the thought never entered my mind to just call it a day. Daniel M came over and asked if I'd eaten. I slurred to him that I had but was still hungry and suggested we go across the road to a seafood restaurant for a change of scenery and a sit-down meal. I told him I would be paying.

I staggered across the road and we sat down at a table near the ablutions. I decided on a double gin and tonic and, as with all my drinks, plenty of ice. I ordered a curry and Daniel M ordered a fish. I asked him if he used to drink "'til he fell off his bar stool" and he laughed and confirmed that he had. I told him about the conversation I'd had with our mutual acquaintance and that he'd mentioned about Daniel M attending some kind of meeting.

He replied, "Yes, I'm an alcoholic and I go to AA meetings on a Monday and Tuesday night each week."

When I told him what I thought AA meetings were all about, he burst out laughing and explained that they were not like that at all.

I then asked if he thought I was an alcoholic, and he told me he couldn't answer that question. I told him that if he, after going to meetings, couldn't tell me if I was an alcoholic, how was I as a lowly drunk going to know? I thought to myself that that was quite a good question, but Daniel M just smiled and shrugged and said I had to come to that conclusion on my own.

I finished my curry, lifted my glass and downed what I thought was the last of my drink. It wasn't! It was the next double gin I'd ordered – neat! I just made the basin in the ladies' toilet; too much in a hurry to check which was which. I filled the basin with both my meals I'd had. It took me five minutes to clean the place up. I paid, and Daniel M had to lead me home across the street; I was too drunk to walk on my own!

The next morning there was a knock at my door at about 10:30am. Earlier on, I had shivered and staggered around my building site, set the boys up, done my orders and arrived home to nurse my hangover. Perfect timing, because I might never have got the material he had for me. It must be remembered that at this time, my mind was formulating a plan to relocate to the old Transkei, so my interest in this AA stuff was actually a last clutch at a straw.

Daniel M's 'enthusiasm' still tickles me pink today! He barged in, slapped a dark blue paperback on the kitchen nook and said, "Read that! Answer the questions in that brochure, but don't tell me what your answers are because I don't want to know! Oh yes, use a pencil because you are going to lie, then you can do it again when you decide to be honest! Cheers!" That was that, and he was gone.

The first thing I thought was, "How dare he say that I'm going to lie?" I was determined there and then to be as honest as I could and answer the questions to the best of my knowledge, just to prove him wrong. (I think that may have been his evil ploy all along!) There was definitely divine intervention in the way Daniel M approached me. He wasn't trying to save me from my misery. If he had, I'm sure I would have thought the whole thing a crock of s*** and bolted!

I got twelve out of twenty questions answered 'yes' and felt quite chuffed with myself, until I read the bottom piece: "If you have answered YES to any three or more, you are definitely an alcoholic." To back up this bold claim of theirs, it added in brackets, "The above Test Questions are used by John Hopkins University, Baltimore, MD, in deciding whether or not a patient is alcoholic." A huge breakthrough occurred there and then; I became convinced in my mind that I was an alcoholic! I had toyed with that thought many times before, but now I knew.

I read Bill W's story starting on page one of that dark blue book *(Alcoholics Anonymous)*. The second breakthrough occurred here; my story was identical to his! Not in the events or anything, but in his description of how he felt and perceived things. This story had been written over seventy years earlier, so no one could be trying to pull the wool over my eyes. We must have been feeling the same. Bill W got sober; maybe I could too. Excitement and hope gripped me as I read the pages. This was mind-blowing stuff here, I thought, until I saw the fourth chapter entitled, "WE AGNOSTICS"!

"Here we go again with this religious stuff!" I thought. I wanted to turf the whole thing. I had done the whole 'God and church' thing and had failed miserably at that. The God I thought I knew was not going to help me with this drinking problem. But I believe that the first paragraph or so saved my life. It said that the Program was not a religious one but rather a deeply spiritual one. It said that we should keep our minds open to the fact that there might be a being greater than ourselves who could possibly be able to help. Reading this made me just curious enough to read on. I praise God that I pressed on with reading the book. It suggested that instead of listening to other people's perception of who God is, why didn't I choose my own perception of Him? They hinted at the idea of thinking of God as one's own, not as other people's. That way God could be seen in the way that you wanted to see Him, and at least you were acknowledging some form of greater being or spirit. This I could do; I decided my God would be loving, forgiving, understanding, patient, graceful, supportive and able. When I look at a portrait of Jesus these days, He is all those things and more! The only thing I had to do was give Him the problem with complete abandon. I am now very grateful to God for the gift of desperation. I was so desperate that I was willing to try anything! I know that I would not have gone through with the Program so wholeheartedly if I were not frantically desperate. I knew I was beaten and could not stop. I had my contingency plan to go to the old Transkei if this Program never worked. So, I let go and did it.

I chose the only God I'd ever vaguely known, the heavenly Father, and said this to Him with all sincerity: "God, if you're there, I need a miracle. My problem is that I can't stop drinking so I'm giving You the problem. I am not going to try. I'm just going to read this book a few times. If I feel like a drink tomorrow, I will just go to the bar and make sure it's a triple, because I can't fight it anymore. I will try to go to one meeting a week and I will be as honest as I can. I will do whatever they suggest I do at the meetings as best I know how, but You've gotta help because I cannot do it alone." Little did I know then that from that moment on I would never feel like a drink again. I climbed into bed and slept soundly. The next day I didn't feel like a drink, but that was normal when I'd had a three-day bender. I asked God to "please help me not to drink today" and I read some of the book. That evening I thanked Him for helping me through the day. The next day, no cravings and I repeated the same pattern as the day before. This carried on and I continued to read; sometimes just a few pages, but mostly a few chapters a day because it was so interesting. I couldn't believe how much sense it all made and how I could relate to each and every story written. I finished the book thrice in five weeks and told Daniel M I wanted to go to a meeting.

The first meeting I attended was on 3rd July 2006 in Margate, and I had been sober for exactly five weeks. Daniel M said that I should not worry if it didn't make sense in the beginning, but I found that it made perfect sense to me right from the start. I was still reeling in the amazement at the fact that I wasn't the only one who felt 'different' and drank to try to feel normal.

The next night I went to another meeting in Port Shepstone, where one of the members was celebrating his 15th year sober. I couldn't believe it! I thought that if I made three months it would be incredible. I listened to his story and once again, it was very similar to my own experience. Two things were said at that meeting, one by him and one by another member, that stuck. He said to me, "You are the most important person at this meeting. We think you can do more for us than we can do for you; you remind us of what it was like for us before. So, take the cotton wool out of your ears and stick it in your mouth. In other words, shut up and listen!" *I'm the most important person there and I'm told to shut up and listen?* Another guy with three years' sobriety said, "Just make sure you keep coming back. The meeting you least feel like attending is the one you most need to be at."

I followed both these pieces of advice and, boy, am I glad I did! They told me to get a sponsor (mentor), so I got three – Daniel M, Blackie H and Rajan I. I owe these men my life. I thank God for giving them to me to be there for me. Raj I said to me, "This is a suggestive Program, so we suggest you do it!" I still laugh at that today and share it at many of my talks. This was how I was introduced to the 12-step Program, and I started doing it as best I could. I remember once feeling a bit down, and I gave Raj a call. I said, "Hi Raj, I'm feeling c*** today." There was a brief pause on the other end, and he replied, "Well then, take your finger out you're a*** and you won't feel it anymore!" I was flabbergasted for a moment and then cracked up laughing. That was all it took, and I had a super rest of the day.

'Three months' came along, and I was very scared a couple of days before 29th August. I knew that this would be the longest stretch without a drink in sixteen years. The guys at the AA group rallied around me with support, jokes and love. I spoke to my God through the Lord Jesus to comfort me, and He did. The day came and went, and I realized then that someone else was in control, that on 29th May 2006, my God granted me my miracle! I can't describe the euphoria I felt when I realized His power, love and amazing grace had been granted me. I felt peace, contentment and excitement at this new-found sobriety. Without a doubt, it is the most incredible experience in my life to date.

The farmer-evangelist Angus Buchan likes to say, "In order for a miracle to occur, the situation must not be difficult; it must be impossible!" I now know this to be true and realize that what my mom said was correct: miracles did happen to me every day. I could have been in serious trouble or killed on many occasions while acting thoughtlessly while inebriated. He had never left me through all those times; what an awesome God!

Looking back, I can honestly say that I am grateful to be an alcoholic. I don't believe I would have been able to find a relationship with God any other way. I have learned so many amazing things as a sober alcoholic that I realize I never would have learned had I not been an alcoholic. It has taught me a new way of thinking; a selfless Christ-like style of living. A very simple phrase mentioned many times in an AA meeting by my Christian alcoholic sponsor Blackie H of thirty years' sobriety has become part of my daily prayer. He says, "Just for today, I want to help somebody. But the big secret is, nobody must know about it!" This so encapsulates a Jesus-modelled Christianity. I have found the following to be true by following that simple phrase:

- It helps me live in the present and focus on what I can do right now.
- It helps me obey the Lord's word (Holy Bible), and thereby fulfil my purpose of glorifying and worshipping Him.
- It assists someone else in need.
- It takes away my self-centredness, because I'm focused on someone else. This in turn takes away any guilt, depression, anxiety and self-pity I might have had. How can you have any of these feelings when you're not focused on yourself?

- It keeps my motives pure. If no one knows that I've helped someone, I can't be applauded.
- I store treasure in heaven, where it counts most, because God sees my heart is true.

Even if this phrase is not understood for all its benefits, the person applying it to their lives will still have a different outlook on life. They will still reap the reward of serenity in their lives, as an unexplainable peace and contentment envelops them. This is the power of the Lord that enveloped me because I was prepared to 'let go and let God'.

In these couple of years that have gone by, I have learned so much and many amazing things have happened for me. I still have to fight resentment (the number one destroyer of alkies), expectations, anger, fear, frustrations, self-centredness and trying to take back control from God. But when I get it right, and I have many slips in-between, He blesses me with an inner peace and joy. This Program is a journey and that's exciting because there is always something to do, with new challenges daily. The thing I really like about it, though, is that I don't have to do it alone anymore.

There was an old man in AA who died last year, a week before his thirty-fifth year sober, who always used to say, "You youngsters that are new here, stick around – things beyond your wildest dreams will come true!" Boy, was he right! I have been able to make and save some good money. I have been single the whole time, but I've recently started dating the most amazing woman in the world. She loves the Lord like I do and I know the Lord will honour us as we obey and honour His word. I have never asked for these things. I have prayed for humility, honesty, love, perseverance and the knowledge and power to do His will for my life.

> *But seek first the kingdom of God and His righteousness, and all these things will be added to you as well.*
>
> *Matthew 6:33*

> *Give and it shall be given to you. A good measure, pressed down, shaken together and running over, will be poured into your lap. For with the measure you use, it will be measured to you.*
>
> *Luke 6:38*

After reading these two passages, I know that God has been truthful in fulfilling His word in my life.

It is a very simple Program – yet I always want to complicate things! Christianity is the same; it is very simple but with huge rewards. I want to have a closer relationship with God. I believe that He wants this and that is why He created us. I feel very humbled when I think how small and insignificant I am and how much I've hurt Him and yet He still wants a relationship with me. I want to help people, and I believe that God Himself has put that desire in my heart. Not because I can, but because I love God and I want to show Him gratitude for what He has done in my life. To me, when I help someone for nothing in return, this is gratitude in action.

All the praise, honour and glory be to the Lord our God! Amen.

The Question

Am I really an alcoholic, or just a heavy drinker?

Anyone who is asking this question will most certainly be facing a drinking problem which I believe to be alcoholism. It has been discovered that alcoholism gets steadily worse over the years, and, indeed, I found this to be true with my own drinking. I never started off displaying alcoholic drinking, although some of my friends reading this might disagree. My drinking was done maybe twice a month with almost never a scene. I would get *happy* but not fall-down drunk. It stayed like this for a couple of years with the odd raucous occasion – nothing to write home about. There were times that I could abstain from drinking for a few weeks, but there seemed to be a spring inside me that would slowly tighten; making me more restless, irritable and discontent as moments went by. It would become so tight that I felt I was on the verge of exploding. I knew that only a few drinks would take away this feeling, and it did. Once I started, though, I could seldom stop, and these sessions would end in trouble on most occasions. The next morning I'd have exchanged the restless, irritable and discontented feelings for depression, anxiety, shame, guilt and dread. The same remedy would follow for these symptoms, with some relief while drinking, but the next day they'd be back, this time multiplied. I would also get physically ill, so I'd have to stop the drinking and recover again. Or I would be the opposite and I'd feel on an absolute high. It would start with me having finished a good week's work where I'd achieved a lot in a short space of time; I'd even get a compliment every so often. I felt like I was riding high on the crest of a massive wave with the world as my oyster. (This may sound like feelings of mania, but that is for discussion later on.) But this wonderful feeling was never enough; I wanted to feel even better. So, I would "just have a few drinks", and off I'd go again. I'd dream up amazing ideas of what I would accomplish, and then talk long into the early hours of the morning about how I would set about achieving these feats. These cycles would get longer and longer and the intervals between shorter and shorter over the years.

When I was first told by my father that I drank too much and that I might have an actual problem, I thought he was being ridiculous: I went to the pub and drank, and so did all the friends I knew. When I went to a wedding, braai[17] or any other social event, people drank. So, if my father, who never drank, was saying that I had a drinking problem, then in my mind, so did the rest of the population. It's funny how I never noticed that they went home after an hour or so, or that they only had one or two drinks in the evening; they were drinking and that was all I noticed.

Other than my father and other Christians, I was sure everyone drank. The conviction of this thought was certainly one of the reasons I never pursued the idea that I might be an alcoholic. I was convinced that I was just a bit 'wilder' than my mates. For me, it was more about striking the balance between having fun and not causing too much trouble rather than drinking too much. The reason I believe that anyone who is asking questions about their drinking has a problem is that non-alcoholics don't think about booze with the same obsession as we alkies do. As a problem drinker, however, I thought that my preoccupation with alcohol was normal practice for everyone. You can imagine my horror at a social when someone turned up having forgotten to bring something to drink; that was just selfish and inconsiderate on their part. Never mind, I would sometimes remedy the situation by retrieving my spare bottle from the car, provided, of course, that I had enough for myself.

In my dealings with alcohol and alcoholics, I found that many things lead a person to believe that they are not alcoholic. However, looking back on my life now, I think the most important factor for me was that I did not want to have a drinking problem. Drinking had become my very real solution, and I just did not want to think of my solution actually becoming my problem. Deep down I had a fear that my solution was turning sour, but the booze helped to keep that feeling suppressed inside me where it belonged. I couldn't have that horrible thought rearing its ugly head in my mind.

Another thing that kept me in disbelief was my circumstances. I never had a girlfriend, I was battling financially, people never understood me, I was lonely, I was bored, there was some tragedy (like when my sister

---

[17] barbeque

died), I never had a decent car, I wasn't earning enough money yet, I was stressed, I needed a holiday to relax and couldn't take one, my family were ignoring me, my boss was horrible to me, and so on. There were a few more, but these were actual excuses I had used with the utmost conviction over the years. My circumstances changed in each of the situations and feelings mentioned, but my drinking did not. There were more excuses; for instance, when I did get a girlfriend and the drinking never dissipated, the excuse just changed to the fact that the girlfriend I had was a mean person – "You'd also drink if you had one like mine."

Then there was the way I drank. Surely, alcoholics drink every day? I didn't drink every day and some nights I went home after three beers. But alcoholism is progressive; the days between drinking became fewer and the stints grew longer. I never drank spirits, just beers. Then, when I did drink spirits, it wasn't white spirits. When it became white spirits, at least it was the more expensive brands.

Can you see the pattern of excuses?

Also, most alcoholics said they could happily drink alone; I never drank alone – yet. I never drank first thing in the morning, only after 12 noon. Then when I did drink before noon, it was only after a breakfast. Then when it was before breakfast, it was because it was weekend. And when it was not the weekend, it was to make me feel alive, get rid of the hangover and calm the nerves. I don't know what I thought the reason alcoholics drank in the morning was for, but I felt sure it was not for the same reasons I did.

There was also my status and lifestyle. I had a good education, a job, rented a place, had a car, had cool clothes, shaved and bathed daily, bought people drinks, drank mainly in bars and bought pricey drinks. I asked myself, "Do alcoholics have and do all of those things? No, they never shave and they drink from suspicious-looking brown bags on park benches."

You see, I believe that it is not what type or form of alcohol you drink, not how much you drink, not how often you drink, not where you drink, not what you do when you drink; it's what it does for you when you drink that makes a person an alcoholic. I wasn't cleverer, nicer, more generous, funnier, cooler, more charming, richer, more good-looking or stable than anybody else. But when I took a few drinks, I felt I was all those things. Some might say, "But I don't think all those things of myself!" – I said the same thing while drinking. But I know now that subconsciously I thought those things and booze allowed me to feel the things I thought.

I drank because it took away my worries, fears, irritations and frustrations; and I had many. After a few drinks, even people I disliked seemed OK. But even this was not entirely true in the end; as I always say, alcoholism is progressive towards the negative end of the scale.

I like to think of myself as a reasonably intelligent person. I knew that the drinking was but a temporary respite, and that the hangover was not going to be worth this brief cure. Despite this knowledge, though, I did it anyway. Why? Because no matter how bad the drunken state was, inside I still felt better than when I didn't drink. That is why I believe it is so hard for an alcoholic to stop drinking. We love the feeling it gives us. A non-alcoholic drinker will have a few drinks, start to feel dizzy and a little out of control. He doesn't like this feeling and stops. An alcoholic has a few drinks, starts to feel comfortable and even in good spirits; he feels in control. So, I think this is another fundamental difference; an alcoholic's system converts alcohol differently to a non-alcoholic's.

Something I've come to understand about myself and other alcoholics is how very touchy we are. I have come to realize that I am an extremely sensitive person. This can be a very positive attribute as far as showing empathy towards other people goes – not so nice when someone runs me down. This happens more often than not without any malice from the other person. For example, my boss comes to check my building site and informs me that he would like me to tidy the site up a bit as it is looking messy. Immediately, the thought flashes through my mind, "What does he mean? Is he trying to imply that I'm a messy person, that I can't do my job? Does he know how much pressure we're under with that breakdown?" The fact of the matter is that he does understand; he is not necessarily cross, he is merely doing his job and pointing out something that needs attention. When I take a few drinks, I lose this sensitivity and the issue becomes 'water under the bridge'. When I sober up and am back at work, however, the feeling returns and intensifies as I say to myself, "You see, he's at me again; he hates me!" I realize there's no 'bridge' for the 'water' to flow under. Instead, then, I often grab hold of a big, fat, juicy resentment to comfort me. In this way, I was often treading on dangerous ground as my reaction to this resentment could cost me my job.

What of control? I am such a perfectionist that it makes me unlikable at times to some people. I believe that there is an element of perfectionism in the character of an alcoholic. This may come as quite a surprise for the non-alcoholic to hear, who may have found a drunk in a messy room rolling in a bed full of vomit from the night before, missing their work, with a bashed car parked askew outside, with the door open and the keys in the bush. But that's just the point; I know that this perfectionism drives people crazy – it drives *me* crazy. People just don't want to cooperate with me. A drink takes this away and I feel quite the opposite. If it works well enough, we don't feel anything at all. By the way, I'm not saying perfectionists are alcoholics, because they're not. I'm also not saying all alcoholics *are* perfectionists; but it does help! (That's a joke, by the way.) It's just that I have noticed this tendency of perfectionism in myself and in other alcoholics I have had dealings with. This causes immense frustration and irritability for the alcoholic, who probably understands he's being unreasonable but cannot get rid of that feeling, yet he knows a few drinks will take it away.

I have a very cynical view of the world and life, and it is one of the things I have to take to the Lord daily in prayer. I see the world as one big horrible mess; a den of liars, cheats, murderers, rapists, child molesters and people who are just out to do everyone else in. I don't want to be a part of that kind of world. When I drink, however, I think the world a marvellous place, and I get right there in the middle; bumping and grinding and loving it all. Now that I'm sober, I don't read the papers or watch the news anymore, and this helps. I know quite a few alkies over the years that have divulged this very same sentiment to me, which I feel is another common attribute of an alcoholic. This feeds our egotistical feeling of separation from life: "I don't belong as part of this world."

People's views of alcoholism are very diverse around the world. I understand this and do not criticize. These are just some of the things that I have observed, understood and experienced; and this has helped incredibly in my recovery.

The Truth

The truth about the problem

I am now going to sound a bit philosophical, or 'silofosical', as I used to say in my drinking days. I once again reiterate that I am no expert and that these thoughts came to me via reading and experience; through the Holy Spirit, I believe. I have been told so many times that I had a drinking problem. I was very proud of my humorous retort, which went, "Yes, I do have a drinking problem; two hands and only one mouth!" Truth be told, I did have a drinking problem, but that was not the *problem* (there's my Irish blood coming out again!) Drinking was my *solution* to the real problem, and this solution had long stopped working and had turned sour. Why, then, could I not just stop if it wasn't my problem? I believe, like many do, that it is because alcoholism is a disease. However, it is not proven to total satisfaction, so I will call it the disease *concept* of alcoholism. Sounds interesting, doesn't it? Let me explain...

Consider the case of an autoimmune deficiency disease. Usually, when a dangerous foreign substance enters the body (such as a bacterium), the body detects it and produces antibodies to 'capture' the foreign substance, which is then destroyed. However, when a person has an autoimmune deficiency disease, their body does not produce these antibodies effectively, so the person finds that they get sick more easily and for longer periods of time.

Alcoholism is similar. Normally, when a person starts drinking, their body begins to sense the danger. After a few drinks they feel they are beginning to lose control and instinctively stop. This is their defence mechanism to protect themselves from consuming too much of a dangerous substance. Not so with the alcoholic. For them, this defence mechanism is broken, so they find themselves battling the effects of too much alcohol more often and for longer periods of time.

This is not a perfect analogy or medical science, so I apologize to all the medics out there, but I found this a helpful illustration. With alcoholism, the point at which a person drinking begins to 'sense' something is happening varies from problem drinker to problem drinker. However, the response to this sense is the same in every alcoholic: an intense craving for more. Some have said that this craving for more was with them from the very first drink. In my case, I believe it took about three or four years. It is very hazy when exactly it happens, which is why a lot of recovered alcoholics refer to this 'crossover' as 'the invisible line'. Once this stage has been reached, the alcoholic will always experience this craving for more. We have now lost the ability to control our drinking and the situation is permanent. There were times that I did not drink, and I could keep this up for a while, but I found that over time, the intervals became shorter and the sprees longer. I almost always drank until inebriated. If I had carried on like this, I would have died or gone insane (wet brain). Many of the people I knew over the years have died from alcoholic suicide, drunk driving, drunken brawls, pancreatitis, liver failure or cirrhosis of the liver. I have been to an asylum and seen someone with a wet brain; it is not pleasant.

The solution, one would say then, is not to drink. This brings us to the second part of the disease; the obsession of the mind. This obsession of the mind, I believe, stems from the original effectiveness of alcohol as my solution. You see, it worked! My brain therefore keeps telling me that it has to work again. If I find myself with those old selfish feelings of restlessness, irritability and discontentedness, my brain tells me the solution lies in the bottle. This is where pure insanity takes over, and I start to repeat the same process over and over again to the same effect. This is the insanity that will be mentioned quite often and is not the same as wet brain. It is merely repeating the same exercise over and over again, each time expecting a different result. I want relief from feeling restless, irritable and discontented, but it does not work anymore. My allergy takes me to a place of blackouts and oblivion. When I come to, I feel all those symptoms of guilt, remorse, shame, disgust, fear, anxiety, depression and physical illness. I beat myself on the head and ask why I did it again. I swear I'll never do it again, but when the old feelings of restlessness, irritability and discontentedness come back, I repeat the whole process again. I tell myself with great conviction as I have done the other hundreds of times before that this time will be different, but it never is. I am in *big* trouble. I cannot drink because I'm dying, and I cannot stop drinking because I know no other solution to ease how I feel. As you can see, we cannot fight this battle here; we have to go to where the true problem lies.

As I've mentioned, I believe the problem centres on *self.* In my life, until I worked through the steps of the Program, I was totally blind to my self-centredness. There is a brilliant Irish saying which goes, "He cannot see until he can see." I remember people saying to me how selfish and self-centred I was. This came especially from my father who was always around and close to me. It really used to irk me as a teenager. What did he know? There is a really good joke which goes, "If there is anything in life you want to know, ask a teenager and they'll tell you!" I was exactly like that. In my mind, my problem wasn't self-centredness, it was a lack of understanding on the part of other people. I had a massive ego and thought I was destined for great things. I was a genius with huge potential and I could not understand why other people could not see it. If they were able to see and understand my potential, they would make me captain of the rugby team, or send me overseas to represent the school in debating. My ego never allowed me to just be in the team, I had to be captain; my team mates needed good quality leadership, and I was their man! I felt hard done by; all the others seemed to get the breaks except me. I was always overlooked, and so I set about rectifying the status quo. I think that this is where a lot of my extraverted behaviour stemmed from. I used to do crazy things in order to be noticed, things that I was petrified to do normally, but I did them because people had to see me and what I was capable of. I was noticed, all right, but for all the wrong reasons and I was never selected. I got so frustrated and angry about all this.

I was totally self-absorbed and all I could think about was myself and ways to better my situation. I had even learned from teachers and other adults that I had to stand on my own two feet and fend for myself. They said I had to look after 'number one' because no one else would. I really could not see just how selfish I was, and it hurt me badly when people told me so. I have passed on my experience to many people who wanted help over the years, and this one thing stands out. I can see the selfishness in them but try not to mention it to them because I know they will not see it. But what is wrong with looking after 'number one'? After all, if everyone did that, the world would surely be perfect? I believe it all has to do with our design; our make-up.

I have a beautiful illustration which came to me from God, I believe. You will read all about my sequestration[18] later in the book, but one of

---

[18] declaration of insolvency

the things my wife and I needed to do was buy a car in her name. The blessings God places on us are truly awesome sometimes. Through a friend, we were able to buy a diesel Audi for a good price and in an immaculate condition. We had had a petrol car before, which the bank was going to come and reclaim. I remember going to fill the new car up and reading "Diesel Only" written somewhere. It took me back to a time once when a petrol attendant had put petrol into the tank of a car with a diesel engine. My friend drove a little way with the car jerking and spluttering until it cut out and stalled at the side of the road. We had to get it towed to a garage where they drained the petrol and flushed out the engine before they put in diesel and my friend could fetch his car. What a waste of time and money! I thought to myself how nice this Audi looked and how fast it could go. I realized, though, that it would go nowhere if I filled it with petrol, never mind how good it looked or what potential it had. I had always preferred petrol cars; they were quieter and didn't smoke as much. I had the habit of always putting petrol in my car, and if I hadn't seen the sign that said, "Diesel Only", I would probably have put in petrol. You see, the manufacturers of this car designed it to run on diesel. I cannot argue with them and say that they are "mental", that I'll be putting in petrol anyway because that's what I like. It doesn't matter what I like or dislike; if I put petrol in, the car will *not perform*.

It dawned on me that I had previously being trying to 'drive' my own life in this way. You see, before I accepted Jesus, I had been an old petrol car that had been going on petrol the whole time. This 'petrol' was actually my self-will. When I accepted Jesus' death on the cross and believed in His resurrecting power at the age of eight, I became born again and had effectively been given a 'new car'. Only, this one ran on diesel. This new life doesn't run on self-will; it runs on *His will*. This 'diesel', or God's will, we run on is the new commandment:

> *Thou shalt love the Lord thy God with all thy heart, and with all thy soul, and with all thy strength, and with all thy mind; and thy neighbour as thyself.*
>
> *Luke 10:27*

How do I best love Him? It is by obeying Him. In order for me to obey Him, I have to know what He wants, and I find this in His instruction manual, the Bible. For me, one of the most profound instructions given to us by God is found in Matthew 28:19-20:

Go ye therefore, and teach all nations, baptizing them in the name of the Father, and of the Son, and of the Holy Ghost: Teaching them to observe all things whatsoever I have commanded you: and, lo, I am with you always, even unto the end of the world. Amen.

It must be remembered that this commission was given to the disciples after they had received Jesus' teaching. I have learnt in life that we cannot give away what we don't have. What we have received, we should freely give away. God created and owns everything, so we cannot love Him by getting Him a bunch of flowers or giving Him a big hug. The way we can love Him is by obeying what He tells us to do, and that is basically to pass on to other people what has been so freely given us by God through His grace.

As we do His will and help others, the result in others' lives is not all that important to us. We cannot 'save' them; only God can. It works just as much the other way in that we cannot damn them either. It doesn't have much to do with us and the other person at all, actually; it is all about God and His relationship with me. We move into a relationship with God at this point, and this is God's greatest desire; to be in a personal relationship with His creation – us! This is just awesome; that this mighty God wants to be in a relationship with 'little ol' me'. It's much bigger, but similar, to an ordinary chap being invited to have dinner at the president's house by Miss South Africa. When I am doing God's will and helping others, my engine purrs; the car cruises. I am at one with my creator. I am filled with peace, joy and contentment. This is how we are designed to function, and it is no good getting angry with The Manufacturer.

It is not easy for us to get rid of this self-will, this ego; mainly because we cannot see it. I thank God that there is a simple solution to this malady, the one found in this Program of 12 steps. We will, however, need continual maintenance, which, I'm happy to say, is also contained in these 12 steps. As was said by the late Chuck C at his talk at the Parla Mesa retreat many years ago, and with which I wholeheartedly agree, "I believe that we can never fully tame or control the human ego. It is a continual daily surrender." For me, it is my cross that I must take up daily. I am so grateful to God that I saw this after thirty-three years.

It is easy to tell when the ego is rising; I feel uneasy and the pain returns. When that happens, I go straight to what the Program says and rectify the situation. As mentioned before, Chuck C, in his talks, describes the human ego like none other: "It is the feeling of conscious separation from God, good (goodness) and life (world)."

When we are in this state, God cannot help us. This is where self-will starts to take over. As an alcoholic, I believe there is no worse case of self-will running riot than could have been found in me. The alcohol made me feel even more justified in my endeavours; it numbed the pain of guilt and eased the tensions of frustration. It allowed me to forget all and dream up even bigger schemes and ventures for myself. There was no place for God, other people, programmes or solutions. In order for me to start dealing with the main problem of self, I *had* to stop drinking. This is the beauty of the AA Program. Having been through the entire Program and having worked with many others who have as well, I believe that no more is needed than a sincere desire to stop drinking. This should be accompanied by open-mindedness, willingness and total honesty.

Letting Go and Letting God

Pain

I was about five or six years old, I guess, when we moved into a new house in Ladysmith. It was small and very old, but it had some really nice trees to climb; what more could a boy ask for? There was one particular tree that I thought was made for me. It grew quite close to the house and had a bough which extended just past the overhang of the roof. It was a perfect access to the roof, and I couldn't wait to get up there. The only problem was that it didn't have many lower branches and I realized it would be a bit of a struggle to climb. I knew I'd do it, of course, and this would mean my younger brother would be too small to make it. As I said – perfect.

There must be a sixth sense about fathers and my dad knew my goal. He told me in no uncertain terms that I could climb any of the trees in the yard, but I was not to climb *that one* (sounds familiar, doesn't it?). He said that it was extremely dangerous and that I could break my neck, or something along those lines; I'm not too sure, I wasn't really paying attention. I spent the next few weeks climbing the other trees, making forts, crawling under the house's suspended floorboards – until I was bored of all that. Then I had to do *the* tree.

I waited until my dad was in his study and was totally engrossed in his work, and then I went for it. I knew I'd only be able to stand on the edge of the roof this time. I'd have to wait until he was out one day to really do a reconnaissance of the entire roof. Up I went. As I had anticipated, the trunk was a mission, but I made it. I sat in the fork of the branch extending out over the roof and gathered my composure. This was it; my plan was to dangle from the branch and move across, one hand over the other. I got halfway and realized it was not going to work. I could not move an inch more, there was just no power left in my skinny little arms. I could not go forwards or backwards, and I'd break my legs or neck if I let go. Panic and fear set in; I was in big trouble.

I bellowed out to my dad at the top of my voice to come and help. He came running outside and stopped under the bough of the tree, then looked up at me with a scowl. There was no time for lectures just now; he couldn't reach me and I was already wailing. So, he told me to let go and he'd catch me.

I glanced down and it looked far. I started crying and kept shrieking in between sobs that he was going to drop me. I really felt that he might not be able to actually catch me. He kept reassuring me that he would not let me fall but that he could only help me if I'd let go.

I couldn't. I hung there crying for another minute or so, which felt like forever. The bark was cutting into my wrists causing extra pain, and my arms were completely lame; I thought they were very close to dislocating. I realized I had no choice; I had to let go. *The pain had become too unbearable* – I was desperate. I closed my eyes, took a deep breath, resigned my fate into my father's hands, and let go.

My dad caught me with ease, put me down on my feet, muttered something about how he wished we kids would just use our ears, and disappeared through the house and into his study.

I picked a few pieces of bark out of my wrists and dusted my front off. I especially remember thinking to myself how easily he'd caught me. I thought about the worry, trauma, pain and anguish that could have been avoided had I let go straight away. Better still, if I had listened to 'my old man' and not climbed the tree in the first place, none of this would have happened. As young as I was, I wanted to kick my own behind for not letting go straightaway.

My recovery from alcohol was similar to this childhood experience in many ways. I had got myself to a point in my drinking where I knew I could not go backwards or forwards and I couldn't let go, because there was no one to catch me. I couldn't drink, but I couldn't stop either. I hung there not knowing what to do; I knew I was headed for certain death. When there was this mention of a recovery programme that worked, desperation made me willing. In the Program they said at one point that I should hand it over to God and let go. I realized that I was facing the same dilemma as when I was a kid; I didn't believe God would 'catch' me if I let go. To this day, I thank God for the gift of desperation the pain brought on. I had no choice any more but to follow the Program's suggestion and let go, because I was dying and there was no cure. I was desperate. I closed my eyes, asked Him to take over, resigned my fate into my Father's hands, *and let go.* I have not had the slightest desire to drink since that day, 29th May 2006. One of my special scriptures is Psalm 37:23-24:

> *The steps of a good man are ordered by the Lord; and He delighteth in his way. Though he falls, he shall not be utterly cast down, for the Lord upholdeth him with His hand.*

I often wonder where I would be if I'd found the Program early in my drinking, but I know that I was far too self-centred and egotistical to ever have listened. God knew I needed the pain to bring enough desperation to actually listen and let go. I thank Him for this, because I would never have been able to establish the relationship I now have with Him without the pain.

In the rest of this chapter, I would like to discuss three fundamental aspects that helped me let go completely. I believe that because us alkies are so ruled by ego, if we were left like this, we'd be back up that tree and trying the same trick again in a few months' time. Pain, as you've heard, is what brought me to the point of being willing to listen. I am truly hoping and praying that you don't need to get to the point of such pain as I felt. Indeed, there are many who have gone way past my point of desperation before they recovered. But I sincerely believe that if you can see yourself on this same 'train' called alcoholism, you'll be able to make the decision earlier, by the wonderful grace of God – this is my prayer.

Honesty

A definition of honest is "fair and righteous (righteous means morally right and law-abiding) in speech and action – not lying, cheating, or stealing – sincere". I can concur with this in my understanding of what it means now, but I certainly could not have done this in my drinking days. I had the idea that as long as you were not trying to hurt anyone, whatever you said did not matter. Once I'd sobered up, the magnitude of the level of honesty that was going to be required of me to get through this Program properly was daunting to say the least. We are talking about a level of honesty at which, when I've done something good that has really helped someone, I can ask myself if I was pure enough in my motive. Did I actually do this thing so that others might think of me as a nice guy? Did I do it because it benefitted me in some way? Did this person perhaps do something good to me first, and do I just want to keep this 'give and take' relationship going? Did I do it to get out of some kind of trouble? Did I even do it because I felt sorry for them? Or did I do it because I am totally grateful for what God has done in my life; that I truly love Him for who He is and I want to show that gratitude to Him by passing it on to another person? It is difficult to buy God a bunch of flowers when He's the one who made the flowers, the money and me.

My motive will never become one of helping people unless I can recognize and confess that this has not been my motive.

Another example of the level of honesty I needed is that I had to be able to admit, "I don't understand," "I don't feel that," "I want to do this but I can't bring myself to," "I don't believe in God," "I don't love that girl," "I can't forgive him," "I haven't worked through the steps thoroughly," "I haven't told you everything," "I haven't made my amends properly," "I still resent them," and so on. Silence can also be a lack of honesty. But if we want to be honest, we have to be *willing* to follow the recovery Program, replacing the word 'alcohol' in the steps with the word 'honesty'.

This was the first decision that got the 'ball of sobriety' rolling for me. It was also the start and key factor in breaking down the barrier I had between God and me. In order for me to connect with God and have a personal relationship with Him, and thus find sobriety, I had to remove the 'me' from the equation. For this to happen, I had to humble myself. When I took the first step by becoming as honest as I could about who I was and what my capabilities were, I started to realize I am nothing without God. The bit of talent which had allowed me to learn a few skills in my life so far was from God anyway. Whatever I may achieve, whether it is while following God's plan or not, it could be taken from me in an instant without His protection.[19] Rich, intelligent, successful, handsome men and women have lost things, or even their lives, in an instant, through forces beyond their control. Honesty brings me to the realization that without God in control of my will, I am set to lose everything.

When we read Jeremiah 5:3, it shows that God is not just casually looking for honesty in us but that he is actually *searching* for it. This implies intensity from God, and intensity shows importance.

---

[19] See Job 1:6-2:10.

The level of importance is such that God struck and crushed His people in order to bring honesty to their lives.[20] The Lord wants fellowship and a relationship with us. This is the reason He created us. Without true honesty, though, there can be no real intimacy in any relationship, let alone with God, and He knows this. We can see here just how much He loves us – awesome!

"We are not saints." How honest a statement is that! I'll bet anyone is capable of being honest enough to make that statement with belief and conviction. Most of us have probably used it ourselves and heard many others use it too.

No one understands this more than God. The task ahead of us seems tough; it's not easy to be truly honest. People can be cruel and despising; we could lose face, friends, jobs, families and even spouses. The thought of it strikes fear into most of us; we don't have the strength or fortitude to face this. We have some comfort when we read 1 Corinthians 10:13, as we see that what we're feeling and going through is not unique; others have been through the same. It says that God will not give us more pressure than we can handle and will always provide a way out.

"So now what?" most of us say. How do we find sobriety without the essential honesty we are told we need? These were the exact questions I asked when I started in the Program of recovery. From as early as I can remember, I had used lying, deceit, manipulation, 'candy coating' and even silence to try to get things to benefit me or work my way. It had become a habit, and now I was supposed to just switch over and become totally honest? It just doesn't work that way.

I became as honest as I sincerely knew how, asking the Lord daily for His help, and that was enough for me to get sobriety. "Amazing!" you might say. Not really, if you understand that honesty does not come from my efforts, but from God when I trust Him. I found that as I *persisted,* more and more of my untruthful ways came to my attention, and so this mist of lies and deceit began to clear slowly. I found that as I became aware of these lies, I was able to ask God for help and I started telling

---

[20] Jeremiah 5:3 (NLT) says "LORD, you are searching for honesty. You struck your people, but they paid no attention. You crushed them, but they refused to be corrected. They are determined, with faces set like stone; they have refused to repent." God was talking to the nation of Israel, but as He has made us His children as well (see 1 John 3), I believe we'd do well to learn from God's response to Israel's dishonesty.

fewer lies. When I did lie, I felt convicted and made amends as soon as I could.

My prayer used to be short, simple, specific and sincere: "Lord, please help me to be honest about the facts when telling a story about the fish I caught. In Jesus' name. Amen." God knows our hearts and wants to give us what we ask for.

> *Ask, and it shall be given you; seek, and ye shall find; knock, and it shall be opened unto you...*
>
> *Matthew 7:7*

This verse says that we should keep on asking, and this means that we may not receive straight away but it *will* happen – don't stop the daily prayer. I find that honesty builds on honesty, and this brings me closer to the Lord.

I found the biggest hindrance for me was indecision. Sure, I wanted to be honest and not have the urge to lie and deceive all the time, but I'd never taken a conscious *decision* to be honest. It was easy; all I did was sincerely say to myself and God, "I now make a decision to be honest. It will not be easy, and I won't get it right straight away, but this is what I want."

There are many things that pull us away from being honest, but I believe that they all stem from *fear*. We may feel shame and guilt, but even these are essentially rooted in fear – fear of what people might think, say or do to us. As with everything in this Program, we pray. In order for our fear to go away, we need to change our way of thinking – look at the situation in a different way. We need to see that God is in control. What others think, say or do is not going to hinder the outcome of God's plan for us. If we are destined to be killed there and then, we can rest assured that we will be going home to be with our heavenly Father for eternity. If this happens, it is part of His plan for us and we have finished what we were put on this earth to do. We may worry about loved ones if we're taken, but God has them in His care – He can look after them just fine without us! If we lose something, including a friendship or favour with others, it may hurt us really badly, but we can be assured that the Lord will be with us at this time.[21]

If we can see and understand that who we are in life is not determined by what others think of us or by power and possessions, we can lose a

---

[21] See Matthew 28:20.

little of that fear already. I personally believe that who we are in this world depends entirely upon our relationship with our Lord God and creator through His son Jesus Christ. So, if we want to get closer to God, we need to become more honest with Him. God will honour and acknowledge as much as we surrender in honesty.

There is a lot to take in, but we need to grasp this properly. Once we understand the importance of honesty, attaining it is relatively simple. We need to make a genuine decision to be honest. Then we need to be as honest as we know how, never neglecting to hand it over to God when we get scared. We must go back and make amends as soon as we are able to do so if we slip up with an untruth. We must just keep this up, no matter what. It is not difficult as long as we don't allow guilt to overcome us; guilt will often be what deters us from pressing on. As we start to be honest little by little, a certain amount of humility creeps into us automatically as we realize how vulnerable we really are. Humility is our next point as we move towards 'letting go and letting God'.

Humility

A definition of humility is "having or showing a low estimate of one's own importance – of modest pretensions". I found I achieved a certain amount of humility once I'd become honest to a fault with myself. For the first time in my life, after I truly looked at myself honestly, I saw all the flaws. I saw all the areas where I was not in control at all. I might be the most careful drug user in the world, for example, but somebody could change the drug as I turned my head for a split second. This could spell the end for me. I could walk out the door the richest and most intelligent man in the world and be killed outright by a speeding car. With this kind of realization, I can humbly admit that I am nothing on my own. This humility naturally resulted from being honest. Can you see how this makes sense?

Once I am humble enough to admit my lack of control, I am more inclined to stop trying to be part of the solution. If I now hand the problem over to God, He is then able to make the change. While I am trying to 'help' things along through lies, manipulation etc., I still do not trust the Lord enough. My humility is therefore only a false humility; I still think I can make a difference to the outcome. I find true humility when I understand that even the talents that I have do not come from my effort in skills development but from the Lord himself. Even the drive and ambition I have is from Him.

> *And the whole earth was of one language, and of one speech. And it came to pass, as they journeyed from the east, that they found a plain in the land of Shinar; and they dwelt there. And they said one to another, Go to, let us make brick, and burn them thoroughly. And they had brick for stone, and slime had they for morter. And they said, Go to, let us build us a city and a tower, whose top may reach unto heaven; and let us make us a name, lest we be scattered abroad upon the face of the whole earth. And the Lord came down to see the city and the tower, which the children of men builded. And the Lord said, Behold, the people is one, and they have all one language; and this they begin to do: and now nothing will be restrained from them, which they have imagined to do. Go to, let us go down, and there confound their language, that they may not understand one another's speech. So the Lord scattered them abroad from thence upon the face of all the earth: and they left off to build the city. Therefore is the name of it called Babel; because the Lord did there confound the language of all the earth: and from thence did the Lord scatter them abroad upon the face of all the earth.*
>
> *Genesis 11:1-9*

This account of the tower of Babel shows who really is in charge...

I once worked for a very rich boss in construction. He was pretty much what the world would term a 'self-made multi-millionaire'. He was a hard man and did not seem to care much for others' welfare. He worked hard and put in long hours, and expected it of others, although he never paid accordingly. For instance, he paid the workers for eight hours a day, but would push nine hours out of them. He used to sit with me (I was a site agent, which means I was in charge of an entire construction site) and tell me how he had started at the bottom with one of the big construction companies. After twelve years he had been made a director, which is impressive, then, not long after this, he had left and started his own company. He told me how he had worked eighteen to nineteen hours per day, how he used to get involved and do the work himself. He said that he had used willpower, determination and self-discipline to get where he was – and I believe him. However, he thought that these qualities were self-made, that the breaks he got in life were of his own working.

Don't get me wrong; I believe he used his skills very well, as did the servant who received ten talents in the Parable of the Talents[22]. However, he seemed unaware of the fact that his skills had been given to him exclusively and that they came from God. He also seemed oblivious to the many gifts he received from God in his daily life; I think he took many things for granted. I don't think he saw self-discipline as a gifting, for instance. I don't believe he understood or saw that his deals falling into place, or the fact that there were no major disasters on his sites, were actual blessings from God. He gave the impression that all these things had been achieved through his own hard work and careful planning. He said he did believe in God, but I don't think whether he was a Christian or not is relevant to these skills and blessings. The Bible says:

> *Before I formed thee in the belly I knew thee; and before thou camest forth out of the womb I sanctified thee, and I ordained thee a prophet unto the nation.*
>
> *Jeremiah 1:5*

It also says:

> *That ye may be the children of your Father which is in heaven: for He maketh his sun to rise on the evil and on the good, and sendeth rain on the just and on the unjust.*
>
> *Matthew 5:45*

These scriptures tell me that God had a plan for us (our free will might have spoilt those plans somewhat), and that what He has intended to give us, He still does, irrespective of whether or not we choose to follow Him or even acknowledge Him. So, what we do or don't do has no bearing on what God does or doesn't do for us. Therefore, how can we claim any accolade?

Simply put, this is what I understand humility to be: *I am nothing but an empty vessel without God.* All that I am and will be is because of God and His power and will. His will allowed me to exercise my will, even if it meant deviating from His plan for me. Humility is being conscious and aware of where my power, ability and the circumstances surrounding me

---

[22] See Matthew 25:14-29.

come from, and giving God the credit for any praise, accolades and blessings that might be thrown my way. If I claim any credit for anything in my life without first understanding and then accrediting it to God, I am the opposite of humble. In one phrase: *I can't, but He can.*

In my own experience, I have come to realize that I only have control over one thing in my life: my will. In the past I have chosen to use my free will in all the wrong areas of self-gratification. This was totally selfish. I found that the alcohol, drugs and sex gave me a false sense of well-being. I had chosen this way; I'd not been forced into it. The addictions had grabbed a hold of me, though. Once I realized that this was all false, I had to let go of all pride, even false pride ("Look how good I am for letting go.") God was the master of my destiny, as He had created me. So, I became humble enough to realize that in order to achieve serenity (peace of mind), I had to *choose* to get my will in line with God's will.

The only thing I found that works for me is to hand my free will back to Him and ask Him to put it in line with His will – daily. This is the active part we play in the process, and it does not always come easily. The battle with self in all aspects of life is an ongoing one. I need to constantly remind myself of the inadequacy I have and hand it over to the Lord. I can then take the 'me' out of the picture, and when this happens, God is able to ring the changes in me.

I would like to discuss something I like to call 'bold humility'. This statement might sound paradoxical; the fact is, though, that we are not exercising boldness because of what we see and believe about ourselves, but in the belief and realization of what God can and will do through us if we let Him. This means that we don't have to be anybody's doormat; we stand our ground in a respectful manner, and yet we can humbly apologize for our wrongdoing in the situation. This we achieve by doing a spot inventory (see Step 10).

I can do all things through Christ which strengtheneth me.

Philippians 4:13

When I read this, my focus is on the fact that it is Christ's strength and not mine. This keeps me humble but knowing God as the all-powerful creator gives me the boldness. How awesome is that!

There is something that I have battled my whole life to understand and have only recently been able get my head around. I could never understand why some people seemed so lucky and others not; although, the real issue for me was more likely, *why am I so unlucky?* This wonder never dissipated when I received the gift of sobriety, but the focus shifted off myself and onto others. I believe that my sobriety was God's grace given to me; what I could not get my head around was why it had been withheld from me in the first place and then so freely given, why it was not given to some others, and why still others received it so early in their addictions. About a year ago I read two books, *What's So Amazing About Grace?* by Philip Yancy,[23] and *Humility* by Andrew Murray,[24] and I found the answers to my questions.[25] Please understand that what I am going to say is a level of understanding that I believe the Holy Spirit has given me personally, so if it does not make full sense to you, just discard it; it has no impact on your sobriety. Remember, when I sobered up, I had no clue about anything that was going on; I was desperate to stop drinking (it was busy killing me) and was therefore willing to do the Program as suggested.

The way I understand grace is: assistance of any kind that is given without merit, without being earned and with no conditions. I had the impression that God's grace was for specific people only, and that the criterion for who would receive it was one of God's mysteries, that whatever was given to me should be accepted with gratitude. The idea of gratitude and acceptance without question sat well with me, but what I could not accept was that a fair and loving God would reserve His grace for some and not for others. In many aspects, as demonstrated in the parable of the talents, this is the case; some people are graced with intelligence, skills, natural drive and ambition, etc., while others seem to have none of these attributes. In fact, some end up with hindrances such as learning disabilities, physical disabilities, low drive or unfavourable situations and circumstances. Paul says, however:

> *Actually, I don't have a sense of needing anything personally. I've learned by now to be quite content whatever my circum-stances. I'm just as happy with little as with much, with much as with little. I've found the recipe for being happy whether*

---

[23] Philip Yancy; *What's So Amazing About Grace;* Zondervan; ISBN 9780310245650

[24] Andrew Murray; *Humility;* Rickfords Hill Publishing Ltd.; ISBN 9781905044405

[25] I thank these writers for allowing God to use them so powerfully in my life.

full or hungry, hands full or hands empty. Whatever I have, wherever I am, I can make it through anything in the One who makes me who I am.

Philippians 4:12-13 (MSG)

Paul has the solution: we are to focus on the right thing as our source of joy, which is God. God is able to give us joy in any circumstances, because our circumstances are not what make us joyful or not; our relationship to God is.

The way I have come to understand it is that grace is given to everybody right from the beginning. All we need to do is to accept it, but this is where the problem starts. You need to be humble in order to accept grace with all its blessings. I say this because of the manner in which it is given. Grace was given to us, in effect, before we were born. (I say 'in effect' as God does not operate within the parameters of time as we do.) Therefore, I cannot do or not do anything to 'up' my grace; it was already given to me in full. I am not deserving of it in any way, I cannot love God more to receive a larger portion, and I cannot do anything more in this world for others to improve my stakes; *God has already given it all to me.* He knew what I would do with my free will right from the start, so He knew I was going to need His help, which comes in the form of grace. That is why I believe that in order to accept such a gift, I have to be humble. No one who has humility and thinks they are deserving of humility, or have worked hard to achieve humility, can truly accept the gift of grace, because their very nature cannot accept something so freely offered with 'no strings attached'. Herein lies the big issue; most people feel that they are humble, or that they can become humble if they set their minds to it. However, the minute one says, "I'm going to be humble from now on," the ego is there, because it's all about what *you* are going to do. That is why my understanding of humility is, "I can't, but He can."

In my case, and certainly in working with people with dependency disorders, I have realised we are riddled with pride, ego and self. I could never see that I was like this while I was an active alcoholic, even when others filmed me and showed it to me the next day. I always had an excuse that generally centred on the theme that I was "hard done by".

So, to sum up my woes: I was busy dying because of my alcohol dependency and needed to stop, but I could not stop without God's help; He had already given me help in the form of grace, but I could not access it because my pride, ego and self-centredness made it impossible for me to do so; I needed humility in order to accept His grace and the blessings and miracles that come with it, but my pride, ego and selfishness prevented me from truly seeing the need for humility.

Here is where the miracle of the Program comes in.

I heard how others had recovered from their dependency disorders, and through the God-given gift of desperation, I was willing to do exactly what they had said they'd done in order to stop their drinking. There was not much mention of grace and humility and the like. I was told that if I wanted to stop drinking, I had to simply work through the Program (the steps), and that they would show me how. I needed to be as honest and thorough as I could be (which wasn't very much initially). This is all I knew and understood, so I did the Program, which took me about six months, and I have never touched a drink from the day I started. What the Program did for me, while I was totally oblivious to even needing it, is that it deflated my ego and pride. I thereby achieved a certain amount of humility, which gave me access to enough of God's grace so that I did not (and do not) have to drink. In all my dealings with problems and character defects, the only approach that has brought me victory has been this Program.

I came to see as clear as daylight just how full of pride, ego and self I was. I still suffer with these things on a daily basis, but the difference is that I can see them now, and this has allowed me to tackle many of my defects of character. The more humility that comes in, the more grace is attainable. After this I could really understand 2 Corinthians 12:9:

> *And he said unto me, my grace is sufficient for thee: for my strength is made perfect in weakness. Most gladly therefore will I rather glory in my infirmities, that the power of Christ may rest upon me.*

Paul realized that the more he accepted his powerlessness, the more of God's grace was available to help him.

I often felt empathy for people who seemed less fortunate than me. This is not in itself a bad thing, but I once sat in an old retired pastor's 'humble abode' and listened as he and his wife shared some of their lives with me. He had nothing, his health was deteriorating rapidly, he had children and grandchildren following their own paths and who really 'sponged' what they could off his meagre pension. Yet he had something that I wanted so badly: an incredible love and relationship with God that brings a lump to my throat even as I sit here and write. He never spoke about the problems around him, only about the wonderful things the Lord had done for him in his life. As he spoke of these, tears of absolute gratitude and love would choke him up and his wife would have to continue with the story. I knew that this old man had more than I could ever dream of having; he had received a large amount of God's grace that was available to him.

We often feel we were given a raw deal when God's 'talents' were dished out to us, when actually we have just been focused the whole time on things that are not important; things that do not bring us peace, joy and contentment in a close relationship with Him. I am starting to understand why Jesus said:

> But seek ye first the kingdom of God, and his righteousness; and all these things shall be added unto you.
>
> *Matthew 6:33*

Humility, although explained in a simple way, is a task that is not easy for us. Self is always rearing up. Humility does not come easily, so we need to keep it in our daily prayers. Our Lord God is the creator and is all-powerful. We need to ask Him daily for His help and guidance.

This understanding brings us to the final point in the move towards 'letting go and letting God': perseverance.

Perseverance

A definition of perseverance is "steadfast pursuit of an aim, constant persistence; continuance in a state of grace". I know that sobriety is a journey and not a destiny; therefore, I am going to need perseverance and God's grace to be allowed to make mistakes and yet continue. I think the key here for me was to recognize that this continuance is "in a state of grace". Without this grace, we would have been damned no matter what. This is what God has granted us through the death of His Son Jesus Christ, and for which I am eternally grateful. I need to show gratitude for this by thanking God daily and by passing this message on to others, which is part of His will for my life and a vital part of recovery.

Many words and actions are closely linked to perseverance: patience, tolerance, long-suffering, self-control, forgiveness, endurance, stamina, courage and focus. A lot of these are the fruits of the Spirit.[26] Perseverance is needed to acquire most of the tools we need in sobriety. Once we're convinced that this is the course of action we need to take, we can make a choice to do so with the comfort that it will be a journey until we leave this world – one we do not take alone, but with the Holy Spirit to guide us and our sponsors and the Program to support us. We have another guarantee in God's word that tells us to rejoice in hard times; it's not always a bad thing or a punishment to go through problems and trials.

> *And not only so, but we glory in tribulations also: knowing that tribulation worketh patience; And patience, experience; and experience, hope: And hope maketh not ashamed; because the love of God is shed abroad in our hearts by the Holy Ghost which is given unto us.*
>
> *Romans 5:3-5.*

Strength of character is what we need to overcome our defects of character. If you are showing strength of character in an area of your life, you won't be defective of character in that area, will you? God tells us that there will be no disappointments when we hope, and this is what really gives me courage to persevere when it's tough!

I believe that perseverance lost its value in the world with the fast pace of technology and a world promoting instant gratification. Some young people became multi-millionaires in the space of a year or two with their computers and the Internet. Programmers and web designers in their teens were leaving school and going into a market which lacked trained computer 'people'. The efficiency of computers and the Internet in business warranted quick change – at any cost. The slogan 'time is money' rang true and was pushed to the limit. 'Takeaway food' became known as 'fast food', with some restaurants even boasting that the food purchased would be given free if not delivered on time! What about life? John Lennon wrote, "Life is what happens to you while you are busy making other plans."[27] Nobody wants to do the 'horrible' bits of life; we try to ignore them, bypass them or speed through them. Why cook when you can get nutritious pre-cooked meals? One saves on time, money and cleaning up all that mess after cooking.

---

[26] See Galatians 5:22.

[27] From the song *Beautiful Boy,* released on the 1980 album *Double Fantasy.*

The character defects that arise in our lives, some of which are directly derived from the lack of proper social interaction caused by everything being sped up, are treated with the same 'fast food' attitude as the rest of our lives. Go and see a psychiatrist and get on some medication for the lack of energy, insomnia, irritable bowel syndrome, depression, anxiety, frustration, anger – I could increase the list ad infinitum. Please note, however, that I am not downing psychiatry or the use of medication in any way; they do have their place. What I am saying is that whilst some of our defective character traits have been learned over a considerable period of time, often as subconscious defensive or coping mechanisms, in other cases the root cause is simple self-centredness – self-will out of control, sometimes due to a lack of adequate discipline and boundaries during childhood.

Whatever the reason, it all boils down to this: the inability to see anything through to the end. *If it doesn't work quickly, bin it and try something else.* The hard truth is that there is no quick fix. It took many years to build up these defects, and it is going to take many years to be free of them. Added to this, we need to realize that this job is our responsibility. We need to take responsibility for our character defects and dependencies, but we do not need to take the blame. And the good news is that we do not need to do it alone. We have the Lord God who is there to assist and comfort us, and the Program and our sponsors for support. We need to make a decision to follow a plan and see it through, no matter what!

I have already touched on a bit of what I believe the world's view of a quick fix is; let's see what the Lord has to say.

> *The Pharisees also with the Sadducees came, and tempting desired him that he would shew them a sign from heaven. He answered and said unto them, When it is evening, ye say, It will be fair weather: for the sky is red. And in the morning, It will be foul weather to day: for the sky is red and lowering. O ye hypocrites, ye can discern the face of the sky; but can ye not discern the signs of the times? A wicked and adulterous generation seeketh after a sign; and there shall no sign be given unto it, but the sign of the prophet Jonas. And he left them, and departed.*
>
> *Matthew 16:1-4*

The Pharisees wanted a sign as proof that Jesus was the Messiah, and we do the same when we expect an instant deliverance or miracle from God. I'm not saying it doesn't happen; in fact, I'm living proof that it does happen. The point here is that the expectation of a quick fix is the one sure way to set ourselves up for a slip or a fall. It often takes a lifetime of hard work to remain victorious over our addiction.

Even though I experienced the instant miracle deliverance a lot of us look for, I was only aware of this three months or so into my sobriety. What wasn't mentioned previously was that six months into my sobriety, I was asking myself the question, "This has been all too easy; am I really an alcoholic?" Stinking thinking! Luckily, I was attending regular meetings and about a week later, I heard a chap give his talk. He'd been sober seven-and-a-half years and had been constantly told by his wife and family that he wasn't really an alcoholic after all; he'd had issues and had now worked through them. He finally bought into this crazy notion one evening at a wedding reception and had a glass of champagne. The next part of his story surprised me but proves the 'patience' of alcoholism. He went on to say that he drank in moderation, a couple of beers every other night, for two-and-a-half years. However, the day came when it all went wrong again and during the course of the next few years, he ended up in four different rehabs and was hospitalized with severe alcoholism three times. It was touch-and-go on one of those occasions. He was four years sober when he told this story but said that it had been twenty times harder to sober up the second time.

In my years sober, I have come to realize something that has been a *huge* breakthrough in my sobriety: the problem does not lie in the alcohol, it lies within me. I had used the alcohol to escape how I felt about myself.

I cannot begin to fathom God's way of doing things. I recommend reading chapters 38 to 41 in the Book of Job. Here is just one part:

> *Then the Lord answered Job out of the whirlwind, and said, Who is this that darkeneth counsel by words without knowledge? Gird up now thy loins like a man; for I will demand of thee, and answer thou me. Where wast thou when I laid the foundations of the earth? declare, if thou hast understanding. Who hath laid the measures thereof, if thou knowest? or who hath stretched the line upon it? Whereupon are the foundations thereof fastened? or who laid the corner*

stone thereof; When the morning stars sang together, and all the sons of God shouted for joy?

Job 38:1-7

With this in mind, how can I have any *expectations?* And since I've established that I am dealing with character defects that were formed while drinking, and indeed many which led me to seek relief in drinking, I now know that there will be no ultimate quick fix. We will need to persevere through the tough times. When we recognize this truth, we are less likely to be disappointed by the difficulties in the recovery process, and more aware of the small victories God gives us along the way. I can trust God, even if nothing materializes for me here on earth. Jeremiah was a major prophet who spoke to the Israelites under God's instruction on many occasions, and they never once listened to him. "What a waste!" we might say! Not so in God's eyes. You see, it's the perseverance in the face of adversity that pleases God. Jeremiah is one of God's beloved in heaven. We see from the story of Job that God later blessed him with double what he had. And he lived a long life.

And the Lord turned the captivity of Job, when he prayed for his friends: also the Lord gave Job twice as much as he had before. Then came there unto him all his brethren, and all his sisters, and all they that had been of his acquaintance before, and did eat bread with him in his house: and they bemoaned him, and comforted him over all the evil that the Lord had brought upon him: every man also gave him a piece of money, and every one an earring of gold. So the Lord blessed the latter end of Job more than his beginning: for he had fourteen thousand sheep, and six thousand camels, and a thousand yoke of oxen, and a thousand she asses. He had also seven sons and three daughters. And he called the name of the first, Jemima; and the name of the second, Kezia; and the name of the third, Kerenhappuch. And in all the land were no women found so fair as the daughters of Job: and their father gave them inheritance among their brethren. After this lived Job an hundred and forty years, and saw his sons, and his sons' sons, even four generations.

Job 42:10-16

I believe everybody should have a special scripture or verse from the Bible that either inspires them or lifts them up. One of mine is:

The steps of a good man are ordered by the Lord: and he delighteth in his way. Though he fall, he shall not be utterly cast down: for the Lord upholdeth him with his hand.

Psalm 37:23,24

The reason that it appeals to me so much is that it is so realistic with regard to everyday life. The best aspect of this verse is that it teaches He delights in *our* ways. God loves me, period.

I have a son and when he was little, he'd get up to real mischief. When I caught him, he'd look so innocent, as if butter wouldn't melt in his mouth. It was in times like these that I felt my heart melt for him and I'd love him to bits. It brought me immense joy. My dad had the same experience with me when I was three years old. He needed to fit the sprinkler head to the garden hose and said I should turn the tap on when he called and said he was done. Apparently, I peered around the corner of the house and saw he was still busy, then proceeded to turn on the tap full blast. My father was drenched, and I ran away laughing my head off. When my dad tells this story, he does so with fond memories of deep love. This is what I feel God sees in me too. He knows that I'm His child and that I want to do the right things, but sometimes in my eagerness, I mess it up. I believe He loves us all the more and it brings great delight to Him. The Lord is also saying here that we are on a journey (the steps), which will require us to persevere; all journeys do. It then tells us that we are human and fallible ("Though he fall…"), which I need to never forget – I've tried it my way and made a right mess of everything in my life. But I can persevere with confidence and not futility because I have God's assurance that I will be held up by Him so that I can continue the journey.

There's an old saying in sporting circles: "It isn't losing to get knocked down. Losing is staying down." We're not going to 'win 'em all', but that isn't the bigger picture. We learn and grow and gain experience by defeats. But are they really defeats when they are providing so much more for us in the long run? I used to play a lot of chess at school and one of my favourite plays was the Gambit. This is when you sacrifice a piece for a far better strategic position or ultimate gain. Many times, this led to winning the game. We have such an advantage as children of God because we have this promise from above and can be assured that defeats are all part of the plan to overcome our defects.

I have reached a point in my life where I have realized that since I have given my life over to God, it is His job to look after me – and I know He can. Even if I doubted that He could take care of me, I can take strength in the fact that I know that I cannot (I've already proved that to myself), and therefore anything that He can do for me is far better than what I had before. This way of thinking allows me to persevere even if a battle is lost. It's a journey and way of life; I can't lose as long as I don't give up. I love getting instructions from the Lord; not because they're easy but because I know then that I am on the right track. Over and above this, obedience is the best demonstration of love, and I want to show God my love.

> *Patient endurance is what you need now, so that you will continue to do God's will. Then you will receive all that he has promised.*
>
> *Hebrews 10:36*

> *We give great honour to those who endure under suffering. For instance, you know about Job, a man of great endurance. You can see how the Lord was kind to him at the end, for the Lord is full of tenderness and mercy.*
>
> *James 5:11*

How wonderful! We are even given a promise of reward in the end. However, I have found through my experience that it is not good for me to keep this promise of reward as my motivation to be patient and endure. I find that I rob myself if I do this. The greatest fulfilment I've found I get is when I do these things for God because I want to – for free. This is love, and it pleases God. The apostle Simon Peter explains the process beautifully:

> *In view of all this, make every effort to respond to God's promises. Supplement your faith with a generous provision of moral excellence, and moral excellence with knowledge, and knowledge with self-control, and self-control with patient endurance, and patient endurance with godliness, and godliness with brotherly affection, and brotherly affection with love for everyone. The more you grow like this, the more*

productive and useful you will be in your knowledge of our Lord Jesus Christ.

2 Peter 1:5-8 (NLT)

This is the work God wants us to persevere with; it is His job to look after us and take care of our alcohol/addiction problem. And while we are persevering with our instructions, knowing that God is there to uphold and guide us, and not interfering with His job of trying to 'fix' us, He takes care of our alcohol/addiction. This is what it's all about. The Lord of Heaven gave us free will and freedom of choice; we chose to give our will back to Him and to hand Him control of our lives, and to persevere through hardships as we do His will. Jesus Christ has told us what God's will is:

A new commandment I give unto you, that ye love one another; as I have loved you, that ye also love one another.

John 13:34

I have read and heard many godly people speak on this, and I have tried many things. In my experience, the best way that we can love someone is to do things for them that they need done, and to do these things because we want to; for free and for the enjoyment.

Nothing in the world can take the place of persistence (perseverance). Talent will not; nothing is more common than unsuccessful men with talent. Genius will not; unrewarded genius is almost a proverb. Education will not; the world is filled with educated derelicts (just remember the ones in the pubs!). Persistence and determination are alone omnipotent. 'Press on!' has been and always will be the answer to every human problem.[28]

Calvin Coolidge

I believe this to be true, provided we are in God's will. Nelson Mandela was imprisoned for twenty-seven years. He could have forgotten everything and rotted away, but instead he studied and became a lawyer, and he wrote books which have inspired a nation, and indeed, the world. He came out of prison and became president of South Africa,

---

[28] *www.goodreads.com/quotes/2749-nothing-in-this-world-can-take-the-place-of-persistence*

and a world icon of peaceful transformation and democracy. You see, it's easy to become discouraged in the face of adversity and not to persevere when obstacles line our journey, but we are privileged to have a loving Father God to be with us. We have our groups and sponsors (someone whom we can call for any help, who is in the Program of recovery – the journey) to encourage us. Being in a Program and having a sponsor has been vital in my journey and is quite biblical.

> *Confess your faults one to another, and pray one for another, that ye may be healed. The effectual fervent prayer of a righteous man availeth much.*
>
> *James 5:16*

This healing is also internal healing from discouragement, fatigue and disillusionment.

We are on a new journey called recovery. It is ongoing and it has its disappointments and setbacks. Once we understand that this is normal and that we will have tough times, we can set our minds to the task of persevering. I have found that this simple formula works for me, and when it doesn't work, I just keep doing it no matter what, until I am through the crisis or trial:

- I pray and ask God to take my problem and deal with it, because I can't.
- I do a personal inventory (Step 10) and make restitution where I see I've gone wrong.
- I pick up the phone and call a sponsor/friend and go for coffee, or just talk to him. I tell him my situation and ask him to pray for me.
- I go to a Program meeting and listen – and share if I get the chance.
- I offer my service to anyone who wants it in recovery. I send words of encouragement to those I am sponsoring and try to help other alcoholics that cross my path by sharing with them and helping them with things they need done (Step 12) – for free and for pleasure.
- I praise and thank God for the many good things He's done in my life and for all the blessings He has given me (there are many if you just think about it and ask the Lord to reveal them to you).

Usually, at this point I feel good and can move on. But if not, I simply repeat this formula over and over again; if nothing else, I feel peace and inner joy while doing this.

I follow this pattern continually as part of doing God's work, but when trials or adversities come along, I do these things with greater intensity and with greater awareness.

Our greatest strength lies in the knowledge that without God we have no strength. I know this because the Bible says:

In Him we live and move and have our being.

Acts 17:28

Amen!

The Simplicity of the Program

Just do it

The simplicity of the Program, for me, came in my realization of my utter powerlessness. Here was something over which I had no control. In this area of my life I was totally defeated. This fact alone, I believe, was my saving grace. In most other areas of my life, with enough willpower and determination, I could attain a reasonable semblance of normality, or so I thought. For seven years I tried to either control or stop my drinking to no avail. These attempts were sincere (as I'm sure many of you can relate to), wrought with determination, good intent, medication, inspirational stimulants etc. I was mainly fear-driven because of where I saw my life headed. But eventually even the fear of where I was going to end up left me, and only the hopelessness remained.

It was in this state that I spoke to God with complete abandon, asking for His help. I had done Step 1 – I'd admitted that I was powerless over alcohol, and that my life was unmanageable. I had also done Step 3 – I'd decided to turn my will and my life over to the care of God, as I understood Him. Because I had grown up in a Christian home, the only God I had understood was the Lord God of heaven and earth through His Son Jesus Christ. However, I did not fully believe that He could restore me to sanity or indeed that I was insane, and therefore my Step 2 was incomplete. I did manage to hand the problem over to Him, which suggests a measure of belief, although in my case I think it was mainly desperation.

I had no faith. I had done the action (Step 3) without the belief (Step 2). In Exodus 14:15-22, and Joshua 3:5-16, both Moses and Joshua had to take the action before the miracle happened. Moses raised his staff and *then* the waters of the Red Sea parted. As the Levite priests under Joshua's orders touched the waters of the Jordan River, the river dried up at this place. Moses and Joshua had enough belief to take the action, and this is essentially all it takes.

This is how I was set free. It was as simple and miraculous as that! In fact, it was so simple and subtle that I was a few months sober before I even realized that I never craved a drink. It was then that I completed my Step 2, as I came to realize that God had restored me to sanity. The obsession was gone, the miracle complete.

Now, I am not under any illusion in thinking that it comes this quickly to all people. Since my sobriety, I have tried to tackle other defects of character in the same way I did the alcohol; that is, I have tried to practise these principles in all my affairs (Step 12) and it hasn't been as easy. However, all is not lost. I have overcome many of these character defects and I am still busy with others, with many to come as the Lord reveals them to me. I use the exact same system of asking for his help with complete abandon.

The added factor now needed, I've found, is *perseverance*.[29] Perseverance is to endure hardships with patience and steadfastness, in spite of opposition or discouragement, and in the face of obstacles during an undertaking. I believe that this is where the battle rages hardest in us. In a society which is always looking for the 'quick fix', where IT teenagers are self-made millionaires, where reality TV shows are turning young people into instant celebrities, we have become extremely impatient as a people. Instant gratification is the order of the day in our society.

There is a wonderful scripture in which Jesus says:

> *But I tell you this – though he won't do it for friendship's sake, if you keep knocking long enough, he will get up and give you whatever you need because of your shameless persistence. And so I tell you, keep on asking, and you will receive what you ask for. Keep on knocking, and the door will be opened to you. For everyone who asks, receives. Everyone who seeks, finds. And to everyone who knocks, the door will be opened.*
>
> *Luke 11:8-10 (NLT)*

The key words here are "keep on asking".

So, the message is clear: if it doesn't come right straight away, we just keep at it. In Luke 9:23, we are instructed to turn from our selfish ways and take up our cross daily and follow Him. For me, the emphasis is on "daily". This suggests a journey rather than a destination.

---

[29] See page 72.

It is the very thought of persistence and struggle that puts most people off. They have tried that and become despondent through the lack of results. I know I had, after trying for seven years!

So how do we motivate ourselves? I found the most amazing thing was that once I'd made the decision and had actually handed it over to God, a subtle, small amount of hope and anticipation crept in on its own. When I felt this, I grabbed onto it with both hands and thanked God for it.

All things come from our heavenly Father, so whatever we lack, He is the perfect person to ask it from. Obviously, it must be in His will for us, but I sincerely believe that sobriety and all the aspects needed in achieving it are in His will for us.[30]

Therefore, should I lack motivation, for instance, I go down on my knees and ask for motivation every single morning. I simply say something like, "Lord, you know my heart wants to be motivated to attend meetings, get a sponsor and follow the Program so that I can achieve sobriety, but I cannot generate the strength to follow it myself. Without your help, Lord, I know that it is impossible to become motivated. So, I am giving this struggle I have to You and I ask that You will do it for me. Be with me, I pray, in Jesus' name. Amen."

I make a decision in my mind to ask the Lord for this every day, regardless of how I feel or what results I see or don't see. This, I believe, is part of what it means to 'take up my cross daily'[31].

This is all that is required of me.

When I started to do it like this, my way of thinking started to change as well. I found that as my way of thinking changed, so too did my attitude towards the problem. It is then that I found the problem went away. But just like Shadrach, Meshach and Abednego said in the Book of Daniel:

> *If it be so, our God whom we serve is able to deliver us from the burning fiery furnace, and he will deliver us out of thine hand, O king. But if not, be it known unto thee, O king, that we will not serve thy gods, nor worship the golden image which thou hast set up.*
>
> *Daniel 3:17,18*

---

[30] See Luke 11:10.
[31] See Luke 9:23.

I am glad I had this scripture at the time, because I made the decision and I was going to stick at it no matter what. This passage of scripture is one of my favourites and always gives me goosebumps! It stirs such passion in me for the Lord (must be my Irish blood). You see, these three men had thrown their lot in with God. I believe that they had clearly seen the folly of following any other way but the Lord's. The other methods had been tried and tested and had failed. They never fully understood all God's methods but were going to stand by Him no matter what.

I had tried my own way for seven years and had failed. I had heard and seen how others had found sobriety through the Lord and was therefore going to stick with it no matter what. But I found, like Shadrach, Meshach and Abednego, that the outcome wasn't as bad as it could have been. In my perseverance, I found a quiet peace and comfort that allowed me to continue. This I came to know as 'serenity'. So, whether I was getting it right or not, the fact that I could hand it over to God *each* day made me feel a lot better about myself than if I were not doing that little bit every morning. This part of the experience is just amazing and inexplicable. It is *that simple!*

I don't let guilt at failure get me down because I know it's not my part of the fight; I know I am doing all that is required of me. If the guilt does want to eat at me, I hand it to God with exactly the same prayer. Amazing!

To sum up the simplicity of the Program:

- I have met with absolute defeat and have no hope or faith.
- I tell God honestly of my helplessness – hand it over to Him in prayer with sincerity – and keep on asking for His help daily, no matter what.

The Lord God is all powerful and He is able to remove your defects of character, as long as your heart is right! Our life and circumstances are what they are. I believe that if we truly knew the life and relationship God has intended for us in eternity, we'd understand and fully accept our situation. There is a plan for us and I believe that our circumstances are part of what is needed to mould us into this plan. The root of this sinful nature, I believe, is self. We don't stand a chance in overcoming anything on our own that has not been preordained for us to achieve. God is our creator and He always knows how to fix our defects and restore us to his original design. The Program is one of lowering ego and asking God to come in and do the work. It is by no means easy because our natures fight the yielding process – but it is simple.

PART TWO

The Recovery Steps

Breakthrough into Recovery

The Importance of the Steps

Nothing is more important to achieving victory in your life than working through the steps of the Program. Yes, there will be things that you need to do in order to maintain your victory, but I believe that nothing effective will be achieved if you choose not to follow these steps. For now, however, just read through what is written about them; this should help you get an idea as to where you are headed. When you do come to working through these steps, it is good to refer back to what is written here about each one as you are doing it; it will help immensely, like having a mentor or a second opinion.

Remember though, that whilst my stories may be different to yours, the most important thing is to see what aspects you can identify with. I will be sharing what I have learned through other literature and have put into practice, as well as lessons learned through my own experiences that I believe have been fundamental in my sobriety. Do not become disheartened if you feel that some of the suggestions will just not be possible for you to do. I believe that if your heart is sincere, and your motive pure, God will give you the strength that is needed. Also bear in mind that nothing is cast in stone, that God may lead you on a slightly different path. The key here is to be willing to do anything it takes.

Being an alcoholic, I am using the *Twelve Steps for Alcoholics*. These steps were originally laid out by the founding members of the organization Alcoholics Anonymous. I have included scripture readings from the Bible that over the years have made sense to me during my quiet times with God. These originate from the organisation Alcoholics Victorious.

The fact that we lack power to overcome or resist alcohol in our lives is probably the reason we are here at this point. We may find this surprising, as we might have been able to achieve a semblance of power in other areas of our lives and maintain it. But as the booze progressively started taking over, so we started to see the 'power' sap from these areas of our lives. In my case, this brought on fear, which in turn brought on desperation as I saw all my best efforts collapse – unsuccessful and therefore in vain. It was this desperation that made me willing to do this work; it was through God's grace that I found the Program.

We are powerless over everything in our lives except our will and freedom to choose. It is the key to our recovery to get a full understanding of this concept. We need to recognize that up to this point we have used this freedom to choose based on our own wants and desires. Remember, this includes good things we have done that further our own agenda or satisfy some need within us. In short, we have been extremely selfish. This is what I believe has blocked us from God's power, why nothing seemed to happen when we cried out in pain with all the sincerity we could muster. I know I was genuinely sincere.

What we need to do is get rid of *self*. My problem has always been selfishness, ego and pride. The problem is that it is impossible for me to consciously rid myself of these defects. First of all, I could never see my selfishness; I don't believe a selfish person ever can. I always felt I was being hard done by and therefore had to take and fight for everything I had and wanted. The second problem was, when I finally *did* recognize my selfish, egotistical pride, I couldn't be rid of it.

I recommend trying the following experiment. Make up your mind to be humble and selfless, remembering that real selflessness has no agenda of its own. If you are like me, you will find that it is impossible. The minute I think I'm humble, I've lost my humility in that instant.

I believe that the reason I work through these steps is to remove *myself* from the equation, so that God is able to step in and do the work in my life that I've been asking Him to do all along. God is unable to interfere with our free will; we need to find a way of humbling ourselves,[32] before He can lift us up. The only way I have found to humble myself is to remove myself from the picture. I had to find a new agenda that did not involve my agenda. Throughout my sobriety, the only thing that has worked for me was to *work through these steps* as willingly, honestly and as open-mindedly as I could.

---

[32] See James 4:10.

Step 1

We admitted we were powerless over alcohol, that our lives had become unmanageable.

For I know that in me (that is, in my flesh,) dwelleth no good thing: for to will is present with me; but how to perform that which is good I find not.

Romans 7:18

What a step! For the first time in my life I was going to have to admit that I was powerless over something, and that basically I could not manage my own life. I had been taught throughout school and other institutions to never admit defeat; I'm quite sure you can relate to this.

You might still be at an early stage in your drinking and not think there is anything wrong. The first telltale sign is when other people around you start mentioning your drinking. As the Bible says:

He that hath an ear, let him hear...

Revelation 2:7

I certainly didn't hear because, quite frankly, I did not want to listen. I suspect many alcoholics will not heed this as a sign – I never did – but I have put it in anyway because I believe the grace of God can touch anyone. If your spouse, family or friends are complaining in *any* way about your drinking, take heed. They can generally see these signs long before we can. If you still can't see it, perhaps your attitude might change after one or two more unpleasant incidences. I still think pain is our best teacher.

I believe that subconsciously we know that there is a problem when our drinking gets going. The big issue we face in admitting defeat is that if the so-called 'solution' does not work, we are doomed. We will also be labelled by others, held accountable by our bosses and possibly shunned and despised by our friends and family. This is, of course, all our own perception. Most of the people around us have been well aware of our 'problem' long before us. And when we became aware of our 'little problem', we thought we could keep them oblivious to it with our excellent disguises and elaborate cons. The joke is on us; people are just not that stupid. However, we cannot seem to see that they have stuck with us through living hell, and that *any* form of positive action is welcome to them. So why not level with them?

We have to believe we are in this class of drinkers before we will look at admitting anything. My suggestion is this: have only two drinks every night, certainly no more than three. Try to keep this up for three months and it will be a good indication as to whether you are in this class.

As you will see in the working section of the book in Step 1, there are twenty questions you need to answer. I believe these tests to be the best proof of all. I remember thinking, after I had answered them honestly, that everyone must be alcoholic according to this test. Now that I look back, most of the people I knew only had one or two drinks at a braai. At the time, I wasn't counting their drinks; I just saw they all had drinks. They also went home after the braai; I went to other places and carried on. I moved in drinking circles as well, so a lot of those acquaintances did have drinking problems, I believe.

If I look back at the unmanageability of my life, I can sum it up quite simply. My life was unmanageable when I could not do the good things I set my mind to doing. These included responsibilities like commitments, appointments, exercising, taking the dog for a walk, bill payments, housework, servicing the car, being on time for work, etc. I cannot mention any spiritual plans because there weren't any; I was functioning on self-will, and it was starting to run riot.

Still, many alcoholics cannot get this first step done because they *just don't want to*. I was like that; I was just having too much fun. I saw God, girlfriends, family, work and everyone else as major hindrances to the way I wanted to live, party and drink. So, when I upset these people and they retaliated, I just dropped them and moved on. I began by dropping God, and it was so liberating, I thought. You see, I found Christianity the most oppressive of all. It challenged my morals, my beliefs and my integrity. Free of this, my new motto was, "As long as I don't intentionally hurt anyone, anything goes." I would tell girls at the first meeting that I was not looking for a relationship. Obviously, this turned some away, but with the ones that said they felt the same, I was able to have a sexual relationship with them for a few months and a bit of companionship. After a while they would start complaining about my drinking and try to control me. I would then say that I needed my space and reminded them of the fact that I had mentioned at the onset I was not wanting a relationship. I believe I hurt many girls over the years, for which I am not proud.

I wanted to be able to manage the things in my life that I realized needed managing, without any effort and time. I would mentally commit to paying a bill, visiting my mom, taking my girlfriend to the movies, going to a function or whatever. The evening before, I'd go for a drink after work and get home at 3am, and so I would end up missing my commitment. I could not manage my life.

The powerlessness went something like this:

I wake up on Monday morning after a hectic weekend, all hung-over. I force myself to work but arrive late, promising that next time I will stop drinking at 12 on a Sunday so that I can recoup and make a better go of Monday. I drink small amounts of energy drink all day and try to keep it down. Then, after arriving home, I take an aspirin with fruit salts and go to bed.

On Tuesday morning, I wake up feeling dull and miserable, but physically stronger. I manage to get a piece of toast down during the day and drink a few glasses of water. In the evening, I feel ravenous and I wolf down a decent amount of food, watch a movie and go to bed.

On Wednesday, I wake up feeling a bit guilty but much stronger. I put in an outstanding performance at work, catching up most of what I've let slip the two days before. I finish work feeling positive and a little proud of my achievement. Then, the powerlessness comes into play once more. I think, "I will just have one little drink to relax after the hard day's work and then go straight home. Last week I stayed long because that pretty blonde chatted to me; this time I will go straight away after one or two." Notice how my thinking has already subtlety changed from "one little" to "one or two". After swallowing the last gulp of my third beer, I stride out the door. "There, you see, no problem," I say to myself, very chuffed for leaving after having just 'one'. "And they say I have a drinking problem... I'd like to see an alkie do that." But truth be told, a little voice in my subconscious is saying, "Jeepers, that was nice; I could have done with one more for the road." I climb into bed and drift off.

Thursday is another cracker at work and I finish at 18:30; extra effort, extra dedication, you know? I get home after 19:00, eat something I find in the fridge, have a nice hot bath and feel totally wiped out.

On Friday morning, I leave to work in high spirits; it's the weekend! The boss makes the fatal mistake of complimenting me on my productivity and on the fact that he noticed I worked late yesterday. It is payday for the workforce at 14:00 and a half-day for me; lovely! The boss is happy, I'm doing well and I feel good. I go to the pub and drain my first draught glass by 14:45; it has taken me twenty minutes to get here. The second goes a bit slower as I settle down to a few games of pool. A win assures me of my first free shot, which I knock back casually. The beer has bloated me a bit, but the shooter is warming my insides. It's now time to switch to my 'medicine'. "Barman, double 'voddi,' beer glass full of ice and a can of Coke, shot," I bark across the bar counter. I can get four of these on a single can of Coke.

On Saturday morning at 07:30, I'm hugging the toilet bowl and vomiting my lungs out. There's only a little blood this time, which makes me feel quite relieved. I feel awful though and have the whole weekend ahead of me. There is only one way to escape this hideousness: back to the pub for a shandy. After that I'll go and get my headlight fixed on the car and visit 'the old man'; I said I'd pop round because he hasn't been well. After the second shandy, I feel like a million dollars; on top of the world and very thirsty. I don't leave the place until 10pm. I cannot talk or walk properly. It takes me five minutes to get the key in the ignition; luckily, I only live a few kilometres away.

I wake up on Sunday morning and repeat the whole process, only this time there's more blood and I start to worry. I have to get rid of this fear and steady the nerves. I manage to keep the third and fourth shandy down, and I'm 'A' for away again. I get home that night at about 9pm, broken. Someone has taken me home and left my keys on the kitchen counter. Darn, I was going to see my dad – was it yesterday or today? What day is it anyway? I hope its Saturday, because I mustn't drink late on a Sunday!

On Monday morning, I've soiled my bedding and puked on the floor. I have to phone the office; "I have a stomach bug and need to see the doc. He'll give me a note and some medicine." Why isn't it Sunday morning? Why couldn't I just stop at noon like I'd planned? My father's not answering my calls; he must be angry. Why do I do this, why can't I just have one or two and go home? *I am powerless!*

When I came to my senses, this step was really easy to explain. In a nutshell, I could not manage things in my life that I put my mind and will to managing, and I was powerless over deciding that one drink wouldn't hurt this time, and thereafter powerless to saying no to the next twenty drinks or to the rest of the bottle. This, I can admit.

I believe the Lord has shown me something quite profound in the beginning of my eighth year of sobriety. I really am thankful to Him that I never needed this clarification to be sober; and neither do you. My new philosophy from God is this:

In my life thus far, I have mistaken God's gift of grace for my self-willed power; and the many talents He has so freely bestowed upon me as my own ability to manage my affairs.

It is only through His gracious gift of alcoholism that I became desperate enough to follow this path to freedom and actually recognize His gifts of grace and talents. That is why I love that good old Irish saying, "A man cannot see until he can *see!*"

Step 2

We came to believe that a power greater than ourselves could restore us to sanity.

And he said unto me, My grace is sufficient for thee: for my strength is made perfect in weakness. Most gladly therefore will I rather glory in my infirmities, that the power of Christ may rest upon me.

2 Corinthians 12:9

I feel that if anyone is going to continue, and work this step thoroughly, they will need to admit to themselves that they are insane. "Are you insane?" you may ask. (I know that was corny, but this Program is fun, and I had to put it in there; I hope you're laughing!) Well, yes, but not in the conventional sense of the word. The insanity they told me about when I came into the Program is the insanity of doing the same thing over and over again, and each time expecting a different result. The best analogy that springs to mind is that of someone switching on a light that doesn't come on. He's most perplexed and stares up at the fitting. He then flicks the switch off and switches it on again, at the same time jerking his head up at the ceiling. Still… nothing! He does it again, slowly, then quickly, in rapid succession; all to no avail. Ten minutes go by and he is still switching the switch on and off with as much enthusiasm as when he first started. If I told you this, you'd say to me, "The bloke's nuts!" and that the men in the white coats ought to come and pay him a visit. A normal person would switch it on and off once or twice and then replace the lightbulb or check the fuse board, for example. In other words, they would do something else to try to achieve the desired result.

My drinking followed the same pattern of insanity. You have already read the description of a typical week in my life in the section on Step 1[33]. I never once said to myself that I must not have that first drink; no way! The insanity of the disease of alcoholism was so strong that after a few

---

[33] page 93

days of recovering, I was able to totally convince myself that one little drink wouldn't hurt, that this time it was going to be different. I must have convinced myself of this literally more than a thousand times in my seventeen years of drinking. Each time, the conviction of this thought, that it would be different this time, was as strong as the last. It was very seldom different; and if it was, it always came with the underlying thought of another drink, followed days later by an even more prodigious bender. In the light of this, I was able to admit a certain degree of insanity, and this was enough to get started.

You will see why it is impossible to do Step 2 without having done Step 1. If I was to believe there could be a power greater than myself, I would have had to have admitted already that *my* power was insufficient to overcome the problem. For me, the saving grace of this step was in the words "came to believe". This tells me that I do not have to *fully* believe in a power greater than myself straight away.

> *And you hath he quickened, who were dead in trespasses and sins; Wherein in time past ye walked according to the course of this world, according to the prince of the power of the air, the spirit that now worketh in the children of disobedience: Among whom also we all had our conversation in times past in the lusts of the flesh and of the mind; and were by nature the children of wrath, even as others. But God, who is rich in mercy, for his great love wherewith he loved us, even when we were dead in sins, hath quickened us together with Christ, (by grace ye are saved).*
>
> *Ephesians 2:1-5*

For me, the last sentence is the key; we can proceed even when we are dead in our sins!

I did not need to give this power a name or have any preconceived ideas or notions about this power. You must remember, at this point in my life I had turned away from Jesus and the church and was now a self-proclaimed agnostic, believing there might be some sort of 'force or being' that all religions were praying to and calling a different name. The 'God, Jesus and the Holy Spirit' in the church had done nothing to help me; I'd begged, prayed and pleaded most sincerely, and nothing had happened. You might be able to relate to this and understand why I was feeling more than a little bit sceptical at this point.

So how did I get over this hurdle? Well, I was asked to keep an open mind to the possibility of a power greater than myself, to be as honest as I could, and to be willing to continue. I got my strength to do this out of sheer desperation – I'd tried everything else I knew – and enough belief in what these people were telling me had worked in their lives. I knew that somehow they had been where I was and yet seemed to have got out and moved on to something much better.

A wonderful story was shared at a meeting by an alcoholic Russian scientist on his coming to grips with a power greater than himself. I was about four-and-a-half years sober at the time and he was new in the Program. I had grasped the understanding of this power greater than myself, but his analogy brought my thoughts into sharper focus. That is one of the wonderful joys of this Program: we are on a journey and learn new things from many different people along the way. What he said was that he would open a bottle of Vodka (what else?), have two 100-gram shots, put the lid back on and put the bottle on the table in front of him. Then he would sit and look at this inanimate object in front of him, containing a liquid that looked like water; and he could not leave it there! He had to pick it up again and finish it. He was totally powerless over this silly bottle and its liquid. It overrode all other thoughts and consumed his being. The craving was so strong that he had to pick it up again and drink more. Boy, do I remember that feeling! He said to himself that if this inanimate object wielded a power greater than the strongest willpower he could muster, how much more so could an actual *force or being?*

I needed to be *willing* to believe. "Came to believe" suggests a journey. We always start a journey, no matter how great or how small, with the first step. This gave me such a hope – to know that I could begin this journey just as I was; the whole me, good and bad. I didn't have to achieve a certain status before this 'power' started doing for me what I was unable to do for myself. All I needed was to be rigorously honest, totally willing and open-minded to the possibility that God, through Jesus Christ and the Holy Spirit, might reveal Himself to me in a way I had never heard of or seen before, that my beliefs and the preconceived notions I'd been taught or thought to be true about our resurrected Lord might have been seen through my own eyes and not through the eyes God wanted me to see them through by His Holy Spirit. The way I see God now is totally different to the way I heard ministers, pastors and other Christians speak of their own experience with Him. I believe God has a unique and individual relationship with each of us. I totally agree with what the pastors say and what the Bible says; I just perceive it all from a unique angle. I believe this has been given to me by the Holy Spirit. All my preconceived ideas and notions of God were actually blocking me from the power of God. My ego was doing the damage. This is the open-mindedness I'm talking about; I have no expectations on *how* or *when* God's going to work; I'm just willing to hand over and give it a go.

The other beautiful thing about this Program, and indeed this step, is that my best doesn't have to be very good at all; it could be horrid, in fact. Everything I have said up until this point might make no sense at all. You could be saying to yourself, "This bloke's on another planet!" It does not mean you can't be sober from right now until the day you die. It does not mean, if you do drink again, that all's lost. You have another ten steps to go. The promise is that this Program does work; with some of us it works quickly and with others slowly, but it does work. My prayer is that God's grace will have allowed you by now to grab onto something that you can relate to, and that this will fuel your hope. All you need is the willingness to continue to the end. Again, remember that this is a journey. The journey is lifelong, but it is one of the most awesome journeys you could ever take; it's exciting! Where I am now, I am glad there is so much more. To me, it's like a good novel or an enjoyable holiday. You are so into it that the thought of it ending is unbearable. I pray it will be like this for you too. The journey, once started, continues for our whole lives, but when we die, it's like the sequel – to be continued in heaven for eternity.

Step 3

We made a decision to turn our will and our lives over to the care of God, as we understood Him.

And he said to them all, If any man will come after me, let him deny himself, and take up his cross daily, and follow me.

Luke 9:23

I faced a dilemma at this point in my recovery: how could I make a decision to hand my will and my life over to something I didn't fully believe in yet?

The first help came from the fact that I had exhausted all other avenues in my attempt to overcome this drinking obstacle in my life. I was desperate to try anything, and I had enough faith in what I read and saw in the Program to prompt me to give it a sincere try.

The second help came from one of my first sponsors (mentors) in the Program. He said that I should not focus too much on understanding and believing in this power, that the decision to hand my will and life over to Him could be enforced by continuing with the steps to the best of my ability. What a relief! I was able to make the decision to turn my will and my life over to the care of God by simply making the decision to see these steps through to the end.

It worked like this for me: as soon as I was able to grasp Step 2 and the possibility of something out there more powerful than me, Step 3 was easy and just had to be formalized.

My understanding of God and how it all works is now very different to what it was when I did this step. Here is a summary of what I now believe:

- He is the *only* God, all-powerful, creator of the universe.
- He is made up of God the Father, God the Son and God the Holy Spirit, yet they are one. I don't fully understand this but believe enough to accept this as so.

- The entire human race has sinned and is doomed to an eternity of separation from our creator. We are unlikely to fully understand the concept of 'hell', but separation is something we can more easily grasp.
- Because of the immense love God has for us (again, something we cannot grasp in its fullness), He provided a way out for us. He made the ultimate sacrifice for us by giving of Himself (His Son), to become a mortal man and live a blameless life amongst us. His Son, Jesus Christ, who had to be blameless, took our sins upon Himself and was put to death. He paid the price for the penalty of our sin. The pain God the Father must have felt to have to turn Himself away from His Son at this point is something else that is hard to fully comprehend.
- Because of Jesus' innocence and power, He overcame the grave and was resurrected to life, and is now seated at the right hand of God the Father. Not only that, but He is speaking and pleading with the Father on our behalf.
- We have to play our part, and Jesus wants to see each one of us make the right choice. Each one of us has to do the following in order to receive the benefit of this enormous sacrifice: we need to confess with our mouths and believe in our hearts that Jesus Christ died on the cross for our sins, that He rose again on the third day, and that He is now seated at the right hand of God the Father and is interceding on our behalf. We also have to ask forgiveness for our sins. Then we will spend eternity in heaven with God. We have no way of fully comprehending what heaven will be like, but it will be joyous, free from fear, worry, heartache, pain, strife and misery. There is nothing more or less that I need to do to receive this.
- The reason God created us was so that He could have a *real* relationship with us. He loves us and has given us the choice to love Him back.

I needed the journey of alcoholism to get me desperate enough to seek God. His grace, through the medium of alcoholism, opened my eyes so that I could see the truth. Then the choice was easy for me, but I still had to make the actual decision.

However, this is a far cry from what I understood God to be back then. Just making the decision, based on the little I knew, to hand over my will and life to Him was enough to set me off in the direction of where I am today; truly joyous and free, and still growing. This is the beginning, and God can remove the desire to drink immediately and instantly; he did it for me. However, he has not worked that way in other people I've known and worked with who have been relieved of their own dependency obsession. Some of them struggled with the 'cravings' and mental obsessions, but all of those who recovered worked through the steps to the end. I believe that had I stopped working through this Program when the desire to drink had left me, I would have picked up drinking again where I'd left off, a few months down the line. These dependency disorders are sly and extremely patient. Paul says to the church in Corinth:

> And lest I should be exalted above measure through the abundance of the revelations, there was given to me a thorn in the flesh, the messenger of Satan to buffet me, lest I should be exalted above measure.

> *2 Corinthians 12:7*

To me, my "thorn in the flesh" is that I am still an alcoholic, and if I pick up a drink, I will be back to square one. This fact means that I have to remain in a relationship with the Lord every day, which is what God wants from me.

Getting to know someone takes time – time you will have to spend with that person. However, you need to make a decision to actually get to know that person. Once you have made that decision, you still will not know them unless you call them up to make arrangements and then go and meet them. In the beginning, you will only know them a little, but the more time you spend with them, the better you will get to know them. You would not expect to know everything about this person from one or two meetings, but you will be moving in the right direction. I believe that 'Satan'[34] (the devil) wanted to take me out with this 'thorn' of alcoholism. However, he did not consider what the scriptures say:

---

[34] You do not need to believe in a conventional devil for these steps, but just have an open-mindedness to the possibility of some force that seems to pull you in the wrong direction at times.

And we know that all things work together for good to them that love God, to them that are called according to His purpose.

Romans 8:28

I feel that the Lord has used the very 'thorn' that drove me away from Him to actually bring me into a relationship with Him that is much stronger and closer than it ever was. But I had to surrender my will over to Him; I had to make that decision myself. Living my own way with my own plans was just not working (remember the diesel Audi story[35]).

We make the decision that God's will shall be done, admit that our way never worked, and then go into action in Step 4.

---

[35] page 56

Step 4

We made a searching and fearless moral inventory of ourselves.

Let us search and try our ways, and turn again to the LORD.

Lamentations 3:40

I thank the Lord for the honesty He has given me in being able to share all the things of my life with you so openly; it's liberating. It was not this way in the beginning. If you are scared to death about bringing all your 'dirty laundry' out on paper, I want you to know that I paddled in that same canoe. In fact, there are things from my past of which I am still not strong enough to share with you in this book. The wonderful thing is that at this stage of Step 4, I never had to in order to find recovery. I was asked to make a searching and fearless moral inventory of myself; not of somebody else, and not by someone else either. I can tell you that the thought of doing this step sent shivers down my spine, but I was desperate and at least I knew no one else had to see it yet.

When it was spelled out for me in this step that I was going to have to 'clean house' in order to recover, I remembered that this was one of the main reasons that had held me back from seeking recovery in the first place. I hated myself for what I believed I'd become and for what I felt I stood for. I now understand that saying, "But for the grace of God, there go I," because I went so low that I dabbled with evil things and I saw how easily I could slip into that lifestyle. It still makes me scared sometimes, because there have been times that I felt the only thing keeping me from these things was God Himself – I know I have no power whatsoever. This step was asking me to bring it all up and put it on paper, and I really did not want to do it. However, once again it was God's grace in the form of desperation that pushed me forwards.

Perhaps through reading my journey into alcoholism, you recognize that you are on the same path. I pray that this will create a sense of desperation in you too so that you are able to work this step before you lose more than you already have.

You will see throughout this book that I often refer to either self, ego or pride as being our main problem and the cause of all our other defects of character. C S Lewis refers to pride as the "Great Sin"[36]. I could not word it better and I see this so clearly now. What I can add from my own experience is that a person suffering with pride cannot see it in himself, no matter how much it is pointed out to him; he simply cannot. This Program was a process for me that brought me to a place where I could recognize my pride. It is easy to see pride in others, but we are not to take another person's inventory; this is very important to remember.

What has all this to do with our searching and fearless moral inventory? Well, it gives us a true source of all our other wrongs. In a nutshell, we will come to see that the nature of our faults of character can be summed up in five words. We are:

- selfish;
- self-centered;
- dishonest;
- afraid;
- inconsiderate.

All these stem from pride, ego and self. We cannot see all this just yet, but this Program is, as the late Charles Chamberlin (a recovered alcoholic) said,[37] a process of "uncover, discover and discard". In this step we are *uncovering*. We want to see how, when, where and with whom we have been wrong, so that we can get on course to rectifying these character defects and the trouble they've caused. It would be pointless to try to fix something if we never knew what was wrong with it. Why do we need to bother with these things, which might be hidden deep in us and painful to extract? It's because they cut us off from the only effective power source (God) that can sober us and restore us to sanity.

There are four areas we are going to break down and look at in the working part of this step, which is at the end of the book. They are our resentments, fears, harms and good qualities. We need to get them down on paper to look at them, and we have to do so as thoroughly as possible. I thought this idea of getting it all down on paper unnecessary, but I did it anyway. I found out I was wrong, and now believe it to be a very

---

[36] C S Lewis; *Mere Christianity;* Fount (September 1978), p.106
[37] Charles Chamberlin, speaking at a men's retreat in Pala Mesa in 1975

important part of the process. Don't worry, everything will be explained and tabled for you; there will even be lists of prompts to help get the memory going.

There are two main objectives that we are trying to achieve. Firstly, we are aiming to establish what these four things effect in us, and secondly, what is the exact nature of what we are doing wrong. Our good qualities may be slightly challenging, in that it is often difficult to uncover our true motive for doing good things. We want good qualities with good motives at the end of the day. If our motives are good but our qualities appear bad, we can rest assured this will be righted, as God is looking at our hearts. I don't want you to feel despondent, though; all of us have genuine good qualities given to us by God. If you can't find them, it is probably because they've been clouded over by the character defects, or they have become warped and exploited by your disease. When we are thoroughly done with this Program, the good qualities will start to come back and new ones will form.

Let us now take a look at each of the four areas mentioned, individually.

Resentments

Resentments are feelings of bitter hurt or indignation which come from rightly or wrongly held feelings of being injured or offended.

I have often heard it said often that "resentment is like drinking poison and expecting another person to die". There was a real 'clown' at one of the recovery groups who went one step further by saying, "Resentment is like pouring petrol all over yourself and lighting it, hoping the other fellow will choke to death in the fumes!" (I'm pretty sure he will have a chuckle about me putting his interpretation into the book.)

The person holding the resentment is always worse off than the person/institution/principle against which the resentment is held. In the book *Alcoholics Anonymous,* Bill Wilson (co-founder) says that resentment is the number one destroyer of alcoholics. The reason I believe this to be so is that in most cases, the person holding onto the resentment is feeling that they are the aggrieved party, that they are the one who has been hurt, rightfully or not. Sometimes, after finding out more facts, they discover that in fact they were not wronged.

For example, consider the case of two office ladies, Anne and Julia, having a conversation. Anne tells Julia something in confidence. Two days later, however, Anne hears another lady from the office, Mary, talking about the same topic. Anne feels very resentful towards Julia for what she believes to be gossip and breaking of trust. After a few days, however, Mary mentions to Anne that the office partition walls are very thin and that she overheard her chatting with Julia. So, was Anne's resentment justified? What if, despite Mary overhearing the conversation, Julia did in fact also go and share the news with her? In this case, some would consider Anne's resentment to be justified, although it depends somewhat on your point of view. What is clear, however, is that, justified or not, Anne was carrying resentment and she was the one suffering because of it.

Any resentment is destructive to you, and you need to get rid of it. For me, justified resentment was the hardest to deal with. I loved brooding and festering over a nice big, fat, juicy 'justified resentment'. If I had had a bad day, I'd get home and 'haul' that old resentment out and play it over and over in my mind until I felt better about myself; ready to really give that 'low-life' a piece of my mind. Just putting it on paper here and reading it now highlights to me how 'insane' I was (and sometimes still am).

When we look at our resentments, we will put each one into a table which you'll see in the working section of the book – all nice and easy. We will look at three things:

- What was the cause?
- What effect has it had on me?
- What was my part in the establishment of this resentment?

The cause is simple; you write what is really 'biting' you about the scenario. The second has a few aspects incorporating your social instincts, your security instincts and your sexual instincts. Don't be too alarmed; in the step-working part of the book these will be broken down and explained in more depth, so you should have full clarity. The third is to check your part against the five major character defects; have I been selfish, self-seeking, dishonest, frightened or inconsiderate? You may have one, all or a combination of a few of these character defects for each of your listed resentments. If you have resentment, you *will* certainly have at least one of these character defects. To a greater or lesser degree, the resentment you carry will have impacted your character.

When I was doing my Step 4 for the second time, I said to my sponsor that I had resentment where I felt I was 100% in the right. I then proceeded to explain. In South Africa, we have minibus taxis. (If you are a South African, you will already be saying, "I know where this is going...") They are an absolute menace on the roads. I would like to check the traffic by-laws of our country one day, because I'm sure there must be two sets of road rules: one for the minibus taxis and one for everyone else. The solid yellow lines on the side of our roads are for emergency vehicles only. For minibus taxis, it's an extra taxi lane in peak hour traffic. They are the cause of innumerable accidents; they swerve in front of cars, cut people off, stop anywhere they like when someone on the sidewalk[38] signals for them to stop, and so on. When they do this in front of me and I have to jam on 'anchors' and swerve with screeching tyres to avoid smashing into them, a 'little' resentment forms. My blood boils over and I start speaking 'French' very loudly, accompanied by a few of the local traffic 'hand signs' which are used for such cases! (I have improved over time and now include them in my prayers – I also have to ask the Lord's forgiveness almost daily, and I thank Him for his gracious mercy.) Someone once complimented a lady for her generous heart by saying, "Gertrude's heart is like a minibus taxi; there's always room for one more." (Just something I thought very funny at the time!)

My sponsor put a scenario to me. He asked if I'd considered that the taxi driver might have had a wife and eight kids to feed; that his boss had said if he didn't do ten trips a day he'd get fired. He asked that if I knew this to be true, would I still feel resentful towards him? I had to answer that I would not; sure, I'd be cross initially, but then I'd probably let it go. I had been inconsiderate of his situation and perhaps a little fearful of the possible danger. (That is not to say that he *does* have a wife and eight kids to feed with his job on the line, but it is possible.)

To illustrate this further, I want you to picture yourself on an overnight bus (not a minibus) travelling from one city to another. A man gets on with his two kids of about six and eight. He sits next to another passenger against the window, while the two kids sit one row back on the opposite side of the aisle. You are a further two rows behind the children. The bus pulls off and everybody settles down to sleep. No sooner has the bus left the city, however, then the kids start with their restlessness: bickering, hitting each other and shrieking. People are

---

[38] pavement

starting to stare in the direction of the father who is sitting with his head against the glass, staring blankly at nothing. He seems completely unfazed by his children's bad behaviour, even when they start running up and down the aisle shouting and screaming. You sit there flabbergasted by the fact that the father is not trying to control his unruly kids.

You've been trying to sleep but cannot, and you've almost had enough, when a woman sitting behind him gets up and angrily taps the father on his shoulder. "Can't you keep your kids quiet? There are people trying to sleep on this bus," she blurts out.

"Too right!" you think to yourself.

The man stands up and says, loud enough for everyone to hear, "I am so sorry and do apologize to everyone. We've just come from the hospital where their mother has passed away; my thoughts have been elsewhere, but I will sort them out right now. I apologize for any inconveniences my children may have caused."

Can you imagine the first thought you'd have? My first thought would be, "Thank goodness I never said anything!" More importantly though, if the kids became unruly again a little later, do you think it would bother you as much? I don't think it would me. I might even try to help by telling them a story or giving them a cookie or something.

What changed? Nothing, except you received information about the situation that you had not considered when you first made a judgement call, and this was enough to remove any traces of resentment you might have felt towards the children and their father. The woman who had 'straightened him out' would surely now be making humble apologies and telling him that it is fine and everything is OK.

In the list of the five defects of character, you had only been inconsiderate, but as soon as more information was given about the situation, you became considerate and the resentment disappeared. Amazing, eh?

So, if we consider a resentment and can't identify that we were selfish, self-centered, dishonest or afraid, then I would say we were probably inconsiderate. We should try to create possible scenarios in our minds in which the behaviour we felt resentful about would be understandable. Note I said *understandable,* not acceptable. As long as you are trying to understand, you are being considerate, and the resentment will probably leave you.

Fears

Fears are feelings of anxiety, agitation, uneasiness, apprehension, etc.

Yes, fear is also sin and will cut you off from God just like the others. Fear is one that I still struggle with immensely. To be more specific, I battle with the fear of rejection. I have come to understand that fear is there in my life because, quite simply, I do not trust God.

One of my sponsors, Mike ('American Mike', as he is affectionately known) told me of his sponsor who lived in one of the southern states in America. Mike would call him up to say he was worried about something or other. His sponsor's response would be, "Michael, you're an atheist!" (I can just hear that good old southern 'twang' as he said 'Michael'.) Mike told me that he would feel most indignant, explaining his good Catholic roots to his sponsor and the fact that he attended regular mass and confessions. His sponsor's retort is what hits home for me. He'd say, "Yeah, but you don't trust God."

Fear is that simple: we do not trust God! I found in my life, though, that overcoming it is *not* that simple. I also found that I had to fight each 'fear' battle on its own; it was not a case of 'one battle for all fears'. However, this is where, for the first time in my life, I had a definite plan of action that really worked – Step 4 – and the step also provided me with a structured framework to work within. The biggest lesson I learnt was patience. I have had many fears; some have been removed and some are being removed. I had a fear of alcohol, crowds, loneliness, boredom, homosexuals, financial insecurity and rejection, to name but a few. As I write now, it has been seven-and-a-half years since I last had a drink, and all these fears have been removed, except for the fear of rejection. The fear of economic insecurity took six-and-a-half years of patience before the Lord gave me victory over it, but that is something I will be going through in more detail in Step 12.

Herein lies the *truth* of my predicament: I find that I do not trust God. All the tough talk, brave posture and all the head knowledge falls to the wayside when, for example, I feel disrespected by my wife. Once again, I am faced with something that I am totally powerless over. No matter how hard I try to reason with myself and think logically, the feeling overwhelms me. Unfortunately, I react in a very 'un-user-friendly' way. My response to the feeling of being rejected is to become angry. As I've mentioned before, I have a mouth like a sewer at times, and people get very hurt and offended by my outbursts – and I can't say I blame them; it is socially unacceptable behaviour.

My eyes were opened to the idea that anger can be a response to fear through my dog. (God works in mysterious ways sometimes!) I have a little Scottish terrier called George; I got him about eight months after sobering up. He had already been named when I got him, and I asked why the name George. I was told it was because the then president of the USA, George Bush, had a little black Scottie… OK, I've drifted off the topic, but I thought that was a cute story! As part of my dog's training, I used to use a rolled-up newspaper. When I smacked him on the backside, it made a loud noise but didn't hurt. As he got out of the puppy stage, he started cocking his leg on the furniture instead of going outside to relieve himself. I would catch him by his collar, rub his nose in it and tap his backside with the newspaper. Instead of yelping, he would growl and try to bite me. I knew he was petrified because he would wet the floor while trying to bite. I realized that it was the nature of a Scottish terrier to react to fear in this way. A Yorkshire terrier or Cocker Spaniel is quite the opposite; they yelp and cower and shiver, sometimes for a long time afterwards. This is their nature. I have come to realize that in the same way, we humans react differently to fear from one person to another.

I need to emphasize that my reaction to fear, and indeed fear itself, is a sin and not condonable at all. My pastor from the coast, Chad, always used to mention that our response is our responsibility. We can be right, but wrong at the top of our voices. I normally owe my wife a huge amends at least once a week (we will get to this in Step 8). My feelings and fears of rejection have nothing to do with her. Her behaviour can be a catalyst, but if I removed that, something else would bring up that fear and its subsequent reaction.

> But those things which proceed out of the mouth come forth
> from the heart; and they defile the man.
>
> *Matthew 15:18*

I have found it vitally important in my recovery to be deadly honest about my sin; I believe sin kept hidden in darkness enables Satan to twist things and work it into something even more evil and difficult to get rid of. Darkness is the devil's stomping ground, but bring sin into the light and he can't mess with you anymore. Don't forget to persevere.[39]

---

[39] See section entitled 'Perseverance' on page 72.

In Step 10 we do a daily inventory (much quicker), and this enables me to make my amends on a daily basis. I believe that the Lord will remove this fear in his own time, and we will discuss this further in Step 7.

When we go about reviewing our fears, the table in the working section of the book will be slightly different to the resentment table. Here we will list the cause of the fear. For instance, "I am scared of spiders because I dislike the way they suspend their bodies and crawl over you with their eight legs," or, "I'm scared of rejection because I can't bear the thought of being left on my own; I get all sweaty and battle to breathe." I believe that fear is a sin because it shows we don't trust God, and this destroys our relationship with Him. I therefore need to make a note to make restitution to God through prayer and meditation. My personal reaction to fear of rejection leads to the next point: our harms.

Harms or hurt

Harms are wrong acts which result in pain, hurt feelings, worry, financial loss, etc. – this includes self.

Harms we have done to people, principle and institutions can be divided into sexual harms and non-sexual harms. (I thought this an interesting split when I first saw it, as my sexual encounters were by mutual consent.) We will look at these two areas separately.

When it comes to dealing with harms, I found that I had to ask for God to open my eyes. As a child growing up, and even as an 'adult', I never saw myself as one that harmed, but rather as on the side of the aggrieved party. One gift I am very grateful for, that I believe the Lord graced me with at birth, is that I am not a vindictive person. My heart goes out in compassion to people who suffer with that deep-seated vindictive and bitter hatred, because I believe it holds them in bondage a long time; it's not their fault, and many times they really have been aggrieved. If you are such a person, know that I care and pray for you; you need to be rid of it, so keep on willing God to remove it through prayer. In most of my conflicts and disagreements, when I had been really hurt or hard done by, I simply wanted nothing more to do with the person. I never wished them any ill or blessing, nor felt joy or jealousy at either their failure or success; I just totally cut them off. Cutting them off was not right, but at least I didn't compound the problem or interfere. In as much as the bridge might have been damaged, it wasn't burnt, so to speak. If the person came back to me and made a sincere apology, I was, and still am, quick to forgive and make restoration, with no grudges. Once again, I am extremely grateful to the Lord for this gift. This meant that in my resentment towards someone for something they might have done to me, I very seldom did anything disrespectful towards them. In other words, I did not harm them. I did harm my relationship with God though, and harmed myself – silly, eh?

When I was studying (not philosophy) I came up with a philosophy that as long as I did not intentionally hurt somebody, I was in the right and therefore a good person. I have come to understand that this philosophy was nonsense, to put it mildly. It meant that I never had to try to get along with or understand anyone. It got me into a lot of hot water over the years, as I stepped callously on people's toes and didn't care. Most of the harms and hurts I created in others' lives were out of total inconsideration. When I drank, I used to say the most inappropriate things at the most inappropriate times, and this used to hugely offend people.

I was once at a student friend's twenty-first birthday celebration in Pietermaritzburg. His mother had bought a pig on a spit which was on the rotisserie in the garden; head 'n' all. I was drunk and got all on my high horse about this pig head. I stood watching the eyeballs sizzling, which I found disgusting, and blurted out as much. I moaned very loudly about how I could not believe someone would do such a thing and not cut the head off, at least. Apparently, the mother was highly upset and embarrassed, because it had cost her a large sum of money and she had done her best. Some of the other people there got irate with me and told me to "push off". But I thought I was fully within my liberal right to have voiced my opinion.

At another twenty-first birthday celebration, this time of another friend, Debbie, I was once again very drunk. She had a swimming pool where we were braaing, and even though her parents and grandmother were present, I decided it would be funny to haul off my kit and dive into the pool in my birthday suit. Well, there were mixed reactions from the oddest people: granny could not contain a chuckle, her old man raised an eyebrow, there was a roar from the younger crowd, but mommy broke down emotionally. She went to the kitchen in tears to wash the dishes. I put a towel around my waist and sauntered into the kitchen to help her with them, but I was kicked out onto the street and told never to return to that house again. The next time Debbie's mother ever spoke to me again was at her wedding, well over a decade later. I got a real chance to make my full amends though, and the fact that I had not touched a drop of alcohol in a year helped in her acceptance of my apology, I'm sure.

One time I did do a 'planned harm' to a nasty school teacher; but to be truthful, I did it more because it was naughty than because of an actual grudge. My friend and I used to walk home after school when we lived in Ladysmith. I must have been about thirteen years old, and our route home took us past the school hostels. This particular teacher used to park his car in the fenced-off parking lot of the hostel grounds during the day, and our footpath took us right along the fence. We got ourselves syringes and brake fluid and sprayed it through the fence onto his car's bonnet. Of course, the brake fluid ate the paint and discoloured the bonnet. There were big announcements and inquiries made at school the following day, but it was difficult for them to know who it was and we were never caught. It sounds funny now but those people were really hurt.

Most hurts occurred through what I said. I could say some really hurtful things, especially when drunk, which was most times in the end.

When it comes to sexual harms, my view is totally in line with what the Bible says. As far as I'm concerned, any sexual encounter outside of marriage to that person is harm. There is a very powerful bond that we are not always fully aware of which forms between two people that are intimate on a sexual level. This is God's design.

> *[Jesus] answered and said unto them, Have ye not read, that he which made them at the beginning made them male and female, And said, for this cause shall a man leave father and mother, and shall cleave to his wife: and they twain shall be one flesh? Wherefore they are no more twain, but one flesh. What therefore God hath joined together, let not man put asunder.*
>
> *Matthew 19:4-6*

These are very powerful words for very powerful bonds. I went into these sexual harms having heard this scripture but not having paid too much attention to it. At the time, I am sorry to say, I was only interested in fulfilling my desire or 'need'; if the woman happened to enjoy it, well, lucky for her and it was a boost for my ego as well. I believe now that by creating this bond, I was hurting any future relationships or marriage she might have planned, and indeed my own. That is why I believe it is vitally important to get these all down on paper.

In our harms, both sexual and non-sexual, I need to include myself. I have unwittingly inflicted all these hurts and afflictions that others experience on myself as well.

We need to view the harms in the same way we reviewed our resentments. We start by putting down in one sentence how we actually harmed the person. For instance, "I robbed them of their freedom by sexually interacting with them," or, "I destroyed their reputation at work through gossip." We also have to see what has been affected in us, in relation to our social, security and sexual instincts. We then need to see the very defective nature of our harms: where was I selfish, self-seeking, dishonest, afraid and inconsiderate? And, as always, I harm the Lord God more than anyone else, so I need to make a note to make amends to Him through prayer.

Good Qualities

I would like to discuss another aspect of our moral inventory which often eludes us because it hides under the auspices of our good qualities. What makes it even more subtle is that very often we receive high praise and accolades from other people for these so-called good qualities. What I am talking of here is motive, the heart.

As human beings we are very result-oriented. We often praise people who have succeeded in gaining power, wealth, a following, a wife, etc. We also want to see evidence of charitable deeds: is he helping the poor, is he kind to children, does he love animals, etc. Such a person is often considered to have good qualities. The true motive for someone 'doing good' can, however, actually be bad. (I am not going to give examples, so that I avoid hurting anyone, but I'm sure you can think of many in the secular world.)

In order to see just how subtle people's motives can be, read the story of the prodigal son in Luke 15:11-32. The end of the story is here below:

> [The older son] was angry, and would not go in: therefore came his father out, and intreated him. And he answering said to his father, Lo, these many years do I serve thee, neither transgressed I at any time thy commandment: and yet thou never gavest me a kid, that I might make merry with my

> *friends: But as soon as this thy [younger] son was come, which*
> *hath devoured thy living with harlots, thou hast killed for him*
> *the fatted calf. And he said unto him, Son, thou art ever with*
> *me, and all that I have is thine. It was meet that we should*
> *make merry, and be glad: for this thy brother was dead, and*
> *is alive again; and was lost, and is found.*

> *Luke 15:28-32*

What I want to focus on in this parable is the older son. On the surface he appears very honest, loyal and hardworking, but note his reaction when he hears that his brother is back and his father has taken him in with a robe, a ring and a feast. He tries to use the old 'martyr routine' about what's fair. He's not interested in his father's well-being or happiness; he's worried that what he's expecting to inherit from his father one day is being depleted. You see, he wants his father's things, just like his younger brother; only, he's 'being good' in order to get them. His heart is purely self-centred.

In my past, I'd go to school with a packet of sweets I'd got for my birthday. I would open the packet on the playground and let all the kids take one. I wouldn't even have one myself. The kids would say thank you and mention what a sharing chap I was. This is why I did it; to be liked by the other kids, not to give happiness and joy to them. My motive was purely self-centred.

The irony is that in both these stories, the one who looked 'good' lost out. The eldest son never went into the feast and probably never received his full inheritance; and the next day at school, the kids didn't want to know me. If our motives had been right, in the end we would have got some enjoyment and no heartache or disappointment.

God is not impressed by results or outward appearances. He looks at our heart.

> *...for the Lord seeth not as man seeth; for man looketh on the*
> *outward appearance, but the Lord looketh on the heart.*

> *1 Samuel 16:7*

Perhaps surprisingly, a good heart does not always produce a good outward result. There is a story of a little old granny standing on the side of the road, hunched over her walking stick, facing the traffic going by. A young man walks by and decides to help the poor old lady across the busy road. He is on his own and his only motive is that he feels compassion for someone in need. Greeting her cheerfully, he announces his assistance and whisks her briskly across the road by her arm. When they stop at the other side, she tries to swat him with her handbag as she shrieks, "What are you doing, you naughty man? I was waiting for my bus, and there it goes!"

I was coming out of a pub one evening many years ago, in a jovial mood but not drunk. I walked to the car park and saw a man laying into a woman. She was screaming and crying as he held onto her hair, punching at her face. I rushed over and wrenched him off, then proceeded to rough him up a bit. The woman proceeded to jump on my back and started clawing at my face and trying to bite me. She was screaming, even more than before, for me to leave her poor husband alone. I had had no intention of gaining anything; I was just trying to help someone being assaulted. They walked off to their car in each other's arms and I sat down feeling stupid!

I suspect that this kind of outcome is rare – the exception to the rule – and I'm sure our heavenly Father enjoys the humorous side to our attempts. If your motive is in any way for your own benefit, you are probably on the wrong path. If it is for others or, better still, for God, you are on the right track.

Please understand that I'm not talking about being a martyr or a doormat; you do need to look after yourself as well. What use would you be to anyone if you were ill or dead? The point is that your heart (motive) needs to be one of pleasing God and helping others, not for self-gain.

If you feel weak at the thought of doing all of this, ask for God's strength in a simple prayer:

"Lord, I am too weak and scared to go any further. Please give me the strength to continue with this step. Thank you. I ask this in the name of Jesus. Amen."

Once you've said this prayer, don't sit back. Read through the step and start by doing what you can; start with the easy ones. If you are asked to list your resentments, list the ones that come easily to you. You may resent your old school for making you wear funny hats to the sports days. Write it down! Then think of the next easy one. You may be resentful towards a work colleague who spread rumours about you so that he could win a promotion position over you. Write it down! Continue like this. Remember that you need to start *doing* something, and if you're doing what you can, the rest will follow.

Even so faith, if it hath not works, is dead, being alone.

James 2:17

I suggest you look up that scripture and read the whole chapter; it really gives clarity and understanding.

This is the first step where action is needed. We are now going to start sorting out the mental, emotional, physical and spiritual wreck of our past, up to and including the present day. Don't be overwhelmed when you look at it; we take things one day at a time in this Program. Do you know how to eat a whole elephant? (Sorry to the animal lovers; it's just a figure of speech!) One bite at a time. The point is this: it does not matter how long it takes, it's that you do it that counts.

You do not necessarily need to complete the Program before you stop drinking. God is all-powerful, and if your heart is right, the obsession of the disorder can be removed straight away. However, to stop drinking was not a problem for a lot of us; it was staying sober that was the problem. It often happens in the Program that someone feels completely liberated from the desire to drink without having worked through all the steps but does not want to do this work because they think it will hurt too much. They only started it out of desperation. So, feeling liberated, the person decides that the first three steps were enough for them and they are happy where they are. Don't be fooled by the 'pink cloud' experience. If you want to maintain that pink cloud, you're going to have to clean house. Picture a ship being tossed around at sea. That is your life. You find the Program and maybe start the first couple of steps. This is like your ship anchoring in the harbour. Compared to being tossed around in turmoil out at sea, being docked in the harbour is calm and blissful. In my job I've always been told that "good is the enemy of best". I can say the same for this scenario. Being in the Program and experiencing a few months sober without having to white knuckle it feels like heaven. You think to yourself that it couldn't get better than this. If the truth be told, you're actually still scared of working through all the steps, especially continuing with Step 4. I have met so many in the Program that never get past Step 3; we call it the 'three-step waltz', because they would rather go back and do the first three steps again: one-two-three, one-two-three, one-two-three, round and round they go. But they cannot see the beauty and freedom of actually stepping ashore; the freedom and peace that comes with completing the steps. It would be OK to remain like this, if it weren't for the fact that ships leave harbours and sail out to rough seas again. If you're still on that boat, you're going off again. Your sobriety needs to run its full course; you need to step ashore. Moreover, God has something so much bigger in store for you – he has for me too.

This need to work through the steps was daunting for me, especially Step 4. I didn't know where to start. As I mentioned, this is one of the great motivating factors for me writing this book. Over the years, I have developed some systems (guidance from the Holy Spirit, I believe) that have worked for me, and have found worksheets that I've modified, breaking this step into very doable 'bites'. You might not understand all aspects of the steps because you are probably on your own, and although I'll try to answer your email queries, it might still be confusing for you. That is why I have tried to go into great detail, cramming in as many suggestions as possible.

Do not lose heart. I suggest you follow the action steps like you would a cake recipe; that's how I did it because I was totally confused in my recovery. I am so glad I did it that way, because I feel I got the best foundation possible. In a cake recipe, it will say "a cup of white flour", for instance. You look in the pantry and you see you only have three quarters of a cup and decide that will do. It says "5 tablespoons of white sugar" and you only have brown, so you use it. It says "3 eggs" but you like eggs and decide to add four. It says "bake at 180°C (sorry, USA, I don't know what that is in Fahrenheit…) for 30 minutes", but you are now hungry and don't want to wait, so you push it to two hundred degrees for fifteen minutes. When your cake comes out, I guarantee it will be a flop. It's the same with the Program. Follow each suggestion precisely. I have aimed to put as much into the steps as possible. If the recipe said three eggs, I have tried to give you the actual size of the eggs as well, so to speak. You will encounter things about which you are just not sure; pray and ask God for direction and then do what you think is most right. The Lord sees your heart, and He can sober you even without your effort. I believe He really wants to see that you are honest and sincere. If you are, it will come.

I am convinced that a dependency disorder will strip a person of everything, and in the end, will take their sanity or life. In Chapter 1, I mentioned a guy who had a funny slur when he was intoxicated (the one who knew Daniel M). That guy drove home from the pub one night when it was raining. He was as 'drunk as a lord' and drove into a ditch on the side of the road. The ditch was filled with water, and on impact, the door came open and he tumbled headfirst into the ditch and drowned. His death was recorded as an MVA (motor vehicle accident), but truth be told, alcohol had killed him. There are millions of deaths and hurts around the world written up as MVAs, domestic violence, rapes, falls, suicides, etc., that were actually due to various dependency disorders. Even the victims' 'incidents' are caused by these dependency disorders, because they were raped or beaten or killed by someone who was drugged up or intoxicated at the time. If this person had been sober or straight, they would most likely never have done these things. The overeater who becomes so unhealthy that the strain on their heart causes a heart attack or causes depression which can lead to suicide would probably never have suffered these fates had they not been enslaved to an eating disorder. I firmly believe that most of these other fates suffered around the world would be drastically reduced if we could eliminate all dependency disorders. I am not suggesting this is the 'mission'; I am just trying to show you the seriousness of having a dependency disorder. You could leave out this step until it gets really bad, but who knows if you'll get another chance? However, if you are feeling as I did when I was in active alcoholism, you will probably not be enjoying your life anyway. Whatever your conviction may be, I pray that you will be able to make this inventory as best you can.

Step 5

We admitted to God, to ourselves, and to another human being the exact nature of our wrongs.

Confess your faults one to another, and pray one for another, that ye may be healed. The effectual fervent prayer of a righteous man availeth much.

James 5:16

"Rory, how free do you want to be?"

This was a question my sponsor asked me over and over during my inventory, and it is my question to you. I was privileged to have a sponsor to go through Step 4 with me the second time; however, the first time, I did it on my own with a couple of pointers from a sponsor. When the time came for Step 5, I did not know which "human being" to pick to share "the exact nature of [my] wrongs" with. Choosing the right person to do Step 5 with is very important, and there were some things I felt I could not share with my sponsor yet.

We first need to understand why it is so important to have to admit to ourselves, to God and to another human being the exact nature of our wrongs. By writing everything down in Step 4, I have essentially admitted them to myself; I might just need to read through them again. I think I knew most of my wrongs, but the inventory helped me to put them into perspective and identify their actual nature.

When dealing with God, I believe He wants us to communicate with Him, even if we recognize that He knows everything. For instance, when we decide to become His child, the scripture says:

...if thou shalt confess with thy mouth the Lord Jesus, and shalt believe in thine heart that God hath raised him from the dead, thou shalt be saved.

Romans 10:9

Why would He want us to confess with our mouth to Him when He is omniscient (all-knowing)? There are two reasons.

The first is that we quickly put things out of our minds that we don't really want to think about. Truth be told, we *know* that God knows everything, but we *do not want* Him to know our wrongs; we want Him to think we are better than we really are. If we are not sitting down and actually confessing out loud our wrongs to God, we have a remarkable tendency to squash them down into our subconscious and forget about them. In this way, I think humans are very much like ostriches with their heads in the sand; as long as we are not looking at something, then it is surely not there! If we know that God sees these defects of our character, there is a certain amount of godly fear in us, and this is a huge motivator for us to really want to change. For me, there was also a bit of shame in the fact that I disappoint God so often, even though I really do not want to.

The second reason involves Satan himself, and is because of the very fact that he is *not* omniscient. The devil trembles at the thought of God, and when he knows that you are open with Him about your wrongs, it is far more difficult for him to use lies on you. It's like when I was a kid playing at home and I accidently broke a window. I was scared to tell my dad and thought it would be better to say nothing and 'play dumb' if he asked me. The problem was that my friend from next door saw me break the window and reminded me of how my dad would discipline me if he found out. "You'll get the hiding of your life if you tell him," he assured me. I realized my 'friend' would have one over me if I lied to my dad, and that I would pretty much have to do what he told me in order to keep him from telling my dad the truth. I plucked up courage that evening and told my dad the truth, and he was surprisingly proud of the fact that I was honest; he forgave me and got the window fixed. The next day the boy next door started taunting me, but he could not scare or threaten me at all; he had no power. I believe it works the same with God and the devil. It is important to know that, unlike God, the devil cannot read your thoughts. This is why it is so important to confess aloud; when the devil hears you confessing your iniquities to God, he tends to leave you alone.

I have also discovered that when we confess our sins, the guilt seems to vanish, and we attain a certain level of peace.

When it comes to sharing the nature of our wrongs with another human being, we really need to know why we have to. After all, if God knows, what has it got to do with anyone else? This part is probably one of the most crucial aspects leading to the success of the Program.

The first benefit is a certain amount of accountability. Although he is not your boss and you owe him nothing, having someone ask you how it is going from time to time keeps those things fresh in your mind. This stops us from pushing our wrongs back down inside us so easily. For me, one of the biggest reliefs I had was the fact that somebody knew about *all* my wrongs and it was OK. *It was OK!* I never lost my job, my dignity, my reputation, my life, etc.; it was OK. What an amazing weight off my shoulders. I could walk up straight, look the world in the eye and know it was all OK. This does not mean that you won't lose any of the things I mentioned, but I believe you will still feel a weight taken off – those things are replaceable, and God has things in store for you that are in line with His plans for you.

I feel one needs to reveal *everything;* if you know there is something you can never tell, that is the thing you must be *willing* to tell. As I said before, though, if you have a sincere desire to be straight and honest, but cannot at present, do not be discouraged; it will come. Show your commitment by telling the person everything you can and mention that there is something you are not ready to speak about. God sees your honesty and He will work in your heart.

The person you choose to share the exact nature of your wrongs with can, in theory, be anyone. If you have a sponsor, that is usually a good choice. However, you might feel that there are things that you somehow know they will not be able to handle objectively. This was the case with my sponsor. As much as he helped me, he had a religious belief and a cultural stance which I believed would prevent him staying open and objective towards me, even if he wanted to, after I'd shared some specific wrongs with him.

The person whom I was most afraid to tell was my mother, and for some reason she was the one I blurted out my Step 5 to the first time. I knew I wanted to tell someone, and I was totally willing to, just so long as I knew it was the right person. I prayed and asked God to present someone to me, telling Him I was willing and ready. Little did I know it would be her! I had come to visit her one day, probably about six months into my sobriety, with no intention of doing my Step 5 with her. While we were talking, though, I had a sense of peace and it all came out. She hugged me and said she was so glad we could have an open relationship once more. She never said anything else, and this is important too; we are not looking for advice or help, just a human ear.

This is why it is so good to ask God ("your will, God, not mine") to bring someone across your path. But remember, you must be totally willing, with enough self-honesty to know you are not trying to procrastinate; otherwise, when God does bring the right person along, you might overlook them. Other types of people you may choose are doctors, lawyers, clergy, counsellors, close friends or even a total stranger. Just remain willing and the Lord will bring the right person.

Because my answer to the question at the beginning of Step 5 was, "Very free," I had to 'let it all hang out'. There were always two things that I'd never wanted to ever get out, but I shared them somehow. I have felt nervous to share them here in this book and had to ask my wife if I could – we never share things that might hurt or injure another, including their reputation or credibility; the world can be a harsh and judgemental place. But she was happy for me to do so. There are many people who battle with similar scenarios to mine, and, if this is you, I believe that the Lord wants you to realize it's also *OK*.

One night I was diving back home as drunk as a lord – I was *seriously* inebriated. My speech was a slur and I could not walk straight. I was driving at about 40 kph and I came to a sharp left bend in the road. It was a double lane road in my direction and I was in the left lane. (We drive on the left-hand side of the road in South Africa.) There was a hidden entry road on the left bend and a car was indicating to turn right. In my drunken state, I decided to stop and let the guy turn across me. This was inappropriate considering that the traffic was light in the evenings. The car just waited for me, so I stuck my arm out and waved him on. I guess he thought this was all rather crazy but didn't want to sit there all night, so he went across me. It must have been a combination of my lights shining at him and the fact that he couldn't see around the bend properly, but neither of us saw the minibus taxi come past me in the right lane. The taxi hit the driver's door of the other car at what must have been about 80 kph. The car spun around and bashed up against the curb. I noticed the minibus taxi had passengers in it as it veered across the road over the curb on the other side and smashed into a solid brick wall of a church. There was no movement from either vehicle, and I first thought of calling the ambulance and then going to check if the people were OK. Then I wondered what would happen when the police arrived and found me in this state. What if someone in the car was 'OK' and told them what

I had done? I did the most despicably selfish thing ever and drove off. That incident haunted me for years and the guilt ate at me often.

The other thing that I couldn't talk about was the fact that I had been sexually abused by older boys when I was six, nine and twelve years old. What made it particularly bad for me later on, I think, was that I can't remember being really hurt. In fact, it all seemed rather secretive and fun at the time. I do, however, vaguely recall being slightly hurt on one or two occasions; it wasn't fun being in the 'big boys' group anymore after that. I was sworn to secrecy, of course, but they fortunately moved to another town at some stage.

My sexual outlook was very messed up and warped in my later life. I could not forgive myself or talk about it because I believed I'd opened up to it willingly. I felt I was to blame. I used to think if I had been badly hurt, I could tell people and they would feel sympathy for me, not revulsion. Anyway, it was all too humiliating to deal with.

These were the things I shared with my mom. She said nothing, and I believe it was the best way she could have handled it. The good thing was that she never changed one bit towards me – it was OK.

By the time I was doing my Step 5 a second time, it wasn't any easier. This time I went for prayer and counselling on this and other things. I believe that if something of a similar nature has happened to you, you too will need deliverance and counselling; it is not your fault, but it is enough for the devil to get a foot in and create a stronghold in your life. Pray and seek guidance as to whom you can go and see; ask the church counsellor or pastor. We want to clear the wreckage of our past. Take courage to know you are not alone and it is not as frightening as you may think.

I asked God for the courage and did it. It was really very liberating; what a load off my mind! I think it also had to do with the fact that I picked the right person to tell; one of my sponsors.

This might be a good time to speak about the benefit of a sponsor and what it means to me. A sponsor can be like a mentor, friend, confidant, sounding board, advisor, helper or guide. This is why in my sobriety, I have a few sponsors. There are some in the Program that swear by only one sponsor, and that works for them – this is the beauty of the Program. You do not have to be too concerned if you don't have a sponsor; I have written this book with the explicit intention of helping those who might not be able to get one. We have already gone over how you can do Step 5 at the end of the book without a sponsor. However, I still believe there are benefits of having a mentor, someone to talk to about honest 'stuff'. I suggest that you go online; there you can get a sponsor who never sees you and you never see them, to deal with your specific dependency or defect of character.[40]

But for everyday things I suggest you actively seek out a friend or mentor.

> *Iron sharpeneth iron; so a man sharpeneth the countenance of [gives moral support to] his friend.*
>
> *Proverbs 27:17*

When I was still living on the Kwa-Zulu Natal South Coast, I had a friend like this who lived just outside of Port Shepstone. He stayed on a sugar cane farm, and I would drive up there three times a week and we'd walk in the cane for an hour or two. He was also a recovering alcoholic but had a firm grip on the spiritual aspect of the Program. We would talk non-stop the whole time about our days, our hang-ups, our relationships, our victories, and pretty much everything we could. We offered each other moral support and gave each other words of encouragement. This was one of the most supportive relationships I had. There were one or two things that he would not share with me, and when I probed, he became very offish. I kept my distance, and soon afterwards my wife and I moved to another city. I've put this in as a real example of a Step 9 amends. Who knows, Colin might read the book one day![41] Another thing I did was join a men's group on a Friday morning before work. We meet in a hotel lobby and drink coffee and share. I am sure you can find something like this in your area. The people don't need to know your situation, but remember that you have many affairs that you need encouragement and support in. The guys in my group do know about my alcoholism, and I am able to make suggestions and help them understand what various people in their lives are going through, who might be afflicted with addictions or dependencies. However you go about it, I know it's not easy dealing with people sometimes. But as the word of God says, we are not meant to be recluses. We are to help others and

---

[40] For suggestions, make a web search for "AA sponsor online". Or try the following: *www.12step-online.com/online-aa-and-al-anon-sponsorship/*

[41] Note to Colin: I just want to say to you that in the past, in my dealings with you, I was self-seeking, afraid and inconsiderate, and I probably hurt you. For this I am truly sorry. Go well, my old friend.

grow in relationships. If it is really tough for you, just remain willing; it will come.

Something else that is important to remember is our obedience to the Bible. The scripture that goes with this step has a condition to our recovery; we have to *confess our sins* (nature of our wrongs) to each other so that we can *be healed* (recover). I found I need not understand any more than this for the healing to come; I just need to obey.

In my recovery, I understood nothing about what was going on in this Program. All I knew was that I was surrounded by a bunch of happy drunks who told me that they had been sober a while by working through the steps and following the Program as honestly, willingly and with as much open-mindedness as they could muster. That was good enough for me because I was desperate. As I am writing now, many years later, one thing stands out more than others as to how the Program worked when all else failed. It brought about a certain humility in my life, and particularly Step 5. I realized that God could not do anything for me while 'self' was in the way. The only way I have ever been able to achieve a semblance of humility is by working through these steps – not perfectly, but to the best of my ability. Few things are more humbling than having to share your dirty laundry with another person. This is why I believe this step to be critical in recovery.

At this point it will be important to go back and make sure you have left nothing out. If there are some things that you do not have the courage to open up about, just hand them over to God and remain willing. Pray and ask Him to reveal anything He wants you to bring to light, those which might have slipped your mind. If you have done this and you feel a peace about doing your best, you will be in a different place in your life right now. If you feel you are still far from where you want to be, look back on your life and take heart from where you used to be. I believe the end is not the goal; the journey is.

Step 6

We were entirely ready to have God, through Jesus Christ, remove all these defects of character.

If ye be willing and obedient, ye shall eat the good of the land.

Isaiah 1:19

This Program is full of surprises, and Step 6 was no different for me. When asked if I was entirely ready to have God remove all my defects, I immediately answered, "Of course!" without much thought; who wouldn't? I thought Step 6 would be easy and straightforward; after all, if I was able to hand over my drinking problem to God and He had removed it, this should be a walk in the park. In essence it is, provided my attitude is right. This step has, however, proved to be one of the more difficult steps; not because it takes time or a huge effort, but actually because it requires no effort. This is harder to do than one thinks because it is natural for us to at least try *something*. Letting go totally and allowing God to guide you will require a miracle in itself.

I have come to realize that each 'battle' has to be fought individually on its own merit. Some character flaws are easy and disappear quickly because we really want God to remove them. Others take time because either we don't really want to let go of them, or we do not trust that God will act. It seems silly that we trust Him in some big areas of our lives, while in smaller areas we find it difficult. Whatever the reason, I have found that the process of learning to trust and really hand over to God is what builds character and forges our relationship with Him. It is truly a beautiful thing if we sincerely follow through with it. I believe that our character is the thing which will determine what we do in eternity.

> *Moreover (let us also be full of joy now!) Let us exult and triumph in our troubles and rejoice in our sufferings, knowing that pressure and affliction and hardship produce patient and unswerving endurance. And endurance [fortitude] develops maturity of character [approved faith and tried integrity]. And*

character (of this sort) produces (the habit of) joyful and confident hope of eternal salvation. Such hope never disappoints or deludes or shames us, for God's love has been poured out in our hearts through the Holy Spirit Who has been given to us.

Romans 5:3-5 (AMP)

I believe this to be the essence of our development. I chose The Amplified Bible here, because it gives a wonderful explanation of the word 'character' ("approved faith and tried integrity"). Character-building starts when we begin to acquire the right attitude, and the right attitude starts when we know and understand more. Knowing and understanding comes when we search in the right places, and God, through the Holy Spirit, opens our 'eyes' (understanding) to things we'd never seen before.

For me to gain the correct attitude towards this step, there were a few things I needed to understand. I will explain these things in the way I believe the Holy Spirit revealed them to me, through the Program and my sponsor. Again, at the time I worked through this step I had no understanding of anything; I just did what I was told with honesty and willingness because I wanted to get sober. I have put down my understanding of how it all worked for me because I think it might bring a bit of clarity to you; but if you don't understand what I'm on about, it won't matter, as long as you do the work honestly and willingly.

The first thing for me was to understand what I was actually expecting God to do for me. Quite simply, I wanted Him to change me. I was getting ready to *repent,* with the firm belief and understanding that only He could help me do this. Under the word 'repent' in the Oxford dictionary, we find the following meaning: "Resolve not to continue wrongdoing in, (action...)" What strikes me about this definition is that we are making a *decision,* a resolve, to turn away from our wrong action. Having got this far in the book, you will know that we do not have the power to do so while maintaining the right motive. For instance, if someone said they'd give me a large sum of money to be nice to someone who is horrible and whom I don't like for an hour, I could easily be as sweet as pie to them for that time. I would 'grin and bear it' for the hour, my motive being the thought of a wad of notes in my pocket. The problem is that with the wrong motive, I could only be nice for a short time, no matter how much I was offered thereafter, because my true feelings and attitude towards that person would come out. Only God can give us the right attitude and enough power to change our defects of character, and this only if certain conditions are met.

The first condition is willingness; we've got to *want* to change. I love the scene from the movie *The Break Up* when Jennifer Aniston says to Vince Vaugn that he doesn't help with the dishes, for example.

He retorts that if she wants him to do them, she must just ask.

She then says that she doesn't want him to just do them, she wants him to *want* to do them.

He replies, "Who wants to do dishes?"

What she really means is that he should have the right attitude towards doing the dishes; that it should be a case of him taking pleasure in wanting to do something that shows he loves and cares for her.

I think God sees it in much the same light. For me, the bulk of this step was becoming willing to have these defects removed.

A gossip will go to the extreme of exposing another's extramarital affair by praying aloud for that person to see the error of their ways. If you ask the person who prayed whether they like a gossip, they'll tell you straight, "No, not at all!" You might wonder why they do it then! Well, this person will probably say that praying for another is not gossip, but rather concerned love and care. I do not believe this to be true, because if they really cared, they would not hurt that person by publicizing their affair. People gossip either because it makes them feel superior to others or because they want the attention as others listen; it makes them feel important. Both reasons are self-centred. However, people know that nobody likes a gossip, so they disguise it as spiritual charity. They often start off by saying something like, "I hate to gossip, but as a Christian, watching my Christian sister going down the wrong path…" They then proceed to rip the other person to shreds.

The point is that if you would ask this person whether they wanted God to remove the defect of gossip in their lives, they'd either say they are not a gossip or they would still want to be able to talk about people "in a loving, helpful way". A person like this would not want to let go of being able to talk about others because when people listen to them, it eases the pain of rejection and being ignored. Do you see how this pans out? The real defect of character is a feeling of rejection. The rejection can be real or imagined but is normally only a perception on their part; it is most often not reality.

I speak here from my own experiences in my life, as I suffered with rejection and enjoyed telling stories that everyone wanted to hear.

There are other defects that are downplayed, such as when we say, "Hate is not murder," or, "Lust is not rape," or, "Comfort food is not gluttony," or, "Ambition is not greed," and so on. However, any of these can become the extreme given the right circumstances. If we are living with defects, even at low levels, and are saying that they are part of us and we are just trying to live with them, we will be miserable and they will just get worse over time.

The reason that we do not want to let go and let God undertake with both the gossip and the rejection, for instance, is that we do not trust that He will remove these defects. We are also not entirely convinced that He is capable of being the comfort we were receiving from the 'attention' invoked by the gossip if He does get rid of them. Does this mean we're done for? Absolutely not. This is where the Program champions over anything else I have ever come across. I never had to understand any of this back then; I just needed *honesty, willingness* and *patience.* Nothing more was required. Desperation had brought me to the Program, the Program told me what to do, and this allowed God to work. Simply tell God that you do not have enough strength to believe that He can remove these defects, that you really want them to be removed because you see them as wrong, but that you feel afraid of being alone and having no one who cares about you and sees you as worthy. Ask God to give you the strength and willingness you will need, and then move on. You do not need to worry about whether it has worked or not. The goal in this Program is the *journey,* not the destination. While we are on the journey, we are finding sobriety, which is the ability to live peacefully, joyfully and comfortably with ourselves. When we are in this state, we are the most useful to God and His plans for us. The destiny, I believe, will be reached in the next life, in eternity.

The next thing, I believe, is that we must be willing to forgive. We must be willing to forgive others, ourselves and even God. Notice that I said we must become *willing* to forgive; we do not necessarily have to forgive straight away. Forgiveness can be very difficult for many people, as some hurts run deep. I put it to you, though, that none of the hurts inflicted on us run deeper than the ones we've inflicted on God.

You might have noticed that I mentioned we need to become willing to forgive God as well. This was no mistake, but I will need to explain it because God is perfect.

We do not and will not fully understand all of God's ways of doing things and will not always think they're fair.

> *For my thoughts are not your thoughts, neither are your ways my ways, saith the Lord.*
>
> *Isaiah 55:8*

> *Yet ye say, The way of the Lord is not equal. Hear now, O house of Israel; Is not my way equal? are not your ways unequal?*
>
> *Ezekiel 18:25*

Consequently, we will be hurt by certain things that come from God which we will perceive as wrong but are not, because He is God and His ways are perfect.[42] Nevertheless, because there are some things we will never fully understand in this lifetime, we can hold onto hurts or resentments towards God which we can only let go of through forgiveness. I do not believe this is being blasphemous because we are truly trying to right our relationship with God as best we know how, and I believe He understands this.

We might wonder why we need to be willing to forgive. The reason is simple. By asking God to remove our defects of character, we are also asking Him to forgive us of our wrongs. In order for Him to forgive us, though, we must first forgive others. I do not fully understand this, but the Bible is clear on this matter:

> *But if ye do not forgive, neither will your Father which is in heaven forgive your trespasses.*
>
> *Mark 11:26*

God knows if we're not strong enough to forgive everyone everything, but as long as we are honestly willing, He will provide the strength needed at the right time. Even if we do not have the willingness to forgive, but are prepared to be honest about that fact, He will work in that area of our lives at the appropriate time.

Here is a summary of the action I had to take. I had to *want* to have my defects removed. Having completed Step 4, I knew that my basic character defects were (or stemmed from) that I was selfish, self-seeking, dishonest, inconsiderate and afraid. When I found that I did not have the

---

[42] See Deuteronomy 32:4.

132

willingness for certain character flaws on my list to be changed, I needed to ask God to give me that willingness. There was nothing more I could do but to continue to ask for that willingness until it came. But I did not just sit and wait for the willingness to come concerning those few character flaws that I did not sincerely want removed; I got on with the rest of the steps. Over time, the willingness did come.

Once more, remember that recovery is the journey and not a specific goal. As long as we are on the journey, we will be exactly where we are supposed to be, regardless of whether we have just started or have been at it for a long while. I love this!

Step 7

We humbly asked Him to remove our shortcomings.

*Humble yourselves in the sight of the Lord, and He shall lift
you up.*

James 4:10

"I can't, but He can."

Once we believe this statement, doing Step 7 is easy. I have discussed
a bit about my understanding of humility in Chapter 4. I would, however,
like to reiterate some points, because it's one of the most vital elements
to attaining recovery.

Why, as human beings, are we so prone to be restless, irritable and
discontented – in a word, miserable? I believe it's because we don't
understand God's will for us and don't trust that He will truly meet our
needs. We are uncomfortable and worried about losing what we have
and also about not getting what we want. Because of this, we want to
control the management of our lives. We may acknowledge that God is
our creator, but we want to tell Him what to do with us.

*But now, O Lord, thou art our father; we are the clay, and
thou our potter; and we all are the work of thy hand.*

Isaiah 64:8

It would be ridiculous if clay was being moulded into a plate and it
suddenly piped up to the potter, "Hey, hang on a minute, pal... I'm not
going to be a plate, I'm going to be a vase, so you had better shape me as
such!" We would laugh at this idea, yet we do it to God all the time.

The cause of this response in us is a lack of trust in Him. As long as
we do not trust Him with our lives, we will try to run them ourselves, or
even try dictating to Him. We come to Him in prayer to meet the needs
that will fulfil our plans, when really, we ought to come to Him each day
expecting direction, guidance and to be equipped for whichever direction
He wishes to lead us in. We need to *trust* that where we are and what we

are doing at this precise moment in time is exactly where He wants us to be and what He wants us to be doing.

> *Surely your turning of things upside down shall be esteemed as the potter's clay: for shall the work say of him that made it, He made me not? or shall the thing framed say of him that framed it, He had no understanding?*

> *Isaiah 29:16*

I cannot run my own life; my creator *has* to. He designed me and I will function best according to the specifications He has laid down for me. He does not hand me the entire manual for each day specifically, but He issues a general manual (the Bible) for the workings of the human being. Just as a small child does not know what it will do each day, so we do not know either. The child has been given certain instructions to follow each day: get up at 7am; wash your face and brush your teeth; get dressed; come down and eat your breakfast etc. For the rest, the child waits expectantly to see what their parent(s) will come up with each day. I believe this is exactly what our heavenly Father wants us to do. This is perhaps why Jesus said:

> *And said, Verily I say unto you, except ye be converted, and become as little children, ye shall not enter into the kingdom of heaven.*

> *Matthew 18:3*

It is vital that we don't know the implementation method of His purpose for our lives, because if we did, we would have a field day trying to orchestrate just how it would need to be done – our egos are just that big. I realized that as long as I thought I had an actual role to play in the running of my life, I could not surrender to God. The irony is that the only role I have to play in my life is the surrender of my will to Him, the only thing God has ever given me control over in the first place. All other control and effect I thought I had was just an illusion. The pursuit of this illusion is what created my defects of character in the first place. God is the creator, He is in control and He has the power to change my life totally. When I can grasp this, I am able to attain a semblance of humility. What God does not have control over is my will; He actually made it that way. With humility in place, I am able to hand my will back to Him, and then I am ready to ask Him to remove my shortcomings.

Motive is very important for this step. We need to again consider why we want these shortcomings removed. An obvious reason can be the realization of the immense pain these shortcomings are causing *you;* this was certainly true for me in the beginning. However, our shortcomings also cause pain to others and to God. Pain is a great teacher, but at this stage of the Program, it is possible to get one's mind focused on a 'purer' motive. I do not feel it is imperative to be able to reach this so-called 'purer' motive in order to achieve initial sobriety, but as we need to continue growing to survive, it will help a lot to see in which direction we need to go. Ultimately, we need to start living a life that is focused on the salvation and well-being of others.

With this in mind, I was able to see that in order for me to even begin to think of others and be of assistance to them, I was going to have to be rid of my shortcomings, my character defects. Being selfish, dishonest, self-seeking, frightened and inconsiderate all point me in the opposite direction to the way God has designed my life to work. If I am to be of any help whatsoever to my fellow man, I *must* be rid of these defects. This understanding really was an immense help to me in having the right attitude (one of humility) towards asking God to remove my short-comings.

Step 8

We made a list of all persons we had harmed, and became willing to make amends to them all.

Therefore if thou bring thy gift to the altar, and there rememberest that thy brother hath ought against thee; Leave there thy gift before the altar, and go thy way; first be reconciled to thy brother, and then come and offer thy gift.

Matthew 5:23,24

I found that Steps 2, 6 and 8 are very similar in that they all require a process that can take time. I'm not saying that they cannot be achieved in an instant, but they most definitely require God's help. In Step 2 we "*came* to believe", in Step 6 we were "*entirely* ready", and in Step 8 we "*became* willing"; all these phrases seem to suggest a process of acquiring a certain 'attitude'. The reason I say that they will require God's help is that if we could attain this way of thinking on our own, we wouldn't be in the pickle we're in! Most of us realised things were going wrong and what was causing it, but we lacked any power to change anything. I am so grateful that God was there with the power needed to get me through these steps; I just had to be willing and ready for Him to work. However, because of the fact that human nature (self, ego and pride) keeps God from working, a process is required to break it down (humility), and this can take time.

What is meant by "make amends"? It sounds simple enough, but is it? I had heard many people refer to Step 8 as 'cleaning their side of the street'. I wish it were as simple as that, but I discovered it isn't.

Just 'cleaning my side of the street' would avoid a lot of embarrassment and would allow me to keep my 'dignity' intact. I put the word 'dignity' in inverted commas because although this is how I perceived it, in fact it was my *pride* that would be kept intact. However, it is pride that blocks me from accepting God's gift of grace – His supernatural power and ability to overcome. What God really wants in making

137

amends is *restitution*. The definition of this word exactly describes what our goal in making amends should be: "A return to or restoration of a previous state or position..."[43]

What we are trying to do with the people we have harmed is to restore our relationship with them to its previous state. I am not naïve enough to think this possible with everyone, but it should be our goal and motive. God can do many things, but He cannot choose for a person; He gave us free will and this gift stops Him from being able to decide for us. There are going to be people who might politely accept our apologies but still not want anything to do with us. We do not try to force them, or even blame them. Due to our behaviour while drinking, we hurt some people deeply and it will require the grace of God in their lives to free them from the bondage of unforgiveness. We need to accept this and walk away. I think this is what was really meant by 'cleaning our side of the street', but it doesn't end there. We need to pray for them, pray that God's love and grace will be made available to them as it was for us. However, we should not feel guilty about what we have done in the past. We are not doormats to be walked on and should not grovel or beg for forgiveness.

Part of making our amends involves asking God for His forgiveness. In fact, this is most important; it is a wonderful thing to know that He *always* forgives us.

> *If we confess our sins, he is faithful and just to forgive us our sins, and to cleanse us from all unrighteousness.*
>
> *1 John 1:9*

I have often found that many of the people who did not want to restore the relationship eventually came back to me and restitution was possible. (I truly believe that prayer helped in these situations.) Sadly though, some relationships are never restored; yet I still believe that praying for these people might help them eventually restore or develop a relationship with God, and this is far more important a relationship than the one we might have with them. In all the amends I was able to make, one person outright wanted nothing to do with me; I still pray for that person, as God's grace allows me to, and my hope is that they too will find serenity in relationship with God. I would say about eighty percent

---

[43] *The American Heritage® Stedman's Medical Dictionary;* copyright © 2002, 2001, 1995 by Houghton Mifflin Company; published by Houghton Mifflin Company

of the amends I made have ended up in restitution and this has given me immense peace in my heart.

The question as to why we need to restore relationships is a key element to our existence, and I feel it will help to share my views on it. The Bible states:

Now ye are the body of Christ, and members in particular.

1 Corinthians 12:27

Everybody on this earth is God's creation, and therefore a potential member of Christ's body.[44] If we take a normal body with its various parts (members) – arms, legs, kidneys, skin, etc. – there is *constant* communication going on in order for that body to function and operate optimally; we can even go as far as to say that each part of the body is working and functioning in *relation* to the others, and they have to, in order to continue proper communication. If there is a breakdown in communication within a body, it malfunctions and does not operate at its optimal design proficiency. The same applies to the body of Christ. There is, however, one major difference, and this is where the comparison falls apart. God has chosen us – those members of his body who are in communication with him – to work to restore relationships with the parts that are missing or malfunctioning. He wants us to help the other person to 'sweep their side of the street', where permitted; not necessarily by doing it for them, but by the example of change they see in us, and by passing on the message of how that happened in our lives.

This is why relationships are so important to God, because He wants the body of Christ to be fully functional. In restoring relationships, we reopen the channels of communication, and God (through the Holy Spirit) is able to once more speak into the lives of others, using *us* as channels. I cannot say for sure why God chose this way to do things, but I believe it could be a way for a person who does not know God to be able to hear His message through another bodily being. It also gives us an opportunity to form a relationship of love and support with another person; but more so I believe that it is so that He can develop a deeper, more meaningful relationship with us personally. My wife and I planned our wedding together, I supplied the funds and she chose what she wanted (just kidding), and in doing it this way we grew to know each other. I delighted her with one or two extra surprises, and I think God

---

[44] See 2 Corinthians 6:18 and Galatians 3:26.

woos us along the way with surprises of His own. This is part of what loving is all about, and God is love and He wants as many ways as possible to express His love, which is why He created us. If we are to be in relationship with Him and part of His kingdom, we need to learn to love and this includes loving what God loves, which is His creation. So, we start first with the people we know, and that is why we need to strive to make restitution with other people during our amends. This is the attitude God is going to place in our hearts. Right now, if we start to grasp this concept and push through with the amends in the next step, God will embed the right attitude in our hearts without us even realizing it.

When you work through the steps in the last part of the book, you will see that I suggest going back to the Step 4 (Harms and Resentment) worksheets and writing down all harms and all resentments for which you can recognize you played a part in another's harm towards you. We often forget two important points as far as others' hurts towards us go. One is that they too are battling with their own character defects. We often fail to realize that we do not have the monopoly on character defects; most people suffer from them as well.[45] The second is that we were probably the first to hurt the other person during our drinking, often repeatedly, long before they ever finally reacted. So many of the resentments we've built up because of what others have done to us are actually due to their reaction to something we did to them during our drinking. We may feel that a person driving a bulldozer through our boundary wall a bit harsh after we only bumped the corner of theirs the night before, but we are not to focus on their wrongs at all. The fact of the matter is that we *did* in fact harm them and we want to make restitution. Before we are able to go to them and ask for forgiveness for our part, we need to forgive them for theirs, even if they do not ask for it.

We are trying to restore and build a relationship with God, and ultimately it will be His forgiveness that is important. Others are required to forgive us in the same manner, but if they do not, God is able to forgive

---

[45] This is why I strongly believe that anyone battling to get rid of any character defects in their lives will be able to achieve this by simply working the same Program in the last part of the book; you just replace the disorder in Step 1 with the defect of character you're battling with and work through the steps in the same manner.

us and remove anything that might bind us. We let that remain between them and Him, but we still pray for that restitution between them and God, and we release them through our forgiveness. I do not suggest we go to them and let them know we have forgiven them if they haven't asked for it; they may feel that they do not owe us an apology, and subsequently build resentment towards us because of what they might construe as arrogance.

Now that we have our list of amends in place and have been able to adopt the right attitude towards the people we have resented and then hurt, we should now be willing to make our amends.

Step 9

We made direct amends to such people whenever possible, except when to do so would injure them or others.

Give, and it shall be given unto you; good measure, pressed down, and shaken together, and running over, shall men give into your bosom. For with the same measure that ye mete withal it shall be measured to you again.

Luke 6:38

Here is a powerful but uncomfortable step. I say 'uncomfortable' because it requires being humbled and that is not fun for us addicts. However, it was after this step that I started to experience the true power of God at work in my life. It was during this step that I became aware of the fact that I was not alone; that 'something' was doing for me what I could never before do for myself. What an immense sense of freedom and peace that gave me! For the first time since beginning the Program, I realized that alcohol wielded no more power over me. I knew after this that I did not *need* to drink anymore. But when I started this step, I had to stick my pride in my pocket and get to it.

Continuing from the previous step: now that we have the right attitude and motive for making our amends, we next need to acquire the most effective means and sufficient courage to make the best amends possible. I was once told by an old pastor of mine, "Rory, you can be right, but wrong at the top of your voice."[46] This cannot be achieved by ourselves or any other human being; we have to go to God. I love this. As usual, I have no other options available but to go to the source of all power, which is God, and His power always comes through for me, as long as I am in His will. I know that I am in His will if I have given everything over to Him and sincerely ask Him to be in His will. From

---

[46] Note to Pastor Chad: Thanks! All these years later, I still remember this saying.

then on in, the process has started; we are where we are, and that is exactly where God wants us to be.

This means that God will orchestrate our amends exactly as they are meant to take place. So, we can really relax and do our best in each case, knowing that the outcome will be in God's hands, and after making the amend, we can leave guilt-free, no matter what the outcome is. Just as God cannot choose for us, He cannot choose the other person's reaction; He can only reveal the truth to them. If there is not a full restitution of relationship after a particular amendment, we can walk away without guilt, knowing that our relationship with God is strengthened. I feel, though, that we should still pray for the other person, that they may find peace and joy in a relationship with God. Very often, over time, the relationship between us and them is restored as God heals their heart.

From my own experience I cannot give any hard and fast rules about how to make each amends, but I can give you a brief overview. As I said before, attitude and motivation are important, but we also need to be true to our heart. What I mean by this is that when deciding on whether to make direct contact or not, we have to search our hearts as to why we want to make any particular amend in a certain way.

Let's look at an example. A man working through this step might decide to tell his wife of an affair he was having many years ago, but upon reflection he realises that the only reason he is doing this is that he cannot bear the guilt. In this case, he needs to consider carefully whether he should make that revelation or not. If his motive, now that he is sober, is to continue his relationship with total honesty and does not want his wife to be embarrassed in public if it is ever revealed, this might be a better motive. However, he needs to truly look at the bigger picture: are there children involved, is she strong enough to handle a revelation of this magnitude, is she the type of person who wants to know this sort of information, etc.? He also needs to bear in mind who else might be affected by the revelation. It might be better to say, "In the past, during my drinking, I have done some wrong things for which I am not proud. I have been dishonest, selfish, and inconsiderate... and I have hurt you. I ask your forgiveness and want you to know that I am truly sorry for my behaviour. I have handed my life over to God and am following a Program of recovery that can set me free from an obsession with drink. I love you and want to rectify our relationship so that I can be someone who will support you and on whom you can rely." Having said this, I believe that if she were to ask him outright if he has had an affair, he should tell her the truth.

Unfortunately, there is very little other advice I can give on how to make your amends. This is why I stress the need to go to God. He knows everything there is to know about the various scenarios and if you hand it over to Him, what needs to be done will come to you. If you feel there is no prompting, maybe leave it a week or so and continue praying. After this, I suggest you 'follow your gut' because a lot of the time this is the way the Holy Spirit prompts us.

Sometimes you might find that the person needs to let off a little steam. Once again, there is no hard and fast rule on whether you need to sit and weather the storm, or if you should 'beetle off' out the door. Personally, I would sit and allow them a little time to vent. If they start getting too heavy or aggressive, I would politely excuse myself and leave. Whatever you choose to do, one suggestion stands: do not argue back and do not bring up their wrongs or harms. I find this easier when I remind myself that they too may be ill and cannot always react in a sensible way. I also remind myself that the harms I caused them can be quite severe.

The order in which to make amends is another debate that has no real right or wrong answers. When I made my amends, I started with the ones that were easiest and closest to where I lived. I left the difficult ones for later, and the ones I felt were impossible I did not think about. I found that as I made the easier amends with little or no ill feeling shown by the other person, it became easier to do the more difficult ones. By the time I had got through the bulk of them, the ones I had thought were impossible now seemed quite doable. Many say this is an obvious progression as a person's self-confidence grows. This could be partly true, but I believe more in divine intervention. I think that as we take the first step 'into the waters of the Jordan river'[47], so to speak, the waters then part and we can walk across the river on dry ground. There is very little we can do but to *start* making the amends. We start with the things that we can do, and as we do so, I believe the power of the Holy Spirit fills us with the strength to get through the others. I always try to keep my primary motive in mind when making difficult amends: I am trying to clear the way so that I can have a relationship with God. It actually has

---

[47] See Joshua 3:13-16.

very little to do with the person or institution with whom I am making the amends.

Step 10

We continued to take personal inventory, and when we were wrong, promptly admitted it.

For I say, through the grace given unto me, to every man that is among you, not to think of himself more highly than he ought to think; but to think soberly, according as God hath dealt to every man the measure of faith.

Romans 12:3

Step 10, in a nutshell, is a combination of Steps 4, 8 and 9 which you do, not for your whole new life every time, but for the recent year, term, day or even moment. Steps 10 to 12 are going to be your new design for living; they will form the basis for the rest of your journey into eternity and you will use them every day.

If you have reached this point in the Program, you almost certainly will have had a spiritual awakening. This could feel like everything or nothing, but it can be recognised in the fact that the desire to drink will have left you. If it hasn't done so, there is something you are holding back, and my suggestion would be to work through the steps from 1 to 9 again (remember the teaching on perseverance in Chapter 4). I have heard many stories (each different to mine) from people who received the power to stop their various dependencies, power which they never had before. We all have 'thorns in the flesh' and 'crosses to bear', especially those of us who have dependency disorders, because otherwise our egos would take our lives back from God's hands again.

Paul said:

And lest I should be exalted above measure through the abundance of the revelations, there was given to me a thorn in the flesh, the messenger of Satan to buffet me, lest I should be exalted above measure.

2 Corinthians 12:7

And Jesus said:

> ...if any man will come after me, let him deny himself, and take up his cross daily, and follow me.

Luke 9:23

I spent a lot of time pondering these words, as most of what I'd heard of God were nice, comfortable things. A 'thorn in the flesh' and 'a cross to bear' both sounded like pain and discomfort to me, and yet both are mentioned as part of being a follower of Christ. What I came to realize was that God wants me in a relationship with Him *all* the time. The problem is that I don't listen too well. In his book *The Problem of Pain*[48], C S Lewis notes:

> We can ignore even pleasure. But pain insists upon being attended to. God whispers to us in our pleasures, speaks in our conscience, but shouts in our pains: it is his megaphone to rouse a deaf world.

Thankfully, God never leaves us without comfort. Jesus said:

> Come unto me, all ye that labour and are heavy laden and I will give you rest. Take my yoke upon you, and learn of me; for I am meek and lowly in heart: and ye shall find rest unto your souls. For my yoke is easy, and my burden is light.

Matthew 11:28-30

This speaks of coming with pain and burden and finding rest, of taking up Jesus' mission *with* Him, learning of Him and finding rest in our souls, and finally that promise that *His* mission and burden are easy and light. Is this not what we are all looking for: rest for our bodies, rest for our souls, and a mission and burden that are easy and light? They can be, if our "yoke" is God's. His yoke (meaning mission, love, passion) is His people, His lost creations.

These days nothing gives me more pain than not being in right relationship with God and nothing keeps me more out of relationship with Him than not being in right relationship with my fellow man. This is why this step is so vital to me. I have to do my inventories continually so that I can right my wrongs with others and gain motivation through seeing my positive growth. This ultimately leads to a continuous

---

[48] C S Lewis; *The Problem of Pain;* Harper One; ISBN 978-0-06-120849-2

unhindered relationship with my heavenly Father. It is an incredible journey. I am sure that as you practise using this step in your life daily, it will come to you habitually, as I find it comes to me.

Once a year I spend some time reflecting on the main events of the past twelve months; it gives me a general overview of my progress and if anything stands out as 'pain', I review who or what caused it, what it did to me inside and how I reacted to it. I look at my part and can go and make my amends. It may seem unnecessary, given that we take a daily inventory. However, I find that I have often overlooked small offences or resentment which have built up over time. This process also allows me to see how my life has progressed with God's help over the last year, and it gives me renewed hope and strength.

Consider a soldier fighting in World War I. He has fought alone for a year in the mud and trenches, winning a piece of ground today, losing a piece tomorrow. By the time a year is up, he must feel like he hasn't done much at all; that it was all an absolute waste of time. What if, once a year, he was taken off the battlefront and shown a map of France? What if he could see on the map that over the last year they had conquered more than a third of the enemy-held country? I am pretty sure this would give the boy renewed hope and energy. Because I have been engaged in spiritual warfare on different fronts during the year, I have often been unable to view the bigger picture. I feel like that soldier must have felt; like I'm swimming in treacle and not going anywhere. I find that an annual inventory is like getting out of the trenches and looking at the map of my advancement. I get renewed hope and excitement at what God is doing in my life.

A daily inventory is more about that particular day's activities and is usually quite easy. You will find, when you start to work the Program, that I have made up a shortened worksheet of Steps 4, 8 and 9. It is easy to use, puts things into perspective very quickly, and shouldn't take more than a few minutes to do. During the course of the day, I might have a worker, let's call him Fabio, who mixes building sand for screeding a concrete floor instead of river sand. I have shown him the difference and shown him which pile is which. The lad is from Mozambique and answers yes to anything I ask him; and I know this. He has wasted four cubic meters of sand and nine 50 kg packets of cement at a very high cost. Instead of explaining to him that this is wrong and that he will have to pay the money back through extra work, I get angry and 'give him a mouthful'. I tell him what I think of him, that he is "as thick as a pile of planks" and shouldn't be working here. Even though I am feeling the pain inside of me because of this outburst, I do not have the peace and calm to recognize my mistake and make amends. (This is what I am striving towards though, and eventually, with God's power, I will not do this at all.) I carry this pain with me the whole day and it puts a bit of a damper on the rest of the day's proceedings. When I get my list out that evening,[49] I write down Fabio's name and what he did. I ask myself if I have resentment. Did I harm him? I then look at where I was defective in character: was I selfish, self-seeking, dishonest, frightened or inconsiderate? I establish whether I owe an amends (most of the time I do) and make it on the phone straight away (if it is early) or first thing in the morning. I then ask God to forgive me for hurting one of His creations, for not reflecting Jesus in my response, and ask Him to restore His relationship with me.

Most of the time, these days, I can make an inventory on the spot. For example, the following scenario happens to me all too often. I finish my time of prayer, reading and meditation with God in the mornings at around 05:15. I feel really positive and uplifted and have set it in my mind that I will not allow the drivers in the traffic to bother me on the way to work. I will continue speaking to the Lord on the way to work and I will have a very peaceful day. Then, after being on the road less than five minutes, my old friend the taxi driver swerves in front of me and stops to pick someone up. Off goes the hooter, up goes the finger and verbal venom spews forth (a bit silly, seeing as he cannot hear me anyway; probably just as well). I feel devastated that all my resolve has gone to pot! The problem is, by the way, that it is just that: all *my* resolve. You see, I made these plans of how peaceful I would be and completely left God out of it. I know I cannot be patient and peaceful on my own; only God has the power to do that for me. Straight away I say, "Lord, sorry for excluding you from my day. I cannot do anything without you. Once again, in my dealings with this taxi driver, I was afraid and inconsiderate. Please forgive me and restore our relationship, in Jesus' name. Amen." I might go past the taxi driver and mouth the word "sorry" and give him a smile and the 'thumbs up'. I feel immediately at peace and my day is really not ruined. Sometimes I have to repeat this

---

[49] These days I have become so accustomed to the list that I can take the harm or resentment through the process in my meditation without pen and paper.

process several times during the course of the day in various scenarios, and it works each time.

This step may sound like a big deal and fuss, but it really works to set one at peace. The more you keep practising it, the more it becomes quite normal and easy. There will be times when the 'madness' is on you, and you cannot do all of this. I guarantee you won't feel good, but do not let guilt get a hold of you. Guilt sucks the life out of a person, I find. You will calm down, and when you do, get to your inventory straight away. Go to God, make your amends with Him and the other person, and you will see how the peace returns to you. As I've said, we are not perfect yet; we are striving towards perfection and God understands this. He loves us and He wants to renew our relationship with Him.

Step 11

We sought through prayer and meditation to improve our conscious contact with God, through Jesus Christ, praying only for knowledge of His will for us, and the power to carry that out.

Let the words of my mouth, and the meditation of my heart, be acceptable in thy sight, O LORD, my strength, and my redeemer.

Psalms 19:14

This step contains our most important mission on earth and one that most people are no doubt striving to achieve in some way or another: to get to know God and to know Him better. There is something inherent in our nature that has this desire to know our creator. I was one that was looking for it in all the wrong places, but I was looking. This fits into the design of why we were created. I've heard it said that God created man to be a companion. Nice, but one should be careful here, because this implies that God might have been bored or lonely or had some other need. I understand that God is *complete* in every way and therefore needs nothing for fulfilment. Rather, God is love and we are an expression of that love. His perfect design for *all* of us is to love Him back; He wants us to have a relationship with Him and, as we know, any relationship requires contact. The more contact we have, the more meaningful and deep the relationship is. Because God is not a being we can see or hear, our main form of contact is through prayer and meditation. Prayer is talking to God; meditation is listening and thinking. However, I have found that the way God speaks to me most often is in His written word – the Bible.

It is impossible to fully understand God's plans and ways. We have seen that as we are His creation, only He knows best how we function and how to fulfil that function at the optimum level.

> *But as it is written, eye hath not seen, nor ear heard, neither have entered into the heart of man, the things which God hath prepared for them that love him.*
>
> *Paul quoting Isaiah in 1 Corinthians 2:9*

So, to pray for what we want or think we or others need, even if it seems good, is not always the best. This is why our safest bet is to pray for the *knowledge of God's will for us.* This is only the first step, though, because it is all very well knowing something but if you are incapable of executing the revealed plan of action, what good is that?

I once saw an accident happen at an intersection; two cars smashed into each other. It was not serious and there were no injuries. I pulled to the side of the road and got out to see if anyone was hurt. There were cars trying to turn but were obstructed by these two vehicles, and the oncoming drivers were not helping because they were slowing down to have a good look. I thought I'd help by stopping some traffic and waving other traffic on, but no one took any notice of me. It wasn't long before there was total chaos and I decided to step aside. Just then, a tow truck arrived on the scene and two men jumped out. One went to the accident and started making arrangements with the drivers. The other, who was wearing a chevron vest, walked to the middle of the intersection and started sorting out the traffic. I watched in fascination as he said a few calm words to one or two of the drivers and then started directing traffic. Within a few minutes the traffic was flowing again and the smashed cars were towed off. I got back into the car, my pride in tatters, wondering how he had managed to get exactly what I had tried to achieve. He was no policeman and yet the drivers listened to him where they had ignored me. As I drove off, it dawned on me that the chevron vest the man had worn had given him the power I had lacked.

You see, despite all my knowledge and quick thinking, my effort was worthless because I never had the power backing me. So, when we ask for *knowledge of His will for us,* we ask too for the power to follow through with His plan. The power needed in any given situation can come in many different ways; I found that it is better for me not to know which way, most times. All I know is that when His will is done, I feel joy, peace and comfort within myself. For interest's sake, I believe the power comes mainly in the form of the fruit of the Spirit.

But the fruit of the Spirit is love, joy, peace, patience, kindness, goodness, faithfulness, gentleness, self-control; against such things there is no law.

Galatians 5:22-23 (ESV)

I know that when I get through the day successfully, it is due to the power of God, and I thank Him. Every now and again, normally in my daily time with Him, God shows me the kindness I might have exercised in a situation that led to its successful conclusion, and I smile and I thank Him for being my God. Moments like those, which happen rarely to me, give me a glimpse of what it must be like to be in constant contact with God.

I would briefly like to share my experience with *prayer, reading* and *meditating.* I knew now that I was to start praying on a regular basis with the intention of forming a closer relationship with God. Some may ask why it needs to be through Jesus Christ, and some may think it a bit formal when they see that all my prayers in this book end, "...in Jesus' name. Amen." The Bible tells us:

Jesus saith unto him, I am the way, the truth, and the life: no man cometh unto the Father, but by me.

John 14:6

So that is what we do. I remember sitting with my mentor/sponsor at this time and asking him what would be the right way to pray. He smiled and told me the Bible had my answer, because Jesus answered that exact same question asked by His disciples in Luke 11:1-4 and Matthew 6:9-13. So, I took the prayer Jesus gave them and I have never looked back; I still pray it today. I have modified it a little; not in its meaning, but in its 'lingo.' My prayer now goes:

"Dear heavenly Father, Holy is your name. Your kingdom come, Your will be done, on earth as it is in Heaven. Give me today my daily bread, both physical as I eat and spiritually as I read Your Word, and forgive me my sins and trespasses [I name the ones I remember], as I forgive those that have trespassed against me [once again, I name the ones I remember]. Lead me not into temptation of any sorts, but deliver me from evil, especially the evils of self, ego and pride, and the evil of not trusting You. For Yours is the kingdom, the power and the glory, forever and ever. In Jesus' name, Amen."

This is the way I interpret the prayer; it says everything that needs to be said in a prayer. Firstly, we acknowledge God as our Father, but also show Him reverence by remembering His holiness. Secondly, we show our hope for God's ultimate plan, and submit our will to His will; this is essential, as I have explained. Thirdly, we are going to God for our needs both physical and spiritual; we are not taking our wants to Him. Fourthly, we are making relationship restitution with God and with our fellow man. Fifthly, we are asking God's protection against things over which we are powerless and asking Him to cleanse our souls. Lastly, and I believe most importantly, we are acknowledging God as the supreme creator of the universe, recognising His omnipotence, and giving Him all the glory, which is rightfully His – this is our true purpose.

When I had found sobriety after seventeen-and-a-half years of drinking, my concentration and patience levels were at an all-time low. By the time I had reached Step 11, probably ten months or so into my sobriety, I found these levels had improved but they were still not where they should be. I found I could only tackle tasks in short spells before my concentration would waver. From as early as I learned to read until my drinking started taking over my life, I was an avid reader – I loved it and still do. After I stopped drinking, I found I could not bring myself to read anything too involved. Even with simple novels, I could only read a page or two before getting bored or tired. My mentor had suggested reading a chapter from the Bible every morning. It is strange how quickly a person becomes estranged from things that once were second nature. I found myself floundering, not knowing where to start reading or how to read. Did I read an entire chapter; should I take notes, or what? It was all too much for me to handle and I found myself slipping into despair.

It is amazing how God works, but I heard in a conversation someone say, "It does not matter with the things of God how much one does or how often you get it wrong; what matters is trying to maintain consistency, even if it is little by little." I remembered it said years ago that the best place to start reading in the Bible is the Gospels, so I started reading from the beginning of the New Testament. I set aside the idea of trying to read an entire chapter or writing anything down and set myself the task of praying the Lord's Prayer and reading one *verse* a day. After reading the verse, I asked God to show me what He wanted me to see and understand, and then went to bed. The whole exercise would take me less than three minutes, but I resolved to be diligent and, come hell or high water, I was going to do this *every day*.

I want to leave it at that and move on to today. My reading, praying and meditating have taken on a life of their own. I read more, pray longer (mostly for other people) and find myself in my thoughts with God, sometimes for hours. In my mind, my resolve is still to read something from the Bible and to speak to God every day. I feel now that I cannot miss one day not speaking to my God, Father and Friend; it's such a beautiful thing.

I have never particularly liked the word 'meditation'; it always seemed so long, so adult, so boring... I guess we all have our ways and styles, but my understanding of meditation is quite rudimentary. To me, it is just thinking and listening to thoughts that come to you. I often find my thoughts drift off to my worries or to my dreams. Before, I used to fight it and think I must be focused on God; now I see it differently, and it brings me a lot of peace and joy. What I do is ask the Holy Spirit to be with me in my thoughts and to speak to me. Thereafter, I let my mind flow and enjoy. I might drift off into a concern about a work issue. I go through the issue and how it makes me feel and how I could handle it. Often resentment wants to spring up, and I go through a quick Step 10. I then ask if my approach would actually work and try to think what I might need to change to make it work. Usually, an idea comes to me that makes sense, and I take that as God speaking to me through the Holy Spirit. Many times, it is an untested approach, and I go and apply it. I find it such fun to see how the whole scenario unfolds for the good; it truly is remarkable. If I find my thoughts wander to my dreams, I let them play out and enjoy them. After my thoughts have drifted a while, I stop and look at where the Lord is in all this, and I find that He is everywhere. I find I have come to a more godly approach towards work issues, and I see how God has shifted my dreams and visions towards being of benefit to others. It is in times like these that a certain beautiful scripture really becomes a reality in my life:

> *Even the mystery which hath been hid from ages and from generations, but now is made manifest to his saints: To whom God would make known what is the riches of the glory of this mystery among the Gentiles; which is Christ in you, the hope of glory...*
>
> *Colossians 1:26,27*

This is what meditation is for me; it's wrapped up in reading God's word, speaking to Him, listening to Him, sharing things with Him – and it is not boring. When I do all these things, I experience exactly what the lyrics of that old song, written by Helen H. Lemmel in 1922, say:

Turn your eyes upon Jesus;
Look full in His wonderful face.
And the things of the earth will grow strangely dim,
In the light of His glory and grace.

Amen.

Finally, as part of my getting to know God, I came to see my need to join a church. It had been a sore point in the past, but a coal taken out of the fire does not stay hot. There are so many people we can love (doing things for them that they need done, for free and fun), and so much encouragement that we need, that we cannot bypass this part. There is no stronger motivation for me than simple obedience to God's word.

And let us not give up meeting together. Some are in the habit of doing this. Instead, let us encourage one another with words of hope. Let us do this even more as you see Christ's return approaching.

Hebrews 10:25 (NIRV)

For me, it is an instruction and I cannot live up to His glory without going to church. I know God delights in it, and the thought of His delighting in something that I can do gives me joy. There is a beautiful scripture in Jeremiah which sums up the importance of this step:

Thus saith the Lord, let not the wise man glory in his wisdom, neither let the mighty man glory in his might let not the rich man glory in his riches: but let him that glorieth glory in this, that he understandeth and knoweth me, that I am the Lord which exercise lovingkindness, judgment, and righteousness, in the earth: for in these things I delight, saith the Lord.

Jeremiah 9:23-24

Step 12

Having had a spiritual awakening as the result of these steps, we tried to carry this message to others, and practise these principles in all our affairs.

Brethren, if a man be overtaken in a fault, ye which are spiritual, restore such an one in the spirit of meekness; considering thyself, lest thou also be tempted. Bear ye one another's burdens, and so fulfil the law of Christ.

Galatians 6:1,2

This step starts off by talking about something I'd never heard of before. The closest I'd come to any kind of 'awakening' was a rude awakening (normally like sticking my head out the bedroom window after a night out, only to see my car had been 'modified' somewhat). I had also heard of a 'spiritual experience', although I never understood it. I have subsequently had a few spiritual experiences, which I count as a touch of love and reassurance from God; not something that happens every day.

One I can remember vividly. I was in church and we were singing a song in which some of the words were, "Holy, Holy are You Lord God Almighty; worthy is the Lamb, worthy is the Lamb; You are Holy..."[50] I was singing along when all of a sudden I got a powerful sense of how awesome and majestic God is, and of how He still had time to think of me and change my life. Now, you can ask my wife or anyone that knows me, I am not a tearful person, but tears just ran down my cheeks as I felt God's love. It was a most incredible experience and I left the church feeling warm and content inside for days.

The spiritual *awakening* referred to here was nothing like that experience for me. It comes as a natural result of the first 11 steps. I have heard of people having spiritual awakenings without the steps but have

---

[50] Agnus Dei

only actually met one. For me, it was a gradual process and was only really realised properly when I had completed Step 9. By the time I had reached Step 12, my awakening had grown, and I find that it is still growing; this is part of the new journey. You realize that you are on a journey here on earth, and that you need to keep growing.

I found that I no longer needed to drink; the booze was present around me, but it had no hold on me. My mind was preoccupied with other things and these things gave me the sense of ease and comfort which alcohol and drugs had previously given me. The difference was that this sense of ease and comfort came without harming others or myself. In fact, my whole attitude was now one of "What can I do for another?" instead of "What can I get from another?" There have been many that I have shared my story with that wanted what God had so freely given me, but they were not prepared to work through the steps as suggested. They could not, therefore, receive this gift – this spiritual awakening.

God cannot deal with anything in our lives while we are still the boss; we have to surrender this right to Him. It is because we have 'been in the way' that we have not had this spiritual awakening before. Because we battle ego and pride, we cannot see these things and cannot stand aside, even if we wanted to. This is why we need to work through the steps. The spiritual awakening began for me as the understanding that God was now in control of my life and was doing for me the things that all along I could not do for myself.

If you are at this step and are not drinking and have an inner sense of peace and comfort with no desire to drink, I put it to you that you are already experiencing a spiritual awakening. You could be experiencing no other difference whatsoever. For each person it is different; some say that they feel totally different inside. But, however you may see it, your desire for whatever you have been dependent on will no longer be there. Whether you realize it or not is irrelevant; God's power, which you lacked before, is now in full control.

Now that we have had a spiritual awakening, we are not to rest on our laurels; we have something to *do*. The first thing this step instructs us to do is to try to carry this message to others. I am glad this step uses the word "tried" here, because people generally have their own agendas, and they are not always ready to hear our wonderful tidings of peace, joy and comfort. Some are eager, but the 'work' is too much. To be completely honest, I don't have a clue as to who, when, how or if anyone will listen and apply the Program.

I'd like to share one of my first experiences of 'carrying the message' with you. The guy was of Danish descent and he must have been about eight years older than me. I shall call him Michael. I must have been about a year sober and was really enjoying following the Program and going to all the meetings. Michael came up to me after one of the Margate meetings and asked if I would be his sponsor. He said he liked what I had shared and could relate to my story quite a lot. I was happy someone had asked me to help them, and so I set up a meeting with him three days later, on the Thursday evening. When I arrived, he was sitting outside at a wire mesh patio table. I remember thinking how the presence of the two-litre glass bottle of Old Brown Sherry in the middle of the rickety wire table made the two crystal scotch glasses look tiny and out of place. I should have left then; my sponsor had always said I should never play nursemaid or companion to a man while he was 'tooting'. Anyway, he seemed to be able to string a coherent sentence together, so I sat down to hear his tales of woe. He told me how his mother had died seven years ago, how his girlfriend had left him many years ago, and how he was all alone. I tried to tell him my story and how I'd found companionship at the meetings, and that he should join in. Truth be told though, he wasn't interested in all that and kept trying to get me to have a drink, which I refused, of course. It dawned on me after an hour or so that he wanted someone to sit and talk nonsense to while he drank. I made a polite excuse and left.

Thereafter, every other day I'd get calls from Mickey in various stages of inebriation. Each time I told him that I'd be happy to come and see him but not while he was drinking. There was a stint of about four days during which time I didn't hear from him and he wasn't answering my calls. I thought, at first, he might have 'got the hump' with me, but something said I should go around his place – I believe it was the Lord. I found him on the bed, locked in his house, and he wasn't moving. I screamed through the burglar guards, but he wouldn't budge. I got the police out and they broke open the bars and called an ambulance. The police found a .22 pistol on the bed, and one of the paramedics said that if he had been found a day later, he would have been dead.

They admitted him to the Port Shepstone government hospital for severe dehydration. The police took his .22 and said I should tell him when he got out. He was in hospital for three weeks and I played the Good Samaritan, bringing him smokes, toiletries, clothes, and visiting him once a day. In the beginning he had bad amnesia and kept asking me to tell his mother where he was. I shared my story with him in that time and was chuffed to be of service.

When he came out, I took him to meetings and he would share how he had nearly died and how well he was doing now. I felt great; I had been able to pass on the message and someone else had recovered. He started driving again, the police gave him his pistol back, and he even got his job back as a security patrolman. After about three months, though, I started noticing he was coming to fewer and fewer meetings and he wasn't calling that often. I tried to phone him a few times but to no avail; I called round his place but they said he'd moved overnight, one evening earlier. About a month later they found him in Southport; he'd put a bullet through his head.

I was devastated, angry and upset all at the same time. I got a hold of one of my sponsors known as Blackie (he used to patrol the Transkei coastline in the police force and his skin got so dark from the sun that that was where he got his nickname from). He had a high-pitched, slow chuckle and when I told him that I would never help anyone again because it doesn't work, he just sat back and gave off one of these long whining chuckles. Once he had caught his breath, he said, in his very Afrikaans accent, one of the most profound things that I've ever heard, which still sits with me today: "Rory, stop trying to play God." I understood what he meant, and the guilt left immediately.

There is another story I'd like to share. I used to go to the local supermarket in Port Shepstone. There was a toothless, inebriate homeless man who often came to harass me for money or takeaway. He would refuse food I bought from the supermarket but used to ask if I had money for him or if I would buy him takeaway food – I never gave him either. He was a drunk of what I then considered the hopeless variety, surviving on methylated spirits and any drug available. But one day I said I would take him to a meeting with me if he wanted to get sober. (If something stirs inside my heart that I know goes against my general nature, it is usually the Holy Spirit.) He said he did, and I picked him up two days later. He was as pickled as a cucumber, as usual; nevertheless, off we went.

At the meeting he kept disrupting proceedings, and I asked another chap to take over while I took him outside. He started swearing and said that everyone looked down on him and that all he wanted was a cigarette. I managed to get him one from a night watchman at the church, and said that I didn't look down on him, that I had felt the same as he did once. I told him that no matter what, I knew God loved Him just as he was right now. He broke down in tears and apologized. That night I booked him into a shelter for the homeless.

The next day I got him into a two-week rehab in Durban where he went through the 12-step Program extensively, and when he came out I got him into a redevelopment programme in Amanzimtoti. They had a church there which he attended a few times a week; they fed and clothed him, and they started teaching him skills in hydroponics; the boy flourished! He even got a new set of 'gnashers' of which he was very proud. I hooked him up with a cell phone and he used to let me know how things were going from time to time.

A year later he wrote down his story and sent it to me and my heart was warmed. I went back to my sponsor to give him the good news of how well this guy had done, and how proud I was of everything. He looked at me and gave me another of those long whining chuckles and his words were exactly the same: "Rory, stop trying to play God."

Right there I had the most incredible clarification that could have only been a revelation from the Holy Spirit. I was not responsible for failure in someone's life, nor was I responsible for success in their life. Blackie was famous for a saying that I use all the time today: "Just for today, I want to help someone, but the big secret is, nobody must know about it."[51] This whole lesson ties so well into what Chuck C said in one of his talks at the Parla Mesa retreat:

To be good for nothing, this is the freedom of life.

In other words, we are good in return for nothing. Our sole motivation is to pass on to others what we have so freely received – *for nothing.*

This 'nothing' actually includes any expected results. But if this is true, why would we do it? It seems ludicrous. Here's where the real plan comes in. We saw in Step 11 that our main purpose is to have a relationship with God and to show Him we love Him. The best demonstration of love we can give God is to obey Him,[52] and this means to try to help others where we've been helped. There are two scriptures which tell us this clearly:

---

[51] Note to Blackie: Thank you for those words. God has blessed you with wisdom.
[52] See Samuel 15:22.

Who comforteth us in all our tribulation, that we may be able to comfort them which are in any trouble, by the comfort wherewith we ourselves are comforted of God.

2 Corinthians 1:4

Heal the sick, cleanse the lepers, raise the dead, cast out devils: freely ye have received, freely give.

Matthew 10:8

(Notice the words "any trouble" in the first verse.)

It is really that simple. The big question may be, why bother if their recovery does not depend on us, and often, because God has given people free will, it doesn't depend on Him either? God's Holy Spirit can reveal the truth to people, but the ultimate decision lies within them. It is amazing, but in the face of all evidence, people often still choose the path of destruction. The reason we continue to pass the message on is that we are showing God our gratitude, and working with others for God's great cause keeps us in a relationship with Him. I know He doesn't need us to help, but I love the fact that he wants me with Him, right next to Him in His mission of "bringing many sons to glory"[53] – that's what it's all about. Two oxen in a yoke are side by side, on the same mission, and that's where He wants us.

Take my yoke upon you, and learn of me; for I am meek and lowly in heart: and ye shall find rest unto your souls. For my yoke is easy, and my burden is light.

Matthew 11:29,30

Once we have this mindset, the rest is easy. I pray in the morning and ask God to show me *anybody* who needs help with anything, and when they come along, I try to help them. It takes a while sometimes before God brings a person across your path that has the same dependency as you, but in the meantime, do what I did: prepare the lunch, clean a colleague's workstation, pick up a piece of litter – do whatever, because you'll feel great. I always remind myself that I am doing it for God because of what He does for me and because I love Him.

If you meet someone who wants your help in recovering from a dependency, you should be glad because this is the Holy Spirit calling you

---

[53] Hebrews 2:10

into a deeper relationship with God. Relax, because it is going to be so simple to help someone; God will be doing all the work, if the other person will let Him. What you will need is patience and time, and you will need to ask the Lord for that. I am going to suggest the entire process of helping someone to you in one sentence. Are you ready for it?

You will pray for their recovery, read through every page of this book with them, and be there when they do the 'Working' part of the book to give prompts, guidance and Step 5s.

I do suggest you get another copy of this book for them to work with you. This process is all I have ever done with those I sponsor. If they fall away, it's OK; some come back, some never do. I can promise you this, though: as you try to help someone, your relationship with God just keeps growing into something more wonderful each day.

The last thing we try to do in this final step of the Program is to "practise these principles in all of our affairs". Which principles are we talking about, and just exactly what is meant by "all affairs"? This one, I am pleased to say, the Holy Spirit showed me directly, and I was able to put it directly into practice. The principles we are talking about are the principles in this recovery Program as laid out in these 12 steps. For me, "all affairs" meant literally everything that affected me in my life; from small to large, from people to institutions to principles.

If you have been reading this book and do not have a dependency disorder, I put it to you that you just might actually have one and that you can break through into recovery from it in just the same way as an alcoholic can from booze. Remember, the first sin ever committed was by Satan, the devil, and it was the sin of self, ego – pride.

> *How art thou fallen from heaven, O Lucifer [Satan], son of the morning! How art thou cut down to the ground, which didst weaken the nations! For thou hast said in thine heart, I will ascend into heaven, I will exalt my throne above the stars of God: I will sit also upon the mount of the congregation, in the sides of the north: I will ascend above the heights of the clouds; I will be like the most High. Yet thou shalt be brought down to hell, to the sides of the pit.*
>
> *Isaiah 14:12-15*

As we have seen, the sin we are most guilty of is just this: self, ego – pride. What makes this sin so deadly is that if we have it, we cannot see it in ourselves at all. How do you rid yourself of something you don't believe you have? The Lord uses pain, however, and this is a good indication of something not being right in us. Once we feel this pain, we can then practise these principles – the 12 steps.

I had been sober for a few years yet had a terrible underlying fear of not having enough money to live – a sense of economic insecurity. I had been sober for just over two years in 2008 when the economic recession hit the Natal South Coast. Business had been booming, people were making fortunes, especially in the building industry, and I was on the bandwagon for sure. I was building holiday homes and complexes for a company and was doing a bit of speculation of my own. To give you an idea of the magnitude of the situation; in a coastal stretch of about 50 km, there were sixty-four individual estate agencies. If you could talk, you could sell. When the economic recession hit globally, it had a huge and almost instantaneous impact on the property market on the Natal South Coast. People stopped buying immediately, as this was surplus money they had been using on holiday homes. I had bought a house in Margate and was in the process of dividing the land and also getting plans passed for building a second house; then the recession hit, and I found I could not sell the house or the separated plot of land. The building of the second house was dependent on the sale of the existing house so there I was, stuck between a rock and a hard place. I then made an exceedingly poor decision. Instead of selling up for what I could get and taking out a mortgage for the balance, I tried to hold out by obtaining overdrafts, loans and credit cards so that I could continue with the mortgage repayments and get my plans passed for the second house. The long and the short of it was that I was stuck in a combined debt of about R1.6 million[54]. On top of this, work was 'as scarce as hen's teeth' down there, and the fact that the company I was working for might not be able to keep me really started haunting me as well.

I got married at the end of May 2009, and this also compounded my financial woes (this 'woe', however, I wouldn't change for the world!) I cannot begin to describe the raw fear that crept into me, and I had to face it sober. "What am I to do?" was the cry.

I went and saw a debt counsellor and went under debt review. This left us scraping the barrel, and 'pap 'n' wors' (stiff corn porridge and

---

[54] roughly equivalent to £100,000 or US$130,000, although as I was dealing in assets, it was more like owing £200,000 or US$250,000

South African farmer sausage) became our staple diet; there was no money for anything else. I went to my sponsor with a plea for help. His first comment was, "Sorry, my Boet[55]," but then he gave me two pearls of wisdom from Step 7 and Step 12 which I had read over and over but had never put to use. He said, "Rory, you have to go to God and you should do the Program with that fear of yours."

I went to God every morning with my fear, and I replaced 'alcohol' in Step 1 with 'fear' so that it read, "We admitted we were powerless over fear – that our lives had become unmanageable." I went through the 12 steps of the Program with fear as the focal point of my powerlessness and unmanageability. However, this fear did not leave me for quite a while.

Eventually the inevitable happened and I had to look for other work. I got a job with a construction company in Pretoria (750 km inland from where we were, in our nation's capital), and I had to leave the family down on the coast for two months while I went to work. The fear gripped me night after night in such a way that I'd wake up sweating in the middle of the night with my stomach in a knot. I would sometimes just pray repeatedly, or I'd get up and sing hymns and choruses. Then the fear would subside, and I'd sleep. Monday mornings were the worst. I'd wake up early with the 'knot' and just ask God to help me through the day and week, and He would.

My wife, Pauline, who worked for a bank, got a transfer and moved up, but the fear persisted. I kept taking it back to the beginning of the Program and going through it again and again. I had left the coast in August 2010, and that December I was docked half my pay. When I inquired, I was told that I was only entitled to six days' leave instead of eighteen because I'd started in August. We have what they call a builders' shutdown in South Africa, which meant the three weeks I was off was forced leave, and therefore it was illegal for a company to allow it as unpaid leave. I took it to God instead of arbitration, and although Pauline and I could only stay at home and were unable to buy Christmas presents for the family, we paid the bills and we spent one of the most meaningful and intimate periods of our lives together.

My financial situation got to the point where I could not keep up payments; the general standard of living was much higher up in Pretoria, and my net earnings were a bit less than I had down on the South Coast.

---

[55] brother

The fear kept coming, and I went to friend who suggested an attorney who could possibly help with a sequestration[56]. I went and saw him, and he said it was the best option available to me, but there were a few concerns; I could not sequestrate until the house was sold for some reason. So, I was advised to continue all payments, sell what I could for whatever I could get, and wait. It was a long and complicated process. Over a year passed and the situation had become critical. I had understood that I would be able to sequestrate after a further two months, but then the attorney told me that he was worried about one financial institution being able to oppose the court order and demand payment in the region of R180,000[57].

It was at this point that another miracle happened in my life. I woke up one morning and the fear was gone. I just knew that no matter what happened, we would be taken care of. It was incredible; after six-and-a-half years of taking this fear to God and working it through the Program, it was gone – just like that. I did not know whether I would be able to be sequestrated, whether an institution would oppose anything, and whether all my debt would be written off. But I had freedom from the fear.

It turned out well. I am now in my third year of sequestration and after the fourth, I can apply for rehabilitation and will be cleared, never having to pay that money back again. My job changed, and I started to earn double what I had before; Pauline was promoted, and her salary has nearly doubled as well. We've been able to buy a car and a house on her name, and all other debt is settled.

I learned that God had to remove the fear before He could change the circumstances, otherwise I would just feel fear every time my financial situation changed slightly for the worse. Now I know I will be looked after, no matter what happens. I got through fear one day at a time with God's help through the Program for six-and-a-half years, and what was different from anything else before was that *I knew that I knew* deep down inside me that He would help me this time. The reason I knew this so emphatically is that He had removed the desire to drink in an instant, and that was a far larger problem in my mind than the fear of not having enough money to provide for myself and my family.

---

[56] declaring insolvency
[57] approximately £11,000 or US$14,000

I still battle constantly with a foul mouth and a grumpy temper, and I take it to God through the Program every day. *I know that I know* he will remove this problem as well, because it is a lot smaller than fear, in my mind.

I previously mentioned that after a year of sobriety, I took smoking through the Program with God's help and that desire left me. There are countless other similar victories and each one of them has been achieved through the same process. Only the time taken for the victory has differed. I often wondered why God could not remove them all in one fell swoop... I think one reason is that we are standing with our pride and ego in front of these individual 'strongholds' and sometimes we are more stubborn and less desperate than at other times. But maybe the more important reason is that God is our Father and He loves spending time with His children. Most of us become too 'busy' for Him when all's well...

PART THREE

Life After Sobriety

My Family and Other People

As one who has not touched a drop of alcohol for nine years, I realize that I am writing to myself as much as I am to you. It is one thing to go to a meeting and talk to a crowd of people, and afterwards smile and chat to them with all the patience in the world. I can sit for hours with someone who is starting his recovery, owing to the fact that he quite often mumbles on about a lot of trivia before getting to the point (as did I), but I tend to battle to show the same patience and tolerance with my friends, sometimes, and especially with my wife and kids.

I got married when I was three years and one day sober and yet my wife and children, who are now young adults, still have to bear the brunt of some of my defects of character that I built up through seventeen years of drinking. I have caused a fair share of sadness and misery at home through my irritability, impatience, foul mouth and 'grumpiness'. I thank the Lord that He has removed all guilt and condemnation from my life, but the remorse and conviction, which is of God, can still be pretty painful. I have no explanation for why it is so difficult for me to treat the ones I most love with *more* tolerance and kindness than others, as I believe it should be this way. I do not make any excuses for my behaviour, and I ask their continual forgiveness and tolerance – thank you, guys, for loving me and putting up with the 'grouch!'

I have heard it said that one person with a dependency disorder affects at least sixteen people around them – I think that the true figure is far higher. The damage we cause to those people around us, especially our families and friends, is not just superficial but often deeply wounding and scarring. I really feel for family and friends who have seen alcoholism (or another dependency) in the one they love result in *them* picking up character defects in their own lives, despite the fact that they have not even put a bottle to their lips (or the equivalent action for another dependency)! Some of these character defects they start to portray like anger, bitterness, deep-seated resentment, a spirit of lying or controlling are often much more difficult to be rid of than the character defects alcoholics have to get rid of. I believe that there are two main reasons for this. The first is that of a victim mentality, which often leads to an unwillingness to acknowledge their defect(s). The second reason is closely linked to the first in that they often feel that they do not need help; they just need to be rid of the person harming them or have the person's dependency disorder 'cured'. I hope that you as the reader do not find this a judgement on the people affected, but rather an empathetic notion of understanding. I have been through a 'victim' situation and know what it can do to a person. I believe, though, that should the person want to recover from what has happened and the character defects they may have picked up, they too can do so using the Program exactly as it is presented in this book. Remember that the non-alcoholic is just as powerless over their alcoholic counterpart's drinking as the alcoholic is. If you work through this Program as laid out, replacing the dependency disorder with your specific defect, I truly believe you will experience the same victory in your life as I did.

It is often sad and embarrassing for me to sit and listen to someone speaking about the damage and destruction in their lives caused by someone with a dependency disorder, because it shows the type of destruction I might have caused in others' lives. Below is a real story written by a woman I will call Sandra, whose life was affected by a person with a dependency disorder. If you have had involvement with, and been hurt or scarred by, someone with a dependency disorder, you might be able to relate to Sandra's story.

> *I was about seven months pregnant the first time it happened. It should have been the first and the last, but there were many more beatings to come. Why couldn't I just leave? It seems logical and simple enough to do, but the truth is I really did love him. Now when I look back, somehow in a strange way I think it's almost as if I was trying to play God. I really believed that as long as I was there, I could try to control things and keep everything together – I believed that I could change him.*

> *He had been out drinking the night before with his friends. He arrived back home at about 10am the next morning. I had hardly slept, worrying to the extent of nausea. Every car I heard pass by, I rushed to the window longing to see him climb out the car and head for the front door. Lying in bed, tossing and turning, I'd pray, "Please, Lord, don't let him drink too*

much tonight and please don't let him get into a fight." There were tons of toxic thoughts keeping my mind captive. Fear consumed me to my wits' end. Why was this happening to me, did I really deserve this?

So, as I said, he finally arrived home at about 10am still drunk. Feelings of absolute relief flooded my being; he was home safe! But at the same time anger and resentment seemed to outweigh the relief I felt. Trying very hard to keep my composure, I greeted him with, "Hi, where have you been, I've been so worried about you?"

I remember the moments that followed so vividly. He lifted his head and looked at me as his whole demeanour changed and his eyes seemed to turn dark and dead in his head. The next thing I knew, he slapped me with such a force that I was down on the floor. I was lying on my side, curled up like a baby, arms wrapped around my tummy trying to protect our unborn child. He continued to kick and punch while I wailed uncontrollably, begging him to stop... this is the undeniable affect that alcohol had on this man that I loved so dearly.

You see, he wasn't always like this. When he didn't drink, he was the kindest, most loving person you could think of. I believe life is all about the choices we make. I really loved this man with all of my heart and was prepared to give him my all. I had made a commitment to him and promised my vows before God. Besides, there was no way I was going back home to mom and dad...

I don't seek pity, but rather I am sharing my story with you to give you an understanding of my state of mind and the severity of the situation. I take full responsibility for my choices and the consequences of these choices. Having said that, I do believe I did my very best in the situation. Maybe there are some of you who can relate in some way to the story of my life which once seemed to be filled with bondage, fear and hopelessness. It is very different to my life now, which is filled with hope, joy and fulfilment.

I'd like to share with you a bit about myself, so that you can get a better picture. I met Rick when I was in my matric[58] year. I fell head over heels and became madly in love with him. I really believed that my 'Prince Charming' had come to rescue me. I dreamed of a perfect life with a white picket fence. He was perfect for me, funny, handsome, witty, charming; the whole package. He told me that he loved me...

My first year out of matric, I fell pregnant, and by the end of that year we were married. Now I haven't mentioned that Rick drank quite a lot, but so did many of his friends. In my naïve state, I really thought that this was what all young guys did, but that they would soon grow out of it. Well, I was wrong. Once we moved into our own place, his drinking seemed to get so much worse. All he could think about was going out drinking, wasting our money on alcohol and gambling. All I wanted was for him to be at home with his new little family.

Early in our marriage, my life became consumed with Rick, but not in a good way at all. I was continuously thinking, "Where is he, who's he with, how much is he drinking and how much of our money is he spending? What time will he be home, is he even going to come home...?" During these times I would worry myself sick. I'd go for days without eating, I'd feel terribly depressed, and would constantly be filled with fear. With all the worry, I became overwhelmed and gripped by fear; I simply started fearing everything. I began to doubt myself, my own capabilities, constantly questioning my worth, as a woman, a mother and as a wife. I literally got to a point where I believed that I was just not good enough. Somehow, I started to believe that I deserved this miserable life. Thoughts, feelings and beliefs began to mould me into someone I couldn't even recognize anymore.

Most of the time, I would try to pretend that everything was okay, desperately trying to keep myself from crumbling and falling to pieces. After all, we had two daughters whom I had to be there for. Rick would drink for months on end, and then

---

[58] the final year of secondary school

stop for a few months. None of his drinking really took place at home. At first, he lived for Fridays, then it didn't matter what night of the week it was. If he'd made up his mind about going out, that was it, his mind was made up. Believe me, I tried almost everything I could think of from planning candlelit dinners, making sure the children were on best behaviour at all times, trying to be the perfect wife, ensuring the household was running smoothly; all those kind of things. Whatever I did or tried never seemed to be enough; nothing was ever good enough to keep him from going out drinking. I even gave up my relationship with my own family for him because he was possessive and jealous. At a stage in our marriage, he asked me to choose between him and my parents.

I eventually got to a point where I just couldn't do it anymore; I genuinely felt like I had nothing more to give of myself. I felt empty and numb, merely going through the motions for the sake of the children. I couldn't share any of this with anyone – can you imagine if it leaked out to him that I had been discussing our lives with other people? So, I bottled this all up inside. Despite me having no support system in place, I continued to constantly reassure the girls that all was going to be okay, making excuses for their dad, trying to candy-coat things, which is something I had become quite good at.

I often thought of taking the children and leaving him, but feared that he would track us down and kill us. His temper made us feel unsafe and his drinking made him dangerous. I never had the guts to go through with it. After all, I had made my vows before God and I took them seriously. I didn't throw in the towel that easily. The only reason I eventually left him was because the last time he came home drunk and beat me up, he threatened to shoot not only me, but the girls as well. The trauma of that day still haunts us. I can only say that it is by the grace of God that we were not harmed. That is the day when I finally realized that I had been doing the same things over and over for the past 16 years, but was always expecting some kind of change.

It was the most humbling thing for me to do to call my parents and tell them that I needed them. Within a few weeks I seemed to have pulled myself together again; I was going to put all of it behind me and like an ostrich that buries its head in the sand, I was to do my best to forget about the past. I managed to get that "it's going to be okay" smile on, but I was feeling extremely fragile.

The girls and I found a lovely church which we started attending regularly. About a year later, I met Benjamin, my real 'Prince Charming', at the same church. I had never met anyone who was so honest and open with me from the word go. He told me that he had battled with a drinking problem and that he attended meetings to help him with his recovery.

At first, I thought to myself, "I don't really want to get involved with another man who has a problem with drink!" I really liked him a lot though and wanted to support him. He invited me to attend recovery meetings with him, which I didn't particularly want to go to because I felt it wasn't my problem; he was the one with the drinking issues. But, being a supportive girlfriend, I went along... After attending a few open meetings, I was told about other meetings which were held concurrently at the same venue; only, the other meetings were for the families and friends of the alcoholics. I was persuaded to attend...

At first, I thought it was a total waste of time; why would I need these meetings? At the end of the meetings, they would say, "Keep coming back, because it works." At first, the steps didn't make a lot of sense to me, but I kept going back. I would sit in the room listening to everyone sharing their stories and then the penny dropped. My life story came together like pieces of a puzzle. I could identify and relate to experiences being shared by various people and it was only then that I realized that Rick was an alcoholic. Before then I knew that our lives had been out of control and totally unmanageable. I knew that Rick drank a lot, and that 'we' could not control his drinking habits.

As I kept going back to these meetings week after week, the steps started to make more sense to me. I realized that these meetings were actually for my benefit, to help me with my buried past that I had managed to tuck away so safely, but that had now resurfaced and was staring me straight in the face. I could never do it before, but I was now ready to expose and face myself.

And so I began to work the steps slowly, just one day at a time. I had to learn the true meaning of letting go of everything and allowing God to take over. For so long I had been trying to keep control of things, but everything seemed to end up in a mess anyway. I figured, what did I have to lose? I realized that some kind of change was desperately needed, and that change had to begin with me. Change is never an easy thing to tackle, but I became willing. I think it has been one of the hardest things for me to work at because I really didn't like who I had allowed myself to become.

All of my so-called 'good traits' which I thought I had, had become twisted as a way to cope with my circumstances on my own. I was relieved to learn that none of Rick's drinking was caused by me, and there was no way that I could have ever controlled his drinking. More importantly, I would never have been able to cure his drinking. If I had known that back then, it would have saved us all quite a bit of pain.

Moreover, as I started doing the work, I realized that I had developed so many character defects, which I was not even aware of until I started doing some 'deep digging' into my feelings, thoughts and behaviours. At times, whilst working through the steps, I became increasingly overwhelmed as I had to relive certain incidents. So, I asked someone to become my sponsor; someone whom I did my Steps 4 and 5 with. These steps brought huge relief to me somehow. I had an amazing breakthrough and a very real reconnection with God as I worked through my list of resentments, feelings of guilt, and as I worked through the list of people I had harmed, both intentionally and unintentionally. This helped me to acknowledge and take accountability for my part in each situation. Then I needed to make amends wherever possible. Words cannot express the huge sense of freedom I experienced as I tackled that obstacle. The situation had made it so easy for me to develop a victim mentality. It wasn't as though I was on a pity party or anything like that; I just got to a place where it was too easy to blame my behaviour on my past. This kind of behaviour and way of thinking is not pleasant for people on the receiving end, especially the ones you love.

As I've grasped the 12 steps of recovery, I have realized that this Program offered me a new way of living and a new way of experiencing life each day. I have so much to be thankful and grateful for. I have regained my sanity. Although I am not the one who had the drinking problem, I allowed the person whom I loved (Rick) who struggled with alcohol to affect me in such a way that I almost lost my life and myself. I have worked on regaining my relationships; firstly, with my heavenly Father through His Son Jesus Christ, and then my children and my mom, which is absolutely amazing. All I know is that the Program is very real, very tangible and it works if you are prepared to put the necessary work into it. There is no quick fix with regard to this Program; it takes a whole lot of dedication and willingness to be open and honest with yourself about you.

I am so grateful for meeting Benjamin, who is now my husband of six years. If it weren't for him introducing the 12-step Program to me, I would still be lost and wrapped up in my own world. Now I am experiencing life without fear, life filled with amazing hope, and a joy which has been graciously restored by my heavenly Father.

I find this story so indicative of God's power, and I relate to many aspects of Sandra's account. I am still so amazed at what God can do in a person's life, even though I know I should be used to it by now because He has done so much in my own.

There are a few general points I would like to highlight that will help you if you have a dependency disorder or are involved in some way in the life of someone recovering from a dependency disorder.

The first is that you will need to pray and hand over your situation and frustrations daily. I have mentioned prayer often for everything we do in this book, and I cannot emphasize it enough. Prayer is talking to God, and He is the source of our strength. We need to pray every day all the time because we either don't believe or we keep taking back what we have handed over. I find this need in my life because prayer keeps me in constant communication with my heavenly Father and it builds trust in me as I see the ease with which He brings me through situations. We need to constantly remind ourselves that He is omnipotent (all-powerful).

> *And I heard as it were the voice of a great multitude, and as the voice of many waters, and as the voice of mighty thunderings, saying, alleluia: for the Lord God omnipotent reigneth.*
>
> *Revelation 19:6*

We are in continual communication with the God who is not only all-powerful, but also in charge. There is nothing we can do and no other place we could go where there would be a more powerful outcome than going to God. In fact, I tried many other options for many years, and the conclusion I come to today is that there are no other real options of lasting effect. When any of us, or others involved with us, become frustrated, sad, hurt, depressed, angry, jealous, bitter, resentful, or just feel totally powerless and overwhelmed, we should go to God first. I have found that if you can get into the habit of doing it daily with everything in your life, you will eventually find that you cannot do without it. Of all the help I can give, I believe that this is the most powerful; the rest I write is mere guidance in finding the true source of power, which is God, through His Son Jesus Christ.

Knowing this, it is important for all to understand that God has either cured us or He has not. It will not help at all to try to control situations and circumstances. Many wives will throw the booze down the sink, while other friends might suggest not going to a place where so-and-so might nip off and buy drugs. None of these attempts will stop the person who has not been relieved of that obsession from doing so, but none of these situations will cause him to stumble if he has been cured by God. If he has not yet been cured and he slips, it is better he and all involved see it sooner rather than later. Often an insight like this will help him take things a bit more seriously.

There is something I'd like to share here which I have been a bit hesitant to share – I trust God will have His hands on our understanding. When I sobered up, I was playing league pool at the time, once a week, in different bars and pubs along the Natal South Coast. As crazy as this may seem, I felt a strong loyalty to my team, Amigo's, and decided to see the league through to the end of that year in November. I used to go to the bars and pubs, stand and drink my Coke, play my games and leave after the last game around 22:30. For those six months I cannot recall getting tempted once. In fact, towards the end of the evening, the others started to get on my nerves with their repetitiveness and general boisterous larks. I was asked recently if I would have stuck the year out had I understood alcoholism as I do today, and my answer was a resounding no! I was treading on very thin ice and it could have gone either way. I do not believe in testing God, as His word says we shouldn't.

> You shall not put the LORD your God to the test, as you tested him at Massah.
>
> *Deuteronomy 6:16 (ESV)*

Jesus Himself referred to this passage in Matthew 4:17 and Luke 4:12, which further emphasizes its importance.

The point I am trying to make is that if we are delivered, we are delivered, and should be able to go anywhere, provided we have the right motive. I was stupid but innocent, and the Lord knew this and protected me. If you want to go and 'steal' a bit of the old life back, you are treading on dangerous ground. Families and friends, don't try to protect your dependent from their disorder, and those of you recovering from a dependency disorder, do not be fearful, but I recommend that you do not 'test the waters'.

Another important point to remember is patience. Time has been a big healer with regard to many of my defects, and all involved should realize and understand this. It took seventeen-and-a-half years of drinking to bring me to my knees, empty of self. It will take a long time to restore my sanity in many areas. It is not that God cannot remove all defects in everyone all at once, but I believe it is more the case that we will not surrender control over certain areas of our lives properly. We may be willing, but stubborn at the same time, and unfortunately my experience shows that God needs to use that little thing called *pain* before we give it over to Him entirely. This will apply to all friends, family and dependents alike. All should try to understand the fundamentals of this gradual change, which should help us exercise the patience and tolerance needed for the healing to complete its process – in other words, don't try to take the bandage off the arm too soon; leave it to heal.

Expectation is another problem I have experienced with family and friends. If I can give a difficult piece of advice to all involved, it would not be wise to have any preconceived ideas as to how life will now be after being restored. Families and friends, I have had many of my own friends and family who I feel wanted me to exercise a certain type of behaviour and to respond to life and situations in a certain way.[59] However, as none of them have actively come out and said as much, I will leave it at that. For me, it has been a huge lesson in life, and one that I am eternally grateful for. It is an ongoing lesson, and I still find myself subconsciously having these expectations of myself and other people, only to have my hopes in these areas dashed. All that one is left with afterwards are feelings of disappointment, anger, frustration, disillusionment hopelessness, etc. – not good. I am reminded of the solution found in that wonderfully well-known scripture:

> *And we know that all things work together for good to them that love God, to them who are the called according to his purpose.*
>
> *Romans 8:28*

So, no matter if I think that a situation could have been handled in a better way, I am reassured that God can work it for our good.

There will be strife and disagreements among family and friends, but there are a few things to remember. One of these is that as an alcoholic, I will need to put the Program second on my list of priorities after God. The reason for this is that if I lose my sobriety, I will lose everything else. While I was still dating my wife, I told her this and asked if she could accept the fact that she would be third in my life. At first, she was none too happy, but after explaining what could be lost, she became content to be number three (remember that one, boys!) I am eternally grateful that she accepted these conditions.

---

[59] Note to my family and friends: Guys, I have let you down by not behaving accordingly, and if that has caused you pain and harm, I am truly sorry for that.

Another thing to remember is that we must not try to hide our past away. So many times I have been able to be of assistance to someone who approached me after they heard me mention that I was a recovering alcoholic, even through a conversation eavesdrop. Family members and friends have been able to help others in exactly the same way. This should be one of the aims we have here on earth, to help as many people as we can in any way we can, provided that they are interested in listening. In personal circles, though, it is not advisable to dig up past issues among one another which have already been dealt with and laid to rest. I battle in this area big time, and when I am having a 'tiff' with my wife or one of the kids, I like to haul out the list of wrongs to substantiate my current disagree-ment and help establish continuity of wrongdoing in the other person. It is something which I struggle with and something that I constantly need to ask forgiveness for. I believe it is getting better, however – praise God!

Just as a lot of people do, my kids lie to get out of things. It really gets to me and I am quite an expert at 'sniffing out' a lie, probably due to the fact that I used to be an expert liar myself. When they ask if I am questioning their integrity, I make it known in no uncertain terms that I am, and then proceed to back it up with lists of occasions where they have lied to me in the past. This does not sit well and causes a break in proper communication for several days. I still struggle to make amends in these situations, as 90% of the time they *are* lying to me again! Nonetheless, short of going to great lengths and heartache to prove that they are lying again, I let it go and I need to make amends for my reaction in the situation if it was hurtful.[60] In most instances I was selfish, self-seeking, afraid, inconsiderate and dishonest myself. God is working with these defects in me. For everyone involved: in a nutshell, don't throw dirty laundry in each other's faces – it stinks!

There was one situation for which a friend never forgave me. It was perhaps twenty years ago, and his brother's girlfriend had wealthy parents. She was having her 18th birthday party at some fancy hotel and had booked out one of the banqueting halls. My friend and I had both been invited and all was merry. I got drunk as usual and drifted into a political discussion that was going on with my friend, the host and a couple of the young guests. It was around the time of the referendum held

---

[60] Note to my children: For all the times I have hurt you and have not made amends, I am truly sorry and ask for your forgiveness.

in 1994 in South Africa, which, by the way, was the last time white South Africans voted on their own. The referendum was on whether we, as white South Africans, wanted the black, coloured and Asian South Africans to have a vote as well. The ballot papers had a simple 'YES' or 'NO' box. You can imagine the discussion, as most of us were students and we were talking on a topic with huge ramifications for the country and our future.

My opinion was asked, and being in an obnoxious drunken mood, I decided to play devil's advocate. I posed the question as to whether any of them would give their car keys to their thirteen-year-old child and send him to the shop to buy cigarettes for them. I asked how they expected forty million people to understand and vote for their future when most had little or no education at all. This got them all worked up, as you can imagine, and they began shouting and arguing and calling me a racist.

I then asked how many of them actually worked with people of colour, who lived near any other races, or who had friends that were black. Most white South Africans lived closed, sheltered lives in those days, and apart from the domestic workers and garden workers, most had very little contact with South Africans of colour, especially the more affluent in society. At least this was my personal finding and understanding; I could be wrong. Needless to say, this last line of questioning caused an immense uproar of shouting and accusations. I stood alone through all this and was quite pleased with myself about that fact.

It was at this point that I decided to make my exit, amidst ever increasing demands that I should leave. I chose to use my most eloquent lines of repartee, and on the back foot shouted, "F*** you all, you bunch of snobs!"

I left hastily that night and the next day when I tried to apologize, my friend said he never wanted to see me again. And that was that.

We did bump into each other again many years later, but it was a "Hi" and nothing after that. I guess some things are not meant to be and all I do is wish all those people whom I hurt and offended the very best. I pray that God will fill their lives with all the love, grace and mercy He so freely granted me.

If we cannot restore these relationships, we still need to make right with God. My primary relationship is with God, and so it should be. Sometimes relationships are not ready to be restored because the aggrieved person still needs to learn to walk a walk with God, but we should always remain ready and willing to restore our relationships when the opportunity arises. I pray for healing in these people's lives and pray that God will maintain the right attitude in my heart towards them in the meantime. Until the day I die, I do not know whom God will restore a relationship with.

Just remain open for the opportunity if it arises.

Starting a Breakthrough Recovery Group

I have been told many times in recovery programmes that if I want to keep what I have, I need to give it away. This is biblical. Jesus said to his disciples:

Heal the sick, cleanse the lepers, raise the dead, cast out devils: freely ye have received, freely give.

Matthew 5:8

So, I obey, and do so out of love. If I am completely honest, however, it is gratitude that motivates me more than anything else. You have heard from my story just how defeated and desperate I'd become. Finally, I realized that it was *impossible* for me to stop drinking, yet when I told God I was defeated, He removed the desire to drink from me in an instant. I followed the Program and thereby set a solid foundation for my sobriety, while also establishing a genuine relationship with God for the first time in my life. This is an indescribable event in my life, and I feel nothing other than gratitude. How can I thank God enough? I simply cannot, but for me, the best way to show my gratitude is to pass it on and try to help someone else who might need it and is willing to take the time to listen.

In my recovery, I found that the group I attended was one of the important factors. I thank all those guys (and still thank the guys in my groups today) who were there for me and who allowed God to work through them to aid me in certain important aspects of my recovery. I was not one who liked groups and in fact, I did not like much help from anyone on anything. This was one of my main problem areas; I thought that I could sort things out myself. I now know that it is actually the opposite, and that there are very few things I can sort out on my own. Any ability or opportunity or successes I may achieve are all God-given and God-sent, therefore all glory *has* to go to God. I am just very grateful that He opened my eyes. I took to a recovery group like a duck to water. These people were *real* with no airs and graces about them. I got hugged solidly (never was a 'huggy' guy) and did not feel awkward because it was genuine. Never before in my life had I come across a bunch of people who were so happy to see me and yet expected nothing from me; they just wanted to help. I cannot explain how odd and appealing that felt all at the same time; it was a place I wanted to be, and these guys had what I wanted. I too got in on the hugging thing. I used to hug the people and tell them I loved them, because I did. This was so out of my character, but when you feel the love God has placed in others, it is hard not to join in and pass it on.

Three or four years ago, one lad in his early thirties celebrated a year of sobriety. He was a well-built, burly kind of a chap of around five foot ten with a toughness about him. During his share, he came to the part in his story when he went to his first meeting. He described our meeting in roughly the following way: "I walked through the doors of this room, and there standing in front of me was this huge bloke over six feet, who walked up to me and gave me a big bear hug and told me he loved me. I was scared out of my wits! I thought the guy might be a 'moffie'[61] but was too nervous to say anything. I found out later it was Rory. And Rory, I love you too, my boet." These guys have been my tangible lifeline to God, along with one or two sponsors along the way.

The last fact is simply this: we are meant to meet together. No man is an island, and God made it this way.

> *Not forsaking the assembling of ourselves together, as the manner of some is; but exhorting one another: and so much the more, as ye see the day approaching.*
>
> *Hebrews 10:25*

What God is saying in this verse is that we should encourage and urge one another on, and I needed this many times. I think it is natural to run out of steam at times, to feel down and lethargic, and this type of encouragement and support is just what we need.

In summary, there are three reasons why a group like this is important:

- You can learn from others.
- You can help and show others the path to recovery.
- You can both support and be supported by others.

---

[61] South African slang for being gay

If you are just two people, you can start a group. We did. If we return to the scriptures, we find confirmation of this principle too:

> *For where two or three are gathered together in my name, there am I in the midst of them.*

Matthew 18:20

So, at a meeting of two, the main member, our God, is present automatically. I started my first group with just the person I was sponsoring and myself. We worked through the steps, shared struggles, read from the word, and prayed for one another and others. Eventually, the group grew and got to about twenty, which is when we started a second group at a shelter. It is amazing what God will do if we let Him. Wayne and I sat many a night on our own in the beginning, but it did not matter; we were staying sober and spending time with God.

Failure or success in terms of numbers has little to do with us and all to do with God. We must just be faithful in carrying the message and willing to share with anyone who wants to listen. Our human nature gets despondent if there are not many people attending, and equally, it is our human nature that wants to take accolades if the place is packed out. Both are wrong.

If you start a meeting, I suggest you do so at your church or another nearby if your own church is not willing. Tell them that you will be fully self-supporting but would like to fall under the church's umbrella of ministries. You would like to help where possible and will respect the church's doctrines.

The structure and format of a meeting can follow these guidelines, or you can follow your own, just as you feel led:

1. *The Opening*
    Use the Breakthrough Recovery Meeting (BRM) worksheet on pages 256-257. You are allowed to scan and copy this page of the book, or download the worksheet from:
    www.onwardsandupwards.org/breakthrough-into-recovery
    If you laminate the worksheet, it will enable you to use it multiple times as the group grows and to preserve the book.
2. *The Reading*
    Anyone can do the reading; normally we take it in turns. You can just read the BRM verbatim and it will prompt you with what to do as you go along.

3. *The 12-step Readings*

   Take a copy of the worksheets on pages 258 and 260 (or download them). Give the worksheet with the *steps* in bold to one of the group members, and the worksheet with the *Bible verses* in bold to another. The one with the steps will begin from the top, reading the first step only. The one with the Bible verses will similarly begin from the top and stop after reading the first step's Bible verse (but not the step again). The first member will then read Step 2, after which the second member will read the Bible verse of Step 2; and so on. If you would prefer to do this in another sequence or format, feel free to do so; this is your meeting.

4. *The Body of the Meeting*

   You could try one of three options I suggest, or you might prefer a different approach altogether.

   a. *Sharing meeting.* Everybody gets to share whatever they would like. I find it better to wait until all have shared and then open the meeting to anyone to share their experience on an issue which might be encouraging to another. It is important not to interrupt or criticize another who is sharing.

   b. *Scripture reading and topic discussion.* This can be done in any way you would like, and normally it takes on the feel of a Bible study. Someone appointed the week before might bring a topic to the next meeting, along with a few scriptures on that topic. He would share some of his or her understanding of the topic and read the Bible verses which he or she has selected as relevant, after which you open the meeting for anyone to share.

   c. *Going through this book together.* This is the format I recommend, because reading helped me the most in my recovery. Start right from the beginning, in the preface, because there is a lot there that will help in preparing for the rest of the book. I feel the meeting should be as close to one hour as possible, and normally take place once a week. Pick someone to read and ask them to stop ten or fifteen minutes before the end of the meeting.

You can then stop and open the meeting for shares. This time is very important for this kind of meeting, as my writing is only an opinion, and every situation and experience is slightly different. Those who can relate to a scenario can share their similar experience, or perhaps a different experience related to that scenario. It is a good time to learn, share and grow. There are no hard and fast rules on any of this, so please do not feel restricted to these formats. If you have other ideas and feel led by the Holy Spirit, by all means implement them. Always remember, though, that this is a Christian group, and always respect the church where you have your meetings.

5. *Prayer*

You will see in the BRM that there is a place for prayer and prayer requests. Some meetings can be given over mostly, or entirely, to prayer. You could pray for circumstances in one another's lives, other people, family, other people caught in a dependency disorder, or whatever you want. Prayer is vital and should never be left out of anything we do; that is why we say a prayer together in the beginning, and one at the end to close.

6. *Closing*

Just follow the BRM in closing or follow your own format if you like. If you feel you want to take a collection for the church or your group, for drinks or food etc., do so. It is not a requirement though.

I wish you all the best with your group. You will find yourself really growing as a person. Remember not to have any expectations of the group though. Leave the results to God and focus on growing in your relationship with Him.

PART FOUR

Working the Program

Preparation

Jesus said:

I am the vine, ye are the branches: He that abideth in me, and I in him, the same bringeth forth much fruit: for <u>without me ye can do nothing</u>.

John 15:5, emphasis added

The words I have underlined are strong words.

Our strength for persevering to the end of these steps and, indeed, the end of our journey here on earth will depend entirely on our handing *everything* over to God. We need to understand that every aspect of our recovery from now on will be completely in our Father God's hands. This includes motivation, courage and endurance. If you work through these steps thoroughly, there are no guarantees of *anything* other than this: you will find serenity and sobriety. Serenity, for me, has been peace of mind, and sobriety has been the ability to live peacefully, comfortably and joyously with myself, no matter what my circumstances are. There are no guarantees for your relationships, finances, work or material possessions. There is not even a guarantee of happiness, as happiness is mostly circumstantial and very different from joy.

Are you ready? Right, let's go to the source of power. I'd like to take a moment to pray with you:

"Dear heavenly Father, I thank you that we have the awesome privilege to come and talk to you directly. Up until now, I have lived a life in which I have tried to satisfy my own needs and ego. I am sick and tired of being sick and tired, and I now want to do Your will. I ask that you will give me the grace to be able to work through these steps to the best of my ability. I want to be rid of self and would like you to take control. I know that I have become so self-absorbed that any conventional attempt to be free of self has failed. I believe that if I am truly open, totally willing and rigorously honest when I work through these steps, that my ego will deflate sufficiently for you to come in and relieve me of *any* and *every* bondage that prevents me from fulfilling your purposes in my life. I want to thank you for this, in Jesus' name. Amen."

To paraphrase an old hand, "This is a serious business (life and death), but it ain't no big deal." From now on, I want you to let go and *enjoy!* Let the Lord achieve for you what you were never able to achieve for yourself; it's an incredible journey.

Let's start...

Step 1

We admitted we were powerless over alcohol, that our lives had become unmanageable.

For I know that in me (that is, in my flesh,) dwelleth no good thing: for to will is present with me; but how to perform that which is good I find not.

Romans 7:18

Go back to page 91 and read about Step 1 again.

Answer the following questions as honestly as you can. You may want to answer them in pencil, as you may feel differently about your answers at a later stage. Remember that this is for you; you need not show anyone or tell anyone about how you fared. Only you can decide for yourself whether you fit into this class of drinker; no one can tell you you're an alcoholic…

Take this 20-question test to help you decide whether or not you are an alcoholic.

(Just answer YES or NO to the following questions)

1	Do you lose time from work due to drinking?	YES / NO
2	Is drinking making your home life unhappy?	YES / NO
3	Do you drink because you are shy with other people?	YES / NO
4	Is drinking affecting your reputation?	YES / NO
5	Have you ever felt remorse after drinking?	YES / NO
6	Have you ever got into financial difficulties as a result of drinking?	YES / NO
7	Do you turn to lower companions and an inferior environment when drinking?	YES / NO

8	Does your drinking make you careless of your family's welfare?	YES / NO
9	Has your ambition decreased since drinking?	YES / NO
10	Do you crave a drink at a definite time?	YES / NO
11	Do you want a drink the next morning?	YES / NO
12	Does drinking cause you to have difficulty in sleeping?	YES / NO
13	Has your efficiency decreased since drinking?	YES / NO
14	Is drinking jeopardizing your job or business?	YES / NO
15	Do you drink to escape from worries or trouble?	YES / NO
16	Do you drink alone?	YES / NO
17	Have you ever had a complete loss of memory as a result of drinking?	YES / NO
18	Has your physician ever treated you for drinking?	YES / NO
19	Do you drink to build up your self-confidence?	YES / NO
20	Have you ever been to a hospital or institution because of drinking?	YES / NO

If you have answered YES to one of these questions, there is a definite warning that you may be an alcoholic.

If you have answered YES to any two, the chances are that you are an alcoholic.

If you answered YES to three or more, you are definitely an alcoholic.[62]

After this; you decide.

If by this point you recognize and agree with certain points but cannot bring yourself to admitting powerlessness over alcohol and/or the unmanageability of your life, ask God to help you. I do not recommend going any further with the steps until you are able to admit these two things; you will likely be wasting your time if you do. Stay here and keep praying until the clarity and willingness come. I have no idea how long

---

[62] The test questions are used at Johns Hopkins University Hospital, Baltimore, MD, in deciding whether or not a patient is an alcoholic.

that might take, but if you are sincere, it'll come. Let me pray for you here:

"Dear heavenly Father, I humbly ask You to open the eyes of this child of Yours who is reading here, so that they may truly see. I ask right now, Lord, for an outpouring of Your precious grace upon them, so that they might be able to make an informed decision on their lives from here on in and can truly admit their powerlessness over their specific dependency disorder and the general unmanageability of the rest of their life. I ask this in the name of Jesus Christ. Amen."

If you are willing to admit your powerlessness over alcohol, and that your life has become unmanageable, let's finish Step 1. Pray a prayer along these lines:

"Dear heavenly Father, thank You that You have brought me to this point in my life. I can now see, and I admit, that I am powerless over alcohol and that my life is unmanageable for me. In the name of Jesus, I pray. Amen."

Step 2

We came to believe that a power greater than ourselves could restore us to sanity.

And he said unto me, My grace is sufficient for thee: for my strength is made perfect in weakness. Most gladly therefore will I rather glory in my infirmities, that the power of Christ may rest upon me.

2 Corinthians 12:9

Go back to page 96 and read about Step 2 again.

- I need to admit my insanity.
- I need to be open to the possibility of a power greater than myself that can restore me to my sanity.

If you understand and can accept this, we can proceed.

Let us pray together:

"Dear heavenly Father, give me the strength to be willing and open-minded towards You without placing any expectations on Your workings. I know that I do not have the power within me to restore sanity into my life. I realize the insanity of my situation and want to trust You to restore me to my sanity, so that I will ultimately be of maximum service to You and can have a personal relationship with You, one that is unique to me. I ask this in the name of Jesus Christ. Amen."

Step 3

We made a decision to turn our will and our lives over to the care of God, as we understood Him.

And he said to them all, If any man will come after me, let him deny himself, and take up his cross daily, and follow me.

Luke 9:23

Go back to page 100 and read about Step 3 again. Remember, you can use it as a reference.

When you have really made the decision in your mind, say this prayer with all the sincerity you have at your disposal:

"God, I offer myself to You – to build me and to do with me as You will. Relieve me of the bondage of self, that I may better do Your will. Take away my difficulties, that victory over them might bear witness to those I would help of Your power, Your love and Your way of life. May I do Your will always. In the name of Jesus Christ. Amen."

Remember, if you do not fully agree with or understand the concept of God as I have suggested so far, it is OK; you may still proceed. (Just remember how I did it in my story.) You only have to be *willing* to believe at this point. The willingness and sincerity of your decision will be shown by you completing the rest of the steps; you need to continue to find recovery.

This is Step 3 completed; quite simple once you make up your mind, but I believe it is one of the most powerful decisions to make.

You may proceed to Step 4, but please remember one important point: you should have no preconceived ideas as to how and when God will work – just work through the steps as honestly and sincerely as possible.

Step 4

We made a searching and fearless moral inventory of ourselves.

Let us search and try our ways, and turn again to the LORD.

Lamentations 3:40

Go back to page 104 and read about Step 4 again. It will be very important for you to keep referring to this step from this source, especially when you're doing this step on your own. In my sobriety, I had to refer back constantly to many things. I was of course blessed with having a sponsor who went through it with me, but I do believe there is enough here to be able to do a thorough job on one's own.

Below is a small glossary of words used and their basic meanings according to my understanding of the words in my recovery. In some cases, I have emphasized the meanings of the words in the context of our working of this step, so the explanations given here may differ a little from dictionary definitions. As such, I suggest you read through them even if you know the meanings. Sometimes something worded differently can add new insight.

Use this section as a point of reference while doing this step if need be. I recommend taking a moment to look back to the meaning of a word in its context here, rather than not being sure and going on a guess. I have found in my own experience that it has given me a sound grasp of the meaning needed in the context of completing this step, and for daily inventories done in the spur of the moment (as will be covered in Step 10).

Glossary and explanation of key words:

Inventories

Resentment(s)	Feelings of bitter hurt or indignation (anger excited by assumptions made) which come from rightly or wrongfully held feelings of being injured or offended (wrong judgement).

Fear(s)	Feelings of anxiety, agitation, uneasiness, apprehension, dread, worry, etc. (wrong belief).
Harm(s)	Wrong acts which result in pain, hurt feelings, worry, financial loss, etc.; these towards others and self (wrong action).
Good qualities	Qualities within us that appear naturally, that generally bless, help, uplift or benefit others to another person's ultimate advantage.
Motive	My true purpose when benefitting someone else (including God); whether with little or no thought to any gain for myself in any way (good motive) or doing something with the intention of gaining something for myself, which could include personal satisfaction (wrong motive).

Instincts affected in ourselves

Social Instinct	My built-in desire to belong to and/or be accepted (companionship) by a community or group of people, wanting to be recognized and/or to be accepted as a leader (prestige). My view of myself, high or low (self-esteem), and my relations with others and the world around me (personal relations).
Security instinct	My built-in desire for money, clothing, shelter, etc., in order to feel secure in the future (material), and my desire to be wanted by others in order to feel at ease (emotional).
Sexual instinct	My built-in desire for sexual intimacy that does not affect my conscience in any way (acceptable sexual relations), and my desire for sexual intimacy that affects my conscience in some way (unacceptable sexual relations), in order to feel sexually fulfilled.
Ambition(s)	My plans to gain or acquire all or some of those things mentioned in our three instincts above, so that I can ultimately achieve my goals for each instinct sometime in the future (sooner rather than later).

Our defects (wrongs)

Selfish	When I am deficient in my consideration of others (can be conscious or unconscious), giving primary attention to my own agenda, while paying little or no attention to anyone else's agenda or wellbeing, or putting mine before theirs.
Self-seeking	Occupied mainly with my own affairs, seeking mainly or solely to further my own interests.
Dishonest	The act of not telling the truth, lying, cheating, stealing, deceiving, telling half-truths, or sometimes not speaking up when I know that the truth might shed light on a subject, thereby changing the outlook or outcome.
Frightened	Being in a temporary or continual state of fear, which includes all or some of the feelings of anxiety, agitation, uneasiness, apprehension, dread, worry etc.
Inconsiderate	Without thought or consideration of others; not taking the time to consider possible scenarios as to why another might behave the way they do in different situations.

We will now deal with each of our inventories one at a time. You might feel that there is a lot of reading and instructions; do not be discouraged, most of it is to help you understand what to do in the best way possible. Your actual work is on the worksheet and is quite short, while the other writings are prompts, suggestions and instructions to help you to complete the worksheets and to be able to get the best possible overview of where you have been coming from.

I want you to know that I love you and have been praying for you in this part of the Program for many years, that the Holy Spirit will open your eyes to where you've been 'missing the plot', just as He did with me.

I recommend that you read everything carefully and do what it says to the best of your ability. You will see that in each inventory, I have given one or two of my own personal inventory examples in the worksheets, with explanations of how and why I came to tick whichever box. I have done this so that you might get a feel of how I produced my inventory. However, if you do yours slightly differently or have a different way of reasoning, that is completely fine. We are all different people and it is amazing that God works with and through us to suit our own unique design. Who better, seeing as He made us with our individual personalities? Throughout this Program, the key is to be as honest, open and as willing as we possibly can be.

INVENTORIES

Resentments Inventory

Download the Resentments Inventory worksheet[63] or draw it up on a piece of paper from the template on page 249. Make as many copies as you need; I had sixty-seven resentments when I did my inventory the second time.

Follow and read quickly through my personal example of the Resentments Inventory list on page 207. As you go through each stage and complete each column, you can refer back to this example; I have tried to put detailed reasoning for each point. Remember that you will not need to write down your reasonings as I have done; you only have to fill in the worksheets. The only reason I put them down is because I wanted to give you an idea as to the way you might need to think about each point. It's only a guide though; you might have a very different outlook and understanding to mine and that is fine. The important thing to remember is to be as sincere and as thorough as you can; God will take care of the rest. Don't get too concerned about doing it 'perfectly'; allow God to guide you. For me, He guided me with a 'niggling thought', an idea or an understanding which I've tried to explain in the example. If I asked my sponsor if I should or shouldn't put something down or answer yes to a point, he would ask, "How free do you want to be?" My suggestion to you will be the same; if you're not sure of something, put it down or mark "yes"; you will understand why in your own way.

- Get your Resentments Worksheet out next to you with a pencil. I did my worksheets with a pencil because it was easy to make changes; this helps when you review what you've written, and avoids a lot of scratching and crossing out, which can create confusion.
- Write down *all* your resentments under the 1st column ("I am resentful towards...") without doing anything to the other

---

[63] *www.onwardsandupwards.org/breakthrough-into-recovery*

203

columns. Your resentments must include any you have had before, which you feel you don't have (or just don't care about) anymore. If you cannot remember a name, fill in something that will remind you of that specific resentment, e.g. "Blonde girl at the village tavern one New Year's party". I suggest that you write down all those that come to mind now.

- After you have written all the resentments you can think of, read through the Resentments Inventory Worksheet Prompts found on page 248, filling in resentments that spring to mind under the first heading (you will see the prompt sheet includes people, institutions and principles.)

I have gone through one of my resentments word for word, taking time to put down my thoughts and feelings. Please don't get disheartened by what seems like a big 'mission'. I took this inventory one day at a time, tackling one at a time. If you set your mind to doing one or two a day and stick to it, you will be staying sober and you will get through it. Personally, it took me two months to work through this Step 4 inventory, but I believe it was vital for me. I drank for seventeen years; a few months' work in order to get in a good solid foundation for sobriety was well worth it. The key to getting through this inventory is to pray every day for the help to keep at it. I cannot guarantee that you will achieve and maintain sobriety if you do this thoroughly (there are many factors involved), but if you do this step to the best of your ability, you will be well on your way to achieving a quality sobriety.

- Write down the reason or cause next to each resentment from column 1 in the 2nd column ("I am resentful because…") without doing anything in the other columns. You really just need a brief summary of what actually got 'under your skin', so that you'll be able to recall the situation in full in Step 5. Take a look at my own example to give you an idea as to how to summarize your cause or reason.

How I filled in the first resentment

Column

1   My mom

2   My mom used to say that she didn't want me at times because she couldn't handle me

3   Under social instincts (I go back to the glossary on page 200 to refresh my memory), did it affect my...
- *Companionship?* – yes, because I was always fearful of people close to me not wanting me (I put a C in that column)
- *Prestige?* – yes, because I felt I would not get noticed (I put a P in that column)
- *Self-esteem?* – yes, because I always had a lower feeling of myself; I didn't match up (I put an SE in that column)
- *Personal Relations?* – yes, because I acted out of character towards my mom and others, being weary of them rejecting me, which caused unnatural personal relations with people in general (I put a PR in that column)
- *Ambition?* – yes, because I curbed and tried to manipulate relations so that people would think I was nicer than I thought myself to be (I put an A in that column)

Under security instincts, did it affect my...
- *Material?* – no, because I don't feel that I suffered or was short-changed in any material possessions or money by my mother's action, or my subsequent resentment
- *Emotional?* – yes, because I was emotionally unstable in many ways because of feelings of being inferior (I put an E)
- *Ambition?* – yes, because I was trying to manipulate people and situations so that I could gain both material and emotional security for my future, due to my feelings of inadequacy and fears of abandonment (I put an A)

Under sexual instincts, did it affect my...
- *Acceptable relations?* – no, because the sexual side never really came to mind as a result of this resentment
- *Unacceptable relations?* – no, I never sought other kinds of sexual relations because of my mother not wanting me
- *Ambitions?* – yes, I did not believe I would settle down with a wife because I thought they would not want me once they got to know me (I put an A)

4   Was I...

- *Selfish?* – no, because being wanted by your mom is a natural desire
- *Self-seeking?* – yes, I wanted to be wanted for myself, not thinking what my mother wanted (I put an SS)
- *Dishonest?* – yes, I was always being false, trying to show myself as what I thought people wanted me to be, such as saying I liked romantic movies because some girl I was trying to impress did (I put a D)
- *Frightened?* – yes, because I had all sorts of fears of rejection and abandonment (I put an F)
- *Inconsiderate?* – yes, because I never considered my mother was 20 years old, stuck in a town more than 1000 km from her family and help, with a child that was riddled with colic and screamed most of the time (I put an I)

5   I express my will to make my amends to God though prayer and meditation (I put PM), and to my mother by some form of amends later (I put MA)

Personal Example of My Resentments Inventory Worksheet

	1. The resentment	2. The reason or cause	3. The effect on me			4. My part	5. Future action
	I am resentful towards (or at)…	I am resentful because…	My social instincts: companionship (C), prestige (P), self-esteem (SE), personal relations (PR) and ambitions (A)	My security instincts: material (M), emotional (E), ambitions (A)	My sexual instincts: acceptable relations (AR), unacceptable relations (UR) and ambitions (A)	Was I… selfish (S), self-seeking (SS), dishonest (D), frightened (F) or inconsiderate (I) in any way?	I will… pray and meditate / think (PM) and make amends (MA)
1.	My mom	She didn't want me as a baby	C, P, SE, PR & A	E & A	A	SS, D, F & I	PM & MA
2.	Girl from England	Broke up with me and left for England the next day	C, P, SE, PR & A	E & A	AR, AU & A	S, SS, F & I	PM & MA
3.	Education system	They don't have proper grants for tertiary education	P, SE & A	M, E & A	-	SS, F & I	PM
4.	God / deity	He's the boss, I must follow the rules but had no choice in being born or not	P & A	M & A	UR & A	S, SS, F & I	PM
5.							

Now work to the end of every resentment line, one at a time, across each of the columns 3 and 4.

- Start with column 3 which asks what the resentment has affected in you. These are broken down into social, security and sexual instincts, with each covering various aspects as displayed in the Resentments Inventory Worksheet on page 249, as well as in the personal example you have just seen. It is important to understand the meanings, and you can refer to the write-up on this step on page 104, the glossary on page 200, or my personal example and explanation on pages 205-207. If a point is appropriate to you, you will use the letter symbol in that specific column, as shown in my personal example. I did this for myself because at the end of Step 4, I had a pretty good idea of each symbol, and as I glanced over my completed worksheet, I was able to pick up my most common issues and mistakes. I could also notice my bigger deep-seated resentments, and it was surprising to see that some resentments which did not consciously seem like a big deal to me had actually had quite a huge impact on my life and wellbeing. If you have no applicable points for a particular column under a specific resentment, just put a dash instead.
- Go on to column 4 and ask yourself what part you had to play in the establishment of that specific resentment. As above, you will mark in the column with each appropriate letter symbol. I do not believe you will leave them all out because I don't believe a person can have resentments without having at least one of the five defects of character. If you cannot mark any, there is undoubtedly something you have not considered (it might even be hypothetical) about the other person, institution or principle. Ask God for His guidance in revealing what it might be and then put down an 'I' for 'inconsiderate' opposite that specific resentment and move on.
- In filling in column 5 we are only making our work easier for Steps 8 and 9. You are not going to do anything here; you are merely displaying a willingness to 'clean your side of the street'. I do not believe we should mark down an amends to the person, institution or principle, if nothing disrespectful was done towards them (i.e. you never harmed them in any way). However, I believe we will always have hurt God, so we show our willingness to ask God for forgiveness through prayer and meditation.

You have now completed your Resentments Inventory. Well done! I know it is a lot, but I found it vital and I urge you to keep going; it gets easier from here on in.

FEARS INVENTORY

Download the Fears Inventory worksheet[64] or draw it up on a piece of paper from the template on page 251.

Follow and read quickly through my Personal Example of My Fears Inventory Worksheet overleaf. As you go through each stage and complete each column, you can refer back to this example. Once again, you will not need to write down your reasonings as I have done, only to fill in the worksheets.

Get your Fears Inventory Worksheet out next to you with a pencil. You will notice that this worksheet does not have 'The effect on me' and 'My part' columns. This does not mean that fear is not a sin; as we have already discussed, it just means that your character defect is fear itself – you don't trust God. Your amends will be made with Him alone.

- Write down *all* your fears under column 1 ("I am fearful of...") without doing anything to the other columns. Your fears must include past fears, which you feel you don't have anymore; they might actually still be there but are not currently activated. I suggest that you write down all those that come to mind now. After you have written down all the fears you can think of, read through the Fears Inventory Worksheet Prompts found on page 250, filling in all fears that then spring to mind under the first heading.

---

[64] *www.onwardsandupwards.org/breakthrough-into-recovery*

How I filled in the first fear

Column

1 Spiders

2 I've heard of spider bites and what they can do to people if the spider is poisonous enough, but I've never actually been bitten. I have seen pictures of bites that have rotted the flesh away. I come over cold and sweaty when I see spiders on the nature programs on television. I had an experience in the bush-veld, where I was doing a conservation practical on random animal counts and went under a low thorn tree. I walked into a thick neon yellow spider web, which pulled this neon blue spider onto my face; it was about the size of my palm. It ran off my face, down my neck and onto my shoulder, where I was able to flick it off. I was finished! I went cold and felt faint. I had nightmares for years afterwards. My logic tells me that nothing will really happen, but I cannot deal with it.

3 I realize that spiders are one of God's creations and that I really do not trust Him much if I think that He could not protect me from a little spider. I need to prepare myself to have Him remove this fear, so I put down PM for prayer and meditation.

Personal Example of My Fears Inventory Worksheet

	1. The fear	2. The reason or cause	3. Future action
	I am fearful of…	I am fearful because…	I will… pray and meditate / think (PM)
1.	Spiders	Their speed, their creepiness and they bite and could have poison	PM
2.	Rejection	I am scared when I think that people will ignore me or laugh at me	PM
3.	Abandonment	I am scared that those I love too much might one day just up and leave me	PM
4.	Hell	I am scared I don't 'make the grade' and end up in hell for eternity one day	PM
5.			

Now you need to complete columns 2 and 3 for each point.

- Write down the cause of your fear in column 2. If you look at the example on page 210, I gave my explanation of arachnophobia, so that you can see that no fear is too stupid. (I'm a six-foot-two guy weighing about a hundred and twenty kilos, and my little wife has to protect me!)

  Follow the explanation of my reasoning and do your own for each of your fears as you go; I suggest actually trying to relive them in your mind and then put in a brief line to sum up the reasoning; this will help you recall or remember it again for later.

- Mark each of the 3rd column spaces "PM" as you make up your mind that you would like to be rid of each fear.

  I need to want God to remove this fear, because I want to have a close relationship with Him, so I mark column 3 with a "PM", for future action through prayer and meditation.

You have now completed your Fears Inventory.

HARMS INVENTORY

Download the Harms Inventory worksheet[65] or draw it up on a piece of paper from the template on page 252.

Follow and read quickly through my Personal Example of My Harms Inventory Worksheet on page 215. As you go through each stage and complete each column, you can refer back to this example. As before, you will not need to write down your reasonings as I have done; you only have to fill in the worksheets. Get your Harms Inventory Worksheet out next to you with a pencil. You will notice that it does not have the column 'The effect on me'. You may, if you like, use column 3 from the Resentments Inventory worksheet to determine what instinct within you was the cause of harming someone else. In my inventory, though, I found it more important to find out which of my defects of character was causing me to harm them.

- Write down all your harms under the 1st column ("I harmed...") without doing anything to the other columns. Your harms must include both sexual and non-sexual.

---

[65] *www.onwardsandupwards.org/breakthrough-into-recovery*

Sexual harms and non-sexual harms are listed separately for good reason. I personally believe that any form of sexual activity outside of marriage is a harm to the person you are engaged in it with and hurts God. So, we distinguish between the two – sexual (SX) and non-sexual (NSX). I suggest that you write down all the ones that come to mind now.

- After you have written all the harms you can think of, go back to your Resentments Inventory worksheet. Go through each resentment and ask yourself if you have done anything disrespectful towards any of these people, institutions or principles; in other words, have you done anything to hurt or harm anyone? It might be physically, verbally or even through silence (not speaking up to protect the innocence of whomever I have a resentment towards.) Write down what you did or how you harmed that person or institution in the 2nd column ("I..."), without doing anything in the other columns. Just put a brief summary of what you actually did, so that you'll be able to recall the situation in full in Step 5. Take a look at my example on overleaf to give you an idea as to how to summarize your cause or reason.

Now you need to complete columns 3 and 4 for each point.

- Start with column 3 and ask what part of your character defects caused you to do the harm or hurt. Then, as shown in the example, mark in the column with the appropriate letter symbol.
- In filling in column 4, we are only making our work easier for Steps 8 and 9. You are not going to do anything here; you are merely displaying willingness to 'clean your side of the street'. In dealing with a harm, no matter the justification of what you did to the person or institution (as put down in column 2), you wronged them. We need to be willing to make an amends to that person or institution (remember, it might be with no actual contact.) Once you are willing, put the symbols PM (prayer and meditation) and MA (make amends) in column 4.

That is the Harms Inventory worksheet completed.

How I filled in the fourth harm

Column

1 Bricklayer

2 In the construction industry, soiling another man's reputation can leave him without work and bankrupt. It is one thing to be asked about the quality of an artisan's work and be honest, but quite another thing when you make it your mission to 'get the guy'; I believe that you are then playing God. I know that he lost work because of my explicit intention of hurting him.

3 Was I...

- *Selfish?* – yes, because I had no thought of the difficulties he might be experiencing (I put an S)
- *Self-seeking?* – yes, I wanted the work done exactly my way with no room for any deviation (I put an SS)
- *Dishonest?* – yes, I made him seem much worse than he probably was. I used statements like, "He's the worst bricklayer I've ever worked with." (I put a D)
- *Frightened?* – no, because I didn't care what he said or thought; I never even thought about his reaction
- *Inconsiderate?* – yes, because I never considered any scenario as to why he couldn't keep up with the building program. If I think about it now, he could have had labour issues, transport problems, personal hassles at home; I never bothered to ask or listen (I put an I)

4 As it is a harm I have done, I will want to make amends to God, which will restore my relationship with Him. I am willing to make amends with the harmed party, which will either restore my relationship with them, or at least clear my side of the street. That is why I will always put PM and MA under harms.

Personal Example of My Harms Inventory Worksheet (Sexual and Non-sexual)

	1. The harm	2. How I harmed	3. My part that caused the harm	4. Future action
	Whom did I harm? I harmed…	What did I do? I…	Was I… selfish (S), self-seeking (SS), dishonest (D), frightened (F) or inconsiderate (I)?	I will… pray and meditate / think (PM) and make amends (MA)
1.	My mom – NSX	Swore at her, heaped guilt and blame on her.	S, SS, D, F & I	PM & MA
2.	Ex-girlfriend – SX	Slept with her, with no thought of her feelings or need	S, SS & I	PM & MA
3.	Old school – NSX	Threw rocks through as many windows as possible	S, D & I	PM & MA
4.	Bricklayer – NSX	Bad-mouthed his name to all other contractors	S, SS, D & I	PM & MA
5.				

215

GOOD QUALITIES INVENTORY

Download the Good Qualities Inventory worksheet[66] or draw it up on a piece of paper from the template on page 253.

Follow and read quickly through my personal example of the Good Qualities Inventory list on page 219. As you go through each stage and complete each column, you can refer back to this example. As before, you will not need to write down your reasoning as I have done, only to fill in the worksheets.

Get your Good Qualities Inventory worksheet out next to you with a pencil.

- Write down all your good qualities you can think of under the 1st column ("I am…") without doing anything to the other columns. I suggest that you write down all those that come to mind now.

  Give yourself free rein and try to think of things that others compliment you on, and also things that you think people don't recognize. You can also put down natural abilities if you feel that they are qualities that might benefit others. You might, for instance, be a good rugby player and you know this pleases your father; put it down. Think also of attitudes towards things that might inspire others to do better; for instance, a passionate approach to your work that gets your colleagues inspired and performing well. Remember that we are going to review motives, so don't think you are boasting by putting things down; we need an appraisal of how we see ourselves. Look at the few examples I have put down to give you a guide. I have tried to pick a variety from my personal inventory.

Rigorous honesty is a must for filling in column 2. I suggest you do as I did, praying and asking God to open your eyes to your motives. Remember, no one need see this part of your inventory – ever. This is between you and God. If you really would like your good qualities to have pure and true motives, you need to get honest with yourself and God. This is what I did, and I can tell you that these days I am more honest because I know that this pleases the Lord, and I believe that my motive has changed on its own; I didn't have to fight it.

---

[66] *www.onwardsandupwards.org/breakthrough-into-recovery*

When doing column 3, it is quite easy to determine a right or wrong motive. If the concern is primarily for my benefit, it's wrong. If my main concern is for the well-being of others or to please the Lord, my motive is right. Try, as I have in my example, to put why you think your motive was wrong or right; it can just be one word. I have found that it has helped me gain more perspective, but it is not a necessity; I had a few right or wrong motives that I couldn't find a word to explain.

The 4th column is much like the other inventories when it comes to prayer and meditation (put "PM"); we will be asking God to change our wrong motives. I also think it is important in the process of recovery to thank and praise God for the goodness He has placed in us (put "PT"). Before the foundations of the earth were created, God had already given us these good qualities, and it is a privilege to show Him gratitude for helping us to keep our motives pure in all we've been through; not through our power, but through His.

You have now completed Step 4. Well done! I promise you it is already having a huge impact on your life.

How I filled in the third good quality

Column

1   Comical

2   I have always had a good sense of humour, and I used to like telling myself that it is because I liked to make people laugh. But after analysing the situation properly, I realized that when people didn't find me funny or ignored me, I used to feel incredibly hurt and upset. This allowed me to understand that I was only seeking attention and had little or no regard for other people's wellbeing or making them happy.

3   My true motive is the 'Wrong' moral standard. As I've mentioned in Chapter 2, any motive that is primarily for the benefit of self is wrong. The ultimate motive is out of love for God, but by helping or benefiting someone else, we are showing God's love to others and this pleases Him. My primary concern was for my interests and feeding my own ego. I was self-seeking, not really interested in whether others were really happy or not.

4   I will pray and meditate, so I put PM in the column. I will ask God for forgiveness for my self-seeking motive and ask Him to instil a new moral standard in my life, whereby I do things for the benefit of others, so that ultimately His glory might shine. I realize this will not necessarily change overnight, so I will continue to pray this prayer until there is a genuine change.

Personal Example of My Good Qualities Inventory Worksheet

	1. The good quality What are my good qualities? I am…	2. Motive What is my reason? I am…, because…	3. Quality of the motive What was my moral standard in this motive? Right or Wrong	4. Future action I will… pray and meditate / think (PM) or pray and thank God (PT)
1.	Honest	Scared of being caught and looking stupid.	Wrong – Self-conscious	PM
2.	Fair	I believe in "do unto others as you would have done to you"	Wrong – Self-interest	PM
3.	Comical	I want people to like me and focus attention on me	Wrong – Self-seeking	PM
4.	Punctual	I know how it feels to have to wait for someone	Right – Considerate	PT
5.	Methodical	People don't struggle later when you've done it right first time	Right – Helpful	PT

Step 5

We admitted to God, to ourselves, and to another human being the exact nature of our wrongs.

Confess your faults one to another, and pray one for another, that ye may be healed. The effectual fervent prayer of a righteous man availeth much.

James 5:16

Go back to page 121 and read about Step 5 again. Remember, you can use it as a reference.

- Get out your Resentment, Fears and Harms worksheets, which you completed in Step 4. Find a quiet secluded spot and start to tell God everything aloud, using your worksheets as a guide. Tell him all your resentments, and what the nature of your wrongs were for each; whether you were selfish, self-seeking, dishonest, afraid or inconsiderate. Do the same with your harms. Then pick up your fears sheet and tell Him all the things you are fearful of, making sure to acknowledge that you know that they are wrongs because you were not trusting in Him.

- When you have finished, pray and ask God to show you if you have forgotten something or left anything out. If you remember anything, write it down on the appropriate worksheet and work through it as in Step 4. You will more than likely remember other things over time. If so, put them in your lists and follow the same procedure as with all the rest.

- Try to find a person to do your Step 5 with who is of the same gender; we've found in the past that this just works better. It is not a prerequisite though, and often someone like a church leader might be of the opposite sex. Pray and ask God, and if you feel a peace, go for it.

- Once you have found the person, explain to them that as part of a Program you are doing, you'd like for them to lend an ear.

Schedule a definite time with them that will suit you both. I used to meet once a week on Tuesdays at 05:30 in the morning, before work. Explain to your listener that you are not sure how many hours it will take and ask if that is OK with them.

- I suggest you sit with them privately and do the same as you did with God. When you mention each cause, try to relate the scenario (the 'whole story') to the listener. For example, rather than saying you have resentment towards so-and-so because they bullied you, try to explain; say something like, "I used to attend such-and-such a high school when I was twelve years old. I was in grade 7 and there was this bloke in my class named Bob who came from out of town. He seemed to have this way about him that he was trying to prove himself. One day on the playground..." Do you see what I'm trying to get at? Especially, try to relate your *feelings* at the time; try to relive the moment of each resentment, fear or harm. This is why I suggested in Step 4 to write down a few key words that would trigger the memory again.

- *Do not try to rush through this.* It is difficult at times, but you need to really try to give your listener the true picture. We call this 'not skimping on the mortar'. With a building, if you skimp on the mortar in between your bricks you are making the walls weak, and the house can come tumbling down later on (I really relate to this, being in the building industry). As an example, my Step 5 took over ten hours to relate, but it was worth every second for the peace of mind I have today.

- I am reluctant to make the following point, as so many of us look for a loophole to get out of doing this part of the step, but I also do not want you to become disheartened. If you have truly done all you can to find someone to do this step with to no avail, do not lose heart; you can proceed to Step 6. (Only you will know if you have really tried. If you are deceiving yourself, I can almost guarantee you the Program will fail; it is your choice.) Bear in mind this is only temporary; you must continue to pray and actively seek to find someone as soon as possible. If your heart is sincere, it will not hinder your recovery and you will eventually find somebody. When you do find someone, do this Step 5 straight away with them. It will not matter where you are in the Program; just stop the other work and finish this Step 5

- Because this step is so important, pray once more and ask God to reveal if there is anything you might have left out. If you feel a calm and peace about it, you are ready for Step 6.

Step 6

We were entirely ready to have God, through Jesus Christ, remove all these defects of character.

If ye be willing and obedient, ye shall eat the good of the land.

Isaiah 1:19

Go back to page 128 and read about Step 6 again. I suggest you use it as a reference.

- Review your defects of character from Step 5. Do you fully agree that you are generally selfish, self-seeking, dishonest, inconsiderate and afraid?

  If your answer is no to having any of the defects of character, I suggest you pray and ask God to reveal them to you. Here is a prayer you can pray: "Dear Lord and heavenly Father, I am once again faced with a dilemma over which I am totally weak and powerless. I hear what is being said, but I do not believe that I am selfish, self-seeking, dishonest, inconsiderate or afraid. Lord, if this is the path to freedom from my dependency/dependencies, please open my eyes to see these defects, if I have them. I want to be totally open with You and I want to proceed without pretending I believe what is suggested I should believe. I ask that You reveal my defects to me. In Jesus' name. Amen." I recommend you do not continue further until you can agree you have all or some of these defects. Once you receive this revelation (I believe you will if you are sincere), you can continue.

- Are you willing and ready for God to remove these character defects?

  If you feel you are not ready to have them removed for whatever reason, you need to pray for that willingness. Here is a prayer you can pray: "Dear Father God, I realize that I have certain defects of character that are ultimately blocking me from Your power which will help me to overcome my dependency disorder(s). For reasons known [name them] or unknown to me, I am not willing to accept that they be removed. However, I believe this could be the way to the relief from my dependency/dependencies, and I ask that You give me a true desire to have them removed by You. In Jesus' name. Amen."

- Once you are able to answer yes to the two questions above, you are ready for Step 7.

Step 7

We humbly asked Him to remove our shortcomings.

Humble yourselves in the sight of the Lord, and He shall lift you up.

James 4:10

Go back to page 134 and read about Step 7 again. I suggest you use it as a reference.

To complete Step 7, all it takes is two prayers.

- For the first prayer, I recommend the following: "Dear heavenly Father, I am now willing that you should have all of me, good and bad. I pray that you now remove from me every single defect of character which stands in the way of my usefulness to you and those around me. Grant me strength, as I go from here, to do your bidding. I ask this all in Jesus' name. Amen."
- The second prayer can be: "Dear heavenly Father, I realize that without You I am nothing. I ask that You continue to keep my motives pure and that You alert me to any change in attitude along my recovery journey. I ask this in Jesus' name. Amen."

You are now ready to continue to Step 8.

Step 8

**We made a list of all persons we had harmed,
and became willing to make amends to them all.**

*Therefore if thou bring thy gift to the altar, and there
rememberest that thy brother hath ought against thee; Leave
there thy gift before the altar, and go thy way; first be
reconciled to thy brother, and then come and offer thy gift.*

Matthew 5:23,24

Go back to page 137 and read about Step 8 again, just to refresh your memory as to the right attitude and motive to adopt.

Download the Amends worksheet[67] or draw it up on a piece of paper from the template on page 254. Check my example on the page opposite of how to choose your 'Name of the party harmed'.

- Go back to your Resentments Inventory worksheet from Step 4 and check column 5 ('Future action') for any resentments marked "MA". On your Amends worksheets, under the 1st column ('Name of the party harmed'), write down all the people/institutions from your Resentments worksheet that were marked "MA" in the 5th column.

- Take out your Harms Inventory worksheet from Step 4 as well, and here on the Amends worksheet, under the 1st column ('Name of the party harmed'), copy all the people/institutions from the 1st column ('The harm').

- If there is any other harm that you might have subsequently inflicted, or some that come to mind that are not on your Step 4 worksheet, write them in, too.

---

[67] *www.onwardsandupwards.org/breakthrough-into-recovery*

Personal Example of My Amends Worksheet

Name of the party harmed	Prayer and meditation	Immediate amends (I) or deferred amends (D – put approximate time and date)	No direct contact	Check when done
My mom				
Girl from England				
Old school				
Bricklayer				

The first 2 names in the first column were taken from my example Step 4 Resentments worksheet and the second 2 from my Harms worksheet

- I suggest praying the following prayer, so that you can be sure that you are not missing any: "Dear heavenly Father, I want to thank You for bringing me this far. I realize the importance of making my amends with all the people whom I have harmed, and do not want to miss any. I ask You to please reveal to me any persons/institutions I might have overlooked so that I can include them in my lists. Thank You for helping me. In Jesus' name. Amen."

You must keep your Amends worksheet with you as you proceed to Step 9.

Step 9

We made direct amends to such people whenever possible, except when to do so would injure them or others.

Give, and it shall be given unto you; good measure, pressed down, and shaken together, and running over, shall men give into your bosom. For with the same measure that ye mete withal it shall be measured to you again.

Luke 6:38

Go back to page 142 and read about Step 9 again. It will refresh your memory as you establish how you are going to approach each amends.

- Have your Amends worksheet from Step 8 next to you and carefully go through my example on page 233. Read the explanations and reasonings opposite the worksheet as well.
- Column 2 can be actioned right away. Go back to the relevant worksheets from Step 4 (Resentments and Harms) and see what the nature of your various harms were. In your prayer, ask for God's forgiveness, for His blessing on the corresponding person or institution, and for His hand to be on the amends process. Here is a prayer you can use:

"Dear heavenly Father, in my past dealings with [name each person from your amends list in here as you pray for each one individually], I realize I was [list all the defects you marked in column 4 ('My part') of your Step 4 Resentments worksheet] and I possibly hurt them, which might have caused them to retaliate. I ask Your forgiveness for hurting You as well as them, and I ask that You bless and protect them. I ask that You relieve them of any bondage I might have caused them, that they might prosper. I ask for You to be in control of this mending process for all parties involved, and I ask that as many relationships be restored as possible. I ask all this in Jesus' name. Amen."

When you are praying this prayer, keep this person in your thoughts. You can do a prayer and amend to God for each person in succession or do each on the day of each amends; it's up to you.

- After praying, take a minute or two to be quiet; God will disclose to you in His own way and time what He wants you to know and understand. Often, He gives you the peace and strength you need to continue through the process of amends during this time. If nothing seems to come, do not be disheartened; you have what you need and it will become apparent in its time. You can now confidently tick the 'Prayer and meditation' box next to this name.

- Now start column 3 – immediate amends (I) or deferred amends (D). I suggest you pray again and ask God for His wisdom and guidance:

  "Dear heavenly Father, I know that You are omniscient (all-knowing) and omnipotent (all-powerful), so I come to You to ask You for wisdom, discretion, sincerity and courage when making amends to [give the person/institution's name]. I thank You for Your help and guidance. In Jesus' name. Amen."

- If you have indicated an immediate amends, pick up the phone and arrange a time with the person as soon as possible. Each person and situation might be different, so I suggest organising and doing the amends with each one as soon as you can, in your own way, without procrastinating.

  Note: You must make sure you do not bring up or refer to the harm the other person might have done; this makes the apology seem insincere and as a result of what they did. It is also important to know that in order for us to restore our relationship with them and God, we cannot be taking stock of their wrongs and harms.

  Here is an example template of what I used to say:

  "_____ [put the name of the person off the amends list here], in my previous dealings with you and/or your company, I was selfish, dishonest, frightened and inconsiderate, and I realize that I hurt you and caused your company a loss of _____ [if that is the case]. I apologize for doing this and would like to pay you back the money in two instalments of _____ each, starting with the first payment on the 30th of this month. [You will obviously make an offer to pay any money back as soon as possible, making sure that your family needs are met, and making sure you do not go into debt. If it is a large sum of money, you may just suggest to the person that you work out a repayment scheme together, that would be amenable to both parties.] I trust this will be acceptable, and I wish you and your company all the best in future."

- Tick off each amends as you do them in the 'Check when done' column.
- If you have an amend to make for which you cannot make direct contact, tick column 4 ('No direct contact'), and then tick column 5 ('Check when done') after you have done your prayer and meditation for this person in column 2 ('Prayer and meditation').
- If you feel that you would like to write a letter or send a message, then keep it short, using the same example as for a direct amends. However, you must be honest with yourself and make sure that it is not fear that is keeping you from making a face-to-face amends.

You can proceed to Step 10 as soon as you have been through your Amends worksheet thoroughly, making sure that you have a definite plan for each amends not yet completed – this should include times and dates for the outstanding amends.

How I filled in the Amends worksheet

Column

Prayer and Meditation	I tick all the harms, under the 'Prayer and meditation' column, because we should always pray and think before we do anything. My main harm was always to the Lord, and I want to restore my relationship with Him. After praying, I spend a bit of time thinking over the harm, and just leave time for God to speak to me. He normally does this through thoughts, and I gain clarity of understanding.
Immediate amends (I) or deferred amends (D)	*My mom* – it is an immediate and direct amends, because she is close by and I want to make restitution (restore our relationship). *Girl from England* – I am married and she might be too. I do not want to make any direct contact with her, as this could cause complications in both our relationships. I therefore put N/A (not applicable). *Old school* – My old school is in another province and the teachers there are not the ones who were there when I was there, so I will write a letter. I will do it in November this year when my work is winding down. *Bricklayer* – I will see him at work tomorrow, and will make an appointment with him at 4pm when the workers are packing up, and make my amends.

Personal Example of My Amends Worksheet

Name of the party harmed	Prayer and meditation	Immediate amends (I) or deferred amends (D – put approximate time and date)	No direct contact	Check when done
My mom	✓	I – immediate		✓
Girl from England	✓	N/A	✓	✓
Old school	✓	D – December this year		
Bricklayer	✓	D – Tomorrow, 4pm		

Step 10

**We continued to take personal inventory,
and when we were wrong, promptly admitted it.**

*For I say, through the grace given unto me, to every man that
is among you, not to think of himself more highly than he
ought to think; but to think soberly, according as God hath
dealt to every man the measure of faith.*

Romans 12:3

Go back to page 146 and read about Step 10 again. Get an idea of
the three main inventories you will do (yearly, daily and momentarily).
Remember, you can do any other inventory you like; weekly, quarterly,
half-yearly etc. They will all be done in a similar fashion to my example
of a yearly inventory.

Download the Personal Inventory worksheet[68] or draw it up on a
piece of paper from the template on page 255.

MOMENTARY INVENTORY

- Make up a small prompt card with just the nine checks written on
  it from the Personal Inventory worksheet that you can laminate
  and carry with you in your wallet or pocket.
- When you've had an interaction with someone or some
  organization that has left you feeling hurt or uncomfortable inside
  yourself, take out your prompt card and go through each
  question, answering honestly to yourself.
  Once you have established the problem (for example, "I am not
  resentful but I have just harmed this colleague") and the character
  defects that caused you to react (for example, "I was self-seeking
  and inconsiderate towards my colleague"), you should make an
  amends directly and immediately. An example of an amend can

---

[68] *www.onwardsandupwards.org/breakthrough-into-recovery*

be: "Listen, Paul. I just snapped at you and that is not cool. I was trying to get my way (self-seeking) and was totally inconsiderate of what you needed. I am truly sorry for that." If you are unable to do the amends for whatever reason (for example, you are feeling too angry), don't get too upset. We are human; move on to the next step and make sure you make right with God. If you are sincere, God will give you the strength for what is needed.

- It does not matter what the outcome is; you have done your part, as long as you recognised your part and were sincere. You need to pray and ask God for His forgiveness, something like:
"Father God, I have just hurt Paul by being self-seeking and inconsiderate, and this led me to snap at him. I know that this is wrong and that it cuts me off from a relationship between him and me, and between You and me. I ask You for forgiveness for doing this, and I ask You to restore a relationship between Paul and me, and You and me, God. In Jesus' name. Amen."

You can do this as often as you need to in a day. Each time should not take you more than a few minutes.

DAILY INVENTORY

- Put your Step 10 Personal Inventory worksheet next to you and carefully go through my example overleaf. Read the explanations and reasonings opposite the worksheet as well. Your main warning sign in your personal inventories is going to be pain. When you've had an interaction of any kind that has left you feeling pain, you will know that you played a part.
- Review your day, paying specific attention to situations and encounters that made you feel hurt, uncomfortable or down. Write each of them down. Remember that if you made your Momentary Inventory during the day and the pain is gone, you need not include it here, but include it if you still feel uncomfortable.
- Follow the 'Personal Example of My Inventory Worksheet' shown overleaf. Read through my example and do the same for each of your listed people, institutions or principles. If an amends needs to be made, do so as soon as you possibly can.

Your daily inventory shouldn't take more than ten minutes or so.

How I filled in the first entry on the Personal Inventory worksheet

Question

Do I have resentment?	Yes – he disobeyed the rules of the road and could have caused an accident and harm (I tick the box)
Have I harmed?	Yes – I verbally abused him (I tick the box)
Was I selfish?	No – I was not thinking of myself
Was I self-seeking?	Yes – I wanted him not to inconvenience me (I tick the box)
Was I dishonest?	No – there was no proper interaction
Was I frightened?	Yes – very frightened as I nearly drove into him (I tick the box)
Was I inconsiderate?	Yes – I never considered anything of what might be going on in his life that may have caused him to do what he did (I tick the box)
Do I need to make amends?	No – it is impractical to do so in the middle of the traffic. If I could, I would say something like, "In my recent dealings with you, I was self-seeking, frightened and inconsiderate, and I might have harmed you with my verbal abuse. I just want to say that I am truly sorry for this."
I need to pray and meditate	Not optional, as I need to restore my relationship with God. I pray something like, "Dear heavenly Father, I come to you to confess that I have been self-seeking, frightened and inconsiderate, and this has led me to verbally abuse one of your creations. I ask you to forgive me for possibly hurting that taxi driver, and I ask that you bless him with all the grace and blessings you give me. Lord, please heal his hurt, and I ask that you restore my relationship with you. I ask, Holy Spirit, for the guidance and strength to hand these shortcomings over to you, as I know I cannot change these things in myself; but you can. I ask this all in Jesus' name. Amen."

Example of My Personal Inventory Worksheet

Daily personal inventory		People, Institutions and Principles			
	Checks	A. Taxi driver	B. Steel fixer	C. Municipality	D. My wife
1.	Do I have resentment?	✓		✓	✓
2.	Have I harmed?	✓	✓		✓
3.	Was I selfish?				✓
4.	Was I self-seeking?	✓	✓	✓	✓
5.	Was I dishonest?			✓	
6.	Was I frightened?	✓	✓		✓
7.	Was I inconsiderate?	✓	✓	✓	✓
8.	Do I need to make amends?		✓	✓	✓
9.	I need to pray and meditate	Done	Done	Done	Done

YEARLY INVENTORY

This is a review so that you can assess your progress. Get out some of your old daily inventories and flip through them if you like.

I found that having done so many daily inventories, I had a pretty good idea which my main defects of character were. I am sure that if you have reached this stage of your sobriety, you too will have an idea of what yours are; they seem to pop up on most daily inventories.

My main three are that I am self-seeking, frightened and in-considerate. Take the time to reflect on yours and see where you can recall acting in a manner that is contrary to your defects. I did not write anything down in this inventory, because I believe that if one has done the other inventories to the best of one's ability, you have quite an accurate picture of what they are.

I also feel that we need to let the Holy Spirit guide our minds to where He wants them focused. A scenario from the past year might come to mind where I would have normally acted in a manner that would have got me something to assist my comfort, and yet I remember actually thinking of gain for somebody else. The situation might be that someone is following me to an event, and the parking lot is full. I spot a parking place and instead of pulling in, I hoot and point to the spot for the person following, and drive to a further section to find one for myself. When you recall an incident like this, just take a second to thank God. Pray something like:

"Dear Lord, I want to thank You for the changes You are making in my life. Thank You that You are bestowing Your grace and nature upon me. I ask You to continue to keep my will in line with Yours. In Jesus' name. Amen."

- Take some time thinking and reflecting on the positive differences in your character compared to the previous year and thank God for them.
- Take the character defect(s) that you still seem to struggle with and commit them to God in prayer for the next year. An example of such a prayer is:
  "Dear heavenly Father, in the past year, as You know, I really have been battling with fear and being inconsiderate of others. I come to You because I know I am powerless over them. I know they are sinful and are blocking me from a more intimate relationship with You. I also realize that they impair my

effectiveness in loving others and showing them Your glory. I ask You to forgive me. I know that You have the power to remove these defects from my character, so I humbly ask You to do so, in order that my next year might be free of these defects, and that this in turn might be a witness to others of Your grace and power. Thank you, Lord. In Jesus' name. Amen."

Step 11

We sought through prayer and meditation to improve our conscious contact with God, through Jesus Christ, praying only for knowledge of His will for us, and the power to carry that out.

Let the words of my mouth, and the meditation of my heart, be acceptable in thy sight, O LORD, my strength, and my redeemer.

Psalms 19:14

Go back to page 151 and read about Step 11 again. Pay particular attention to the way and attitude with which meditation is approached.

- Make a definite time in the morning or evening, or both, for five uninterrupted minutes.
- Start off by saying the Lord's Prayer – think of the meaning of the words as you pray.
  "Our Father, who art in Heaven; hallowed be Thy Name. Thy kingdom come, Thy will be done, on earth as it is in Heaven. Give us today our daily bread, and forgive us our trespasses, as we forgive those that trespass against us. Lead us not into temptation but deliver us from evil. For Thine is the kingdom, the power and the glory, forever and ever. Amen."
- If you find that someone or something comes to mind, you can pray for them as well; it is good to pray for other people. If you have your own prayer, then you can pray that instead of (or in addition to) the Lord's prayer. You may want to thank Him for another day sober; do so.
- Before you start reading the Bible you might say a short prayer like:
  "Dear heavenly Father, as I read Your word, please reveal through Your Holy Spirit exactly what I need to see and apply in my life. In Jesus' name. Amen."

- Open your Bible to the New Testament and start reading from the beginning, one verse a day. If you feel like reading more, do so. My only advice is not to read yourself into exhaustion, because it will kill your resolve to read every day and you might start missing days. When you have read up to the last book of the Bible, Revelation, I recommend you either start the New Testament again or move to the Old Testament. I suggest you do not read Revelation until you are stronger; it can be quite confusing and hard to understand for someone starting on a road to recovery.

- Try to meditate; just think of whatever comes to mind. I believe your experience will be unique; do whatever you feel comes naturally to you. For example, you might walk, drive, lie down or sing. Try to see how this all fits in with God; include Him in your thoughts and plans. Do not get too stressed about this. I find it has a life of its own and God will find His way with you. Relax and enjoy; whether you feel it or not, you are actually getting into closer contact with God.

- Please remember that this is just a start. I don't need to say any more. If you are sincere, your relationship will grow and form on its own.

If you are not in a church, pray and ask God to lead you to a church where He would like you to be. If you struggle, just bear in mind that you are there out of obedience to Him and because you are building a relationship with Him. Try to get involved where you can, even if it feels strange; the Lord will help you. If you are in a church, continue going and try to get involved with an attitude of wanting to help others.

Step 12

Having had a spiritual awakening as the result of these steps, we tried to carry this message to others, and practise these principles in all our affairs.

Brethren, if a man be overtaken in a fault, ye which are spiritual, restore such an one in the spirit of meekness; considering thyself, lest thou also be tempted. Bear ye one another's burdens, and so fulfil the law of Christ.

Galatians 6:1,2

Go back to page 157 and read about Step 12 again. Bear in mind as you read that this is going to form part of your life's journey and your journey is very likely going to be different to mine.

- Sit back and take some time to think about your spiritual awakening. If you've come this far in working through the steps and you are sober with no real desire to drink, I would say that you have had a spiritual awakening, regardless of how you may feel otherwise.

  If you've come this far and are still drinking, I would be surprised, but it is not impossible. In this case, my recommendation is to pray and ask God for an honest desire to willingly redo the Program with an open-mindedness that will allow God to change your life in any way He chooses – that His will be done. I would then, as I did with my 'lack of money' fear, go back and redo the Program. Try to be thorough, and if you know that there is something you cannot do, ask God to give you the stamina to persist until you overcome the problem. You will find it a lot quicker this time, as most of your inventory is done.

- Each morning, before you get up, pray and ask God for an opportunity to help somebody. It can be anyone and under any circumstances. My sponsor suggested a prayer which I have mentioned previously and which you might use. It is very simple:

"Dear heavenly Father, just for today I want to help someone. Please help me be reminded that the big secret is that nobody else must know about it. In Jesus' name. Amen."

- Help anyone with anything that is within your capability without disrupting your important commitments. You cannot take off a day's work to help someone move house, for instance, unless you can do so in the proper way, i.e. request a day's leave that is due to you, in advance. God will guide you.

- If you get a chance to share your story with anyone, even if they are not alcoholic, do so. It is amazing how the Holy Spirit works in the heart of somebody when we share freely.

- If you meet a person suffering with a dependency disorder who is *asking for help* (that is important), set up a time with them at your place or at a neutral venue, and commence to tell them your story. An example of how one would share one's story can be found on page 29 (the 'My Miracle' story); another is the story shared by Sandra on page 172. If he or she wants to talk, then listen; their sharing often gives good insight into their particular situation. I don't want to say too much on what one should do, because I believe that each situation is unique, and I believe in the power of the Holy Spirit to lead and guide you.

- If, after you have shared your story, they show an interest in recovery, I suggest taking them through this book. You could recommend they get a copy or you can let them read yours. When they come to Part Four of the book, you can meet up and go through each step together. You can even sit and read the book together from the beginning. As you do this, I recommend that you share your experiences with them and allow them to do the same. This is what I do when I help someone, and God, through His Holy Spirit, does the rest. Remember that we have no more power over the other's recovery than we had over our own. The power must come from God; we are only vessels. Do not think it silly to take them through the book; it will continually enrich your walk with God and might provide just the courage that person needs at that time.

- If the person is looking for help but does not want to sit with you, suggest they get a copy of the book and go through it on their own. I have specifically tried to write it in such a way that the person can do the Program on their own should they choose to. As God begins to work in their hearts, so they will open up to the right people at the right time – be ready for God to use you again.

- Once you are working with someone, suggest they come to church with you or join one near them. If they are in one already, encourage them to continue and to get involved in helping.

- We previously looked at how to get a Breakthrough Recovery group going.[69] If there already is one, invite the person along; otherwise, why not start one together? One group I started had three of us for three years, then all of a sudden it started to grow. We didn't mind that it took a while; we enjoyed getting together and going through the book and sharing with one another.

- If the person you are working with is not a Christian, just continue with the book and Program as if they were; they will ask the questions when the Holy Spirit prompts them. If they say they are not a Christian, ask them if they would like to become one. If they say yes, take them through the sinner's prayer:
  - Ask them if they believe that Jesus Christ came down to earth and that He died on the cross for their sins.
  - Ask them then if they believe that God raised Him from the dead.
  - Then finally ask them if they are willing to repent and turn away from their old ways.

If they say yes to all of these, lead them through this simple prayer, asking them to repeat after you (or, if you are reading this book on your own, say this prayer yourself aloud):

"God, I believe that You sent Your Son Jesus to earth and that He died on the cross for my sins. I believe that You then raised Him from the dead and that He is seated on Your right-hand side in Heaven. I now repent of my old sinful ways and I choose to follow You. In Jesus' name. Amen."

According to Romans 10:9 in the Bible, they have entered salvation and are now a child of His.

- To practise these principles in all our affairs is to take each of our pains, problems and hindrances through the steps one at a time. You will find, though, that the lengthy work done in Steps 4, 5, 8

---

[69] See page 185.

and 9 will be considerably shorter as time goes on; you will probably go through the steps in no more than a few hours. Most important is to recognize the defect of character as a sin, whether it was caused by you or not. You will right the wrong and you will try to help others. You may need to do this as part of your daily routine, as I do, for many years. Do not lose heart and never excuse sin, no matter what. God's word says He will forgive your sins as often as you ask Him,[70] but nowhere does He say He will excuse our sins. As you experience victory over one sin, another will come up as the Holy Spirit deals with our unrighteousness and moves us ever closer to sanctification and right standing with God. Amen.

Very important: if the person you are helping is showing signs of illness (either mental or physical), do not try to solve that. We are not professionals and you could do more harm than good. Rather, suggest a rehabilitation centre, doctor, psychiatrist, or whatever you feel the Holy Spirit showing you.

---

[70] See John 1:9 and Matthew 18:22.

APPENDIX

Worksheets

Resentments Inventory Worksheet Prompts

People	Institutions	Principles
Father (incl. step/in-laws)	Marriage	God/deity (the creator)
Mother (incl. step/in-laws)	Bible	
Sisters (incl. step/in-laws)	Church	Retribution (vengeance)
Brothers (incl. step/in-laws)	Religion	The Ten Commandments
Aunts	Races (general or specific)	Jesus Christ
Uncles	Law	Satan
Cousins	Authority	Death
Clergy (priests, pastors, etc.)	Government	Life after death
Police	Education system	Heaven
Lawyers / judges	Correctional system	Hell
Doctors	Mental health system	Sin
Employers	Philosophy	Adultery
Employees (if you are a boss)	Nationality	A golden rule ("You must...")
Friends (school, best, life-long)	Military	Original sin (Adam and Eve)
Teachers	Government departments	Seven deadly sins
Co-workers	Rehabilitation centres	Eternity
Acquaintances (sexual & non-sexual)	Hospitals	"Do unto others..."
Girl/boyfriends or spouses		"Turn the other cheek"
Parole/probation officers		
Program and rehab friends		
Creditors		

You might have others that spring to mind because these have triggered a memory. Put them on your Resentments Inventory worksheet.

Template of Resentments Inventory Worksheet

	1. The resentment	2. The reason or cause	3. The effect on me			4. My part	5. Future action
	I am resentful towards (or at)…	I am resentful because…	My social instincts: companionship (C), prestige (P), self-esteem (SE), personal relations (PR) and ambitions (A)	My security instincts: material (M), emotional (E), ambitions (A)	My sexual instincts: acceptable relations (AR), unacceptable relations (UR) and ambitions (A)	Was I… selfish (S), self-seeking (SS), dishonest (D), frightened (F) or inconsiderate (I) in any way?	I will… pray and meditate / think (PM) and make amends (MA)
1.							
2.							
3.							
4.							
5.							
6.							
7.							
8.							

Fears Inventory Worksheet Prompts

Fear of...

Writing an inventory	Dying	Insanity
Rejection	Loneliness	Diseases
Alcohol	Drugs	Relapse
Sex	Sin	Self-expression
Authority	Heights	Unemployment
Employment	Parents	Losing a spouse
Insects	Losing a child	Animals
Doctors/dentists	Police	Jail
Being found out	Stealing	Creditors
Success	Gays and lesbians	Failure
Fear itself	Responsibility	Physical pain
Women	Drowning	Men
Crying	People	Being alone
The unknown	Poverty	Races
Disapproval	Abandonment	Intimacy
Hospitals	Confrontation	Sobriety
Hurting others	Feelings	Getting old
Being alive	Violence	God
Gossip	Government	Gangs
Change	Wealthy people	Guns

You might have others that spring to mind because these have triggered a memory. Put them on your Fears Inventory worksheet.

Template of Fears Inventory Worksheet

	1. The fear	2. The reason or cause	3. Future action
	I am fearful of…	I am fearful because…	I will… pray and meditate / think (PM)
1.			
2.			
3.			
4.			
5.			
6.			
7.			
8.			
9.			
10.			

Template of Harms Inventory Worksheet (Sexual and Non-sexual)

	1. The harm	2. How I harmed	3. My part that caused the harm	4. Future action
	Whom did I harm? I harmed…	What did I do? I…	Was I… selfish (S), self-seeking (SS), dishonest (D), frightened (F) or inconsiderate (I)?	I will… pray and meditate / think (PM) and make amends (MA)
1.				
2.				
3.				
4.				
5.				
6.				
7.				
8.				
9.				
10.				

Template of Good Qualities Inventory Worksheet

	1. The good quality What are my good qualities? I am…	2. Motive What is my reason? I am…, because…	3. Quality of the motive What was my moral standard in this motive? Right or Wrong	4. Future action I will… pray and meditate / think (PM) or pray and thank God (PT)
1.				
2.				
3.				
4.				
5.				
6.				
7.				
8.				
9.				
10.				

Amends Worksheet (Step 8)

Name of the party harmed	Prayer and meditation	Immediate amends (I) or deferred amends (D – put approximate time and date)	No direct contact	Check when done